This is a book about the principles of U.S. agricultural policy and foreign aid. The traditional military–territorial model of the nation-state defines international duties in terms of protecting citizens' property from foreign threats. Professor Thompson replaces this model with the notion of the trading state, which sees its role in terms of the establishment of international institutions that stabilize and facilitate cultural and intellectual as well as commercial exchanges between nations.

The argument focuses on protectionist challenges to foreign aid and development assistance programs, and engages with the views of a variety of economists, commodity organizations, and philosophers on world hunger and development. What emerges is a new interpretation of social contract theory that can determine goals for international trade and development policy.

The Ethics of Aid and Trade will be of particular interest to political theorists, economists, specialists in international trade and development, and agricultural ethicists.

The ethics of aid and trade

Cambridge Studies in Philosophy and Public Policy

GENERAL EDITOR: Douglas MacLean

The purpose of this series is to publish the most innovative and up-to-date research into the values and concepts that underlie major aspects of public policy. Hitherto most research in this field has been empirical. This series is primarily conceptual and normative; that is, it investigates the structure of arguments and the nature of values relevant to the formation, justification, and criticism of public policy. At the same time it is informed by empirical considerations, addressing specific issues, general policy concerns, and the methods of policy analysis and their applications.

The books in the series are inherently interdisciplinary and include anthologies as well as monographs. They are of particular interest to philosophers, political scientists, sociologists, economists, policy analysts, and those involved in public administration and environmental policy.

Other books in the series

The ethics of aid and trade

U.S. food policy, foreign competition, and the social contract

PAUL B. THOMPSON

CENTER FOR BIOTECHNOLOGY POLICY AND ETHICS
TEXAS A&M UNIVERSITY

CAMBRIDGE
UNIVERSITY PRESS

9-15-94

Published by the Press Syndicate of the University of Cambridge
The Pitt Building, Trumpington Street, Cambridge CB2 1RP
40 West 20th Street, New York, NY 10011–4211, USA
10 Stamford Road, Oakleigh, Victoria 3166, Australia

© Cambridge University Press 1992

First published 1992

Printed in the United States of America

Library of Congress Cataloging-in-Publication Data
Thompson, Paul B., 1951–
The ethics of aid and trade : U.S. food policy, foreign
competition, and the social contract / Paul B. Thompson.
p.   cm. – (Cambridge studies in philosophy and public policy)
Includes bibliographical references and index.
ISBN 0-521-41468-7
1. Produce trade – Government policy – United States – Moral and
ethical aspects.   2. Food relief – Government policy – United States –
Moral and ethical aspects.   3. Agricultural assistance, American –
Government policy – Moral and ethical aspects.   I. Title.
II. Series.
HD9006.T49   1992
363.8'83'091724 – dc20
92 – 1036
CIP

A catalog record for this book is available from the British Library.

ISBN 0-521-41468-7 hardback

To my grandparents

O. L. and Dorothy Schuster
Guy and Noveta Thompson

Contents

Acknowledgments

This book would not have been possible without the assistance of many institutions. The project began while I was an International Affairs Fellow with the Council on Foreign Relations. That fellowship allowed me to spend a year at the Agency for International Development in Washington, D.C., and to visit development projects in Ethiopia, Kenya, Mozambique, Botswana, and India. My travel and some subsequent writing were supported by the Rockefeller Foundation. The National Food and Agricultural Policy Center at Resources for the Future offered a resident fellowship to help with the work. At my home institution, Texas A&M University, I received support from the College of Liberal Arts, the Texas Agricultural Experiment Station, and the Center for Free Enterprise, which awarded me the George R. and Maria Julia Jordan Professorship in Public Policy for a term that supported the completion of the manuscript.

Chapter 1 of the manuscript was published under the title "Of Cabbages and Kings," in *Public Affairs Quarterly* 2(1):69–88 (1988). Parts of Chapter 2 were published in "The Bumpers Amendment: Aid and Trade Issues for U.S. Agriculture," *The Social Science Agricultural Agenda Project*, East Lansing, MI: The Michigan State University Press, 1991, pp. 106–113. The rest of the book appears here for the first time.

Kempton Dunn, Duane Acker, Nyle Brady, Phil Church, Ken Farrell, Ed Rossmiller, and Herman Saatkamp each earn my thanks for having facilitated institutional ties. Robert Mathews, Loren Schultz, Robert Stowe, Henry Shue,

Acknowledgments

Glenn Erickson, George Lucas, Doug MacLean, Lain Ellis, and my philosophy colleagues at Texas A&M University have my thanks for their help with the manuscript. David Crocker and Wes Peterson offered many detailed and extremely helpful comments after carefully reading the manuscript. A special note of thanks is owed to Glenn L. Johnson, who undertook my education in economics and was a constant source of encouragement (and creative irritation, I might add). I also received research help from Doug Kutach, Brad Rickleman, and David Kriewaldt. The manuscript was prepared with help from Kelly Hancock and Jerry Arnett. Barbara Stow kept my life organized, allowing me the luxury of concentrating on the book. I would also like to thank my Cambridge University Press editors who gave the manuscript thoughtful attention, corrected many errors, and made the book more readable. All these people deserve credit for much of what is good about the book. I accept responsibility for the errors myself.

Introduction:
Of cabbages and kings

Between World War II and 1988, U.S. foreign policy was dominated by the Cold War. Development assistance policies were constructed against the background of geopolitics. Recent events in Eastern Europe and the Soviet Union present an opportunity to rethink food policy and foreign aid from an entirely new perspective. Like the policies themselves, most previous efforts to assess the philosophical foundations for development assistance to nonindustrialized countries were formulated within a political context dominated by the rhetoric of arms. Developing countries were viewed as clients for North Atlantic Treaty Organization (NATO) or Warsaw Pact nations poised for military conflict. Suddenly, the dominant relationship between the United States and the nations of Eastern Europe is one of trade and investment. The philosophical underpinnings of aid and development now appear to be as influenced by goals of trade and competitiveness as by military power and geopolitics.

The events in Eastern Europe coincided with publication of the consensus report prepared by the World Commission on Environment and Development in 1987. Titled *Our Common Future* and popularly known as the Brundtland report, this document marks a subtle but important departure from previous thinking. Although the report recites much common wisdom on what is to be done to enhance environmental quality and ensure global development, two themes are conspicuous by their absence. One is a geopolitical perspective that places problems of environmental decay and

1

dysfunctional development into the context of ideological dispute about the role of markets, or political alliances with Eastern or Western power blocks. The absence of this theme is particularly serendipitous in the light of geopolitical changes that could hardly have been anticipated while the Brundtland Commission was undertaking its work. The second omission is the North–South conflict that had characterized the Brandt report, published by the Independent Commission on International Development Issues in 1980. Although the Brandt and Brundtland reports share many conclusions and recommendations, the earlier report had placed them within the context of a Northern Hemisphere locked in the ideological contest noted above, and a Southern Hemisphere with radically different needs. This portrayal of global affairs was well suited to philosophical analyses that represented the moral imperatives of the international situation in terms of redistributive rights claims or duties of justice owed from North to South. In place of these themes, the Brundtland report couches its recommendations within a framework that stresses interests, rather than ideology or rights, and emphasizes those interests that all nations (and all people) have in common.

The issues raised by the opportunity to rethink aid and development bring together an extraordinary range of topics. First, they include the general rationale for foreign aid, and for development assistance programs in particular. Focusing on food and agriculture is a promising way to integrate this philosophical question into the realities of international trade. Second, there are goals and policies for U.S. agricultural trade in world markets, a crucial area in the light of General Agreement on Tariffs and Trade (GATT) negotiations during the Uruguay round of talks during the late 1980s. Third, the political strategies employed by domestic producer groups, which are increasingly thrusting their commercial interests into the international arena, demand an alternative to the geopolitical rationale for foreign relations. Fourth, there is the question of how a national government should form its foreign policy with regard to domestic trade interests. What ethical norms should govern foreign policy in the light of trade? Finally, the normative question raises the possibility that political theory and the social contract tradition must be reformed in the light of these new realities.

In point of fact, global trade issues have been important influences on aid and development policy for some time. In May 1986, Congress passed an amendment to the Supplementary Emergency Appropriations Bill restricting funds for foreign aid that might increase foreign production of agricultural commodities that compete with U.S. exports (U.S. Senate, 1986a, p. 56). In sponsor Senator Dale Bumpers's words, the act is to "prevent American tax dollars from being used to help foreign countries who are trying to take our agricultural export markets" (U.S. Senate, 1986b). Under this law, the U.S. Agency for International Development (AID) is required to suspend research and implementation projects that could enable poor foreign farmers to increase commercial production of commodities such as meat, maize, or wheat that are exported from the United States, and also of commodities such as palm oil that are not produced for export in the United States, but may substitute for U.S. commodities. In the current situation, therefore, voices represented by the Brundtland report call for recognition of common interests, and voices represented by this turn in domestic politics stress competition among private interests.

This book draws on recent discussions of conflicting interests in agricultural trade and development policy determination to provoke the more general questions raised by the need to rethink the ethics of development assistance in a world of trading states. Senator Bumpers's Amendment, in particular, is a focal point of analysis. Arguments mounted in favor of the law express the view that is widely held by the lay public, but never defended in the philosophical literature on hunger and development. The view is that domestic interests should never be compromised for foreign ones, even when aid is targeted to the truly needy. The political debate that surrounded passage of the law presents a

3

burden of proof for advocates of development assistance in providing an outline, at least, of the philosophy behind this "domestic priorities first" point of view. Because the debate centered on trade interests of U.S. farmers, it provides a launching pad for more general questions about the link between trade and development.

COMPETITION AND DEVELOPMENT ASSISTANCE

The Bumpers Amendment, as the law is called, may not be particularly significant legislation in terms of its policy consequences. Nevertheless, the politics that led to its passage have important implications for the way that Americans think about the purpose and justification of foreign assistance policy in the United States. In the first instance, the rationale for this sort of legislation appeals to the notion of competitiveness, the idea that helping Americans compete in foreign markets is a public responsibility. A cynic (or an economist) might think that competitiveness is simply a euphemism for protectionism, but competitiveness differs from protectionism both in concept and politics. As a concept, competitiveness presupposes a framework for international exchange that is simply absent in protectionism. Politically, protectionism refers to foreign producers' opportunities in domestic markets, and competitiveness is just the opposite. The political interests served by actions to increase competitiveness are not necessarily the same as those maintained by protectionism. Although the philosophical rationale for protectionism may be relatively well understood, one cannot assume the same for competitiveness. This book does not examine competitiveness as a concept, but elicits the philosophical foundation of important competitiveness arguments on behalf of U.S. farmers.

The Bumpers Amendment is also important because it portrays the trade interests of U.S. producers in conflict with the development goals of U.S. foreign aid. Senator Bumpers attempted to ameliorate this conflict, and was successful with regard to the policy consequences for aid programs.

4

Nevertheless, the overarching tension between self-interest and altruism permeates the episode. Although the conflict between motives of self-interest and motives of altruism is a standard topic in philosophical ethics, there are few policy issues in which they are as squarely and convincingly opposed as in the events that culminated in the passage of the Bumpers Amendment. The episode therefore provides a probe into the way that self-interest and altruism oppose one another at the level of collective decision making and political philosophy.

The opposition of self-interest and altruism is one problem for ethics, where the goal is a normative account of individual human action. It is something else for political philosophy, where the powers of agency are constrained by cooperative agreements, rather than conscience. What governments can do is limited both normatively and functionally by constitutional constraints on public agency. These constraints sometimes take on legal form, as in the separation of powers in the U.S. Constitution. More frequently they are a reflection of real and perceived alliances among citizens and interest groups that wield political power. Two sorts of normative issues arise in connection with constitutional choice, and both are visible in the politics of aid and trade conflicts.

The dominant normative issue in constitutional choice is the question of justifying action in the light of justice, democracy, liberty, and other fundamental norms of government. Competing accounts of these norms make philosophical analysis of constitutional choice unexpectedly subtle. One solution is simply to commit oneself to a philosophy or ideology of state power, and to measure given choices against this standard. The bulk of philosophical work in the social and political fields has taken this tack whenever it has ventured beyond the realm of pure theory. One limitation of this approach is that it ignores a crucial fact of political life: The use of a philosophy or ideology to rationalize, legitimate, or defend a choice in the political arena will only be recognized by those who have already accepted

5

that account of political norms. The alternative is to attempt normative justifications that either undercut competing political ideologies, or that confine themselves to terms on which most contending parties are in substantial agreement. Social contract theory is often advanced under the banner of this second strategy. The contractual justification stresses the basis for rational agreement, and this may be understood as an inquiry into the art of the possible.

The dominant normative issue with respect to trade and competitiveness, then, is to determine whether policies are supported by and conform to philosophical principles that justify the exercise of state power, generally. The political tensions between self-interest and altruism become particularly cogent because alternative accounts of social contract theory would clearly give pride of place to one, rather than another. As a component of political rhetoric, however, foundational arguments can reinforce an opponent's resistance to a policy proposal rather than overcome it. To argue that government power *should be* constrained to pursuit of self-interested goals, or that it *should be* committed to altruistic ones is useful at one level, but if there are policy choices that can be accepted by parties who disagree about the fundamental constitutional issue, it is important to exhibit a rationale that circumvents the more enduring dispute. The argument presented here is aimed at a compromise rationale with regard to aid and trade issues, though more fundamental philosophical arguments are discussed briefly.

The secondary type of normative issue arises because ideological and philosophical justifications become part of the rhetoric used to advance private interests. The institutional constitution of a polity may consist in informal alliances of interested parties, but interests are generally advanced under a shield of legitimating concepts. Policies that happen to serve the interests of U.S. commodity producers, for example, are not publicly defended by noting that they do so. Rather they are defended by appeals to substantive accounts of the broad social norms that underlie

constitutional choice. The political rhetoric of policy formation never admits that naked self-interest is the only reason
for adopting a policy. The policy must be justified by an appeal to principles that will both legitimate the interests at
stake and win allies for the desired policy choices. A different but related art of the possible is at work here. It involves
an account of how the terms of political theory constrain the
process of legitimating private interests.

The politics of the Bumpers Amendment are particularly
cogent to the second sort of normative issue, the use of
philosophically grounded rhetoric in public defense of
private interest. United States commodity producers constructed a plausible and even persuasive defense of the
Bumpers Amendment and convinced themselves, at least,
that their support of the law was a deeply principled appeal.
They appealed to the goal of competitiveness, to be sure,
but their argument cut deeper. Competitiveness was itself
grounded in the contractual notions of social cooperation
that are pervasive in democratic political theory. Those who
might have opposed the law failed to address the principled
argument of U.S. commodity producers almost entirely.

The politics of the Bumpers Amendment, therefore, serves
as a clue to the way that competitiveness might be justified
in terms of more enduring philosophical values. An argument for preferring domestic interests over foreign needs
can be extracted from its politics, and it is an argument that
implies a principled defense of competitiveness as a social
goal. Although arguments have been advanced to oppose
the Bumpers Amendment, most are not principled. They address the alleged self-interested motives of the commodity
producers who supported the law, but do not respond to the
more principled philosophical argument that convinced
these commodity producers of the justice of their cause. This
is an important result, for it indicates the philosophical challenge that still awaits those who would wish to place constraints on competitiveness arguments, not to mention those
who would wish to defeat them altogether.

COMPETITION AND THE SOCIAL CONTRACT

The argument for preferring domestic interests is a contractual argument, at bottom, but in favoring competitiveness so strongly over humanitarian assistance, it arrives at a conclusion that most liberal exponents of the contract tradition will find uncomfortable. Liberal contract theory has constructed ingenious solutions to the problem of economic opportunity for parties to the contract, but the competitiveness argument turns sharply on the assumption that the foreign recipients of development assistance are not party to the agreement that serves as the constitutional foundation of the state. The case, therefore, becomes relevant to the problem of duties beyond borders.

Contract theory attempts to show that political obligations to obey society's laws and to respect the rights of one's fellow citizens are consistent with enlightened self-interest. The rationally self-interested person will, so the theory goes, consent to certain politically imposed constraints and powers because doing so is a good bargain, when contrasted to the alternative. Although the terms of this bargain, and, therefore, of the resulting contract, vary in different versions of social contract theory, it is intrinsic to the bargaining situation that the emerging political obligations are limited to the contracting parties. If, for example, social contract theory entails a political duty to aid the poor, the duty can only be to aid the poor of one's own civil society. Only other parties to the contract can secure direct entitlement as the result of a contractual agreement.

Because its advocates implicitly take social contract theory to lay the foundations for modern democratic states, this conventional view of the limits to contractual obligations entails that political rights and duties not cross national borders, which, in turn, means that social contract theory is ineffectual for clarifying normative international political duties and rights. Yet few are willing to deny that normative considerations are relevant to international affairs.[1] The International Declaration of Human Rights of 1947 documents the importance of normative political principles in international relations, and recent philosophical literature on international justice testifies that political theorists are committed to finding justifications for policies that appear to entail duties beyond borders.

One way to approach the issues is to examine how one might respond to the principled argument of U.S. farmers in supporting the Bumpers Amendment. Although it has been convenient to develop a response in the political language in which the policy debate over the Bumpers Amendment was conducted, the larger goal of the book is to reexamine the problem of duties beyond borders under the assumption that economic, rather than military, competition is the dominant paradigm. This approach provides philosophically grounded international policy guidance by revising the concept of national interest, but does not couple this with a more comprehensive attempt to extend the scope of the social contract. The resulting version of social contract theory addresses the policy problems of transacting with other nations and peoples, but without bringing other nations or their citizens into the initial bargaining that establishes the basis of state power. The key to revising the concept of rational self-interest lies in a comparison of two models for the nation-state. The full details of this argument appear in Chapter 5, but a glimpse follows.

Hobbes's formulation of the social contract in *Leviathan* (1651) presumed that the individual's interest in government was primarily focused on personal security. Correlatively, national interests were defined chiefly in terms of securing national territory against invasion by foreign powers. Richard Rosecrance has shown that the Hobbesian model of the state corresponded fairly closely to the reality of European foreign policy following the Treaty of Westphalia in *The Rise of the Trading State* (1986). These states were relatively self-sufficient in production of staple commodities, and, with a few exceptions, opportunities for exchange with distant peoples were limited. The national interest of these territorial states, as Rosecrance calls them,

9

was in holding territory and protecting citizens' property against capture by foreign powers.

Rosecrance finds the territorial model of the state an increasingly ineffective basis for foreign policy. In contrast, he describes trading states, exemplified by nineteenth-century Great Britain, and by Japan, Taiwan, and states in the European Economic Community today. The trading state defines national interest in terms of its economic interdependence with other states, rather than its ability to protect private property. Indeed, too much emphasis on protection of property is antithetical to economic growth interests of individuals whose quality of life depends on exchange with peoples in distant lands. The trading state is, therefore, more focused on economic growth than on military security. Rosecrance examines the implications of these two models for traditional foreign policy issues, including U.S.–Soviet relations, but these topics do not concern the issues taken up in this book.

As the territorial state fits Hobbes's approach to the social contract, the trading state presents an alternative model. Here individuals are as interested in securing opportunities for exchange as they are in ensuring the security of their property. The analogy to individual self-interest at the level of the state transacting with other states must also be redefined. National interest consists in building self-sustaining economic and cultural relationships with other peoples, as well as in defending the nation against them. The result is a more subtle reading of the contractual mandate for foreign relations, one that emphasizes the importance of treating foreign peoples with respect, but that avoids the logical and conceptual difficulties encountered by those who would simply redefine the scope of the social contract in global terms. The aim here is to show that a more subtle understanding of the links between trade and development can be used in a novel approach to determine the justification for foreign assistance.

By implication, this argument also imposes constraints on competitiveness as a value for legitimating public policy. If the interpretation of national interest that emerges from a sophisticated contractual defense of competitiveness also sanctions respect and concern for the autonomous development of nations and peoples of the Third World, competitiveness must be tempered by a moderating vision of the self-directed interests being sought. Competitiveness does not, in other words, constitute a license for unrestrained greed on the part of the U.S. commercial sector. A more specific account of these constraints must await development of the argument.

THE SOCIAL CONTRACT AND DEVELOPMENT ASSISTANCE

Writing in 1987, Roger Riddell concluded that "a review of the literature on official aid reveals an almost complete absence of a systematic and comprehensive defence of the moral case for aid" (p. 74). By official aid, Riddell means development assistance programs paid for by public funds, and most generally conducted by organizations such as the World Bank, the various governmental aid agencies, and ad hoc organizations, such as the Consultive Group on International Agricultural Research (CGIAR). The emphasis on official aid is crucial, for there is an extensive philosophical literature on world hunger, famine relief, and duties to bring aid. The literature seldom distinguishes between official and unofficial aid, however. The context for developing philosophical arguments relating to the basis for foreign development assistance is divided, with little overlap between the development economics/international relations literature, which focuses on official aid, and the ethics/political theory literature, which focuses on the moral basis of aid without regard to its official or private character.

This is an important gap for this analysis. The Bumpers Amendment prevents AID from assisting foreign nationals. It says nothing about what Americans may or may not do, much less what they should do, when acting on their own. Most development professionals who work at AID would accept the claim that Americans have far more stringent duties to the foreign poor than the U.S. government has been willing to fulfill. Indeed, many have chosen their career out of a spirit of altruism. As government employees, however, they have an obligation to execute the mandate of congressionally approved law and policy. As such, their actions and decisions are far more informed by their ability to interpret the official mandate than by their personal moral views. Doubtless they attempt to interpret the mandate in the light of altruistic values, but laws such as the Bumpers Amendment make this task difficult.

The mandate for official aid emerges from a political process. A government official's first responsibility is to protect the integrity of that process. When the process produces legislation blocking policies that are (in the official's eyes) well supported by moral theory, moral theory ceases to be adequate. The official's more fundamental duty to the democratic process overrides. As such, it is important to have a philosophical approach to development ethics that explicitly acknowledges how much of what gets done will be constrained and influenced by mandates. Although this discussion focuses on public mandates, private development assistance generally depends on a mandate, too (Smith, 1990). A more cogent philosophical literature on hunger and on duties beyond borders would focus on how morality and moral theory bear on the formation of mandates endorsed by a large number of people. This book is the first step.

The analysis that follows is preoccupied with the mandate for official or public aid. The social contract tradition in political theory lends itself to such an analysis for two obvious reasons. First, as a theory of the warrant for state power, it is addressed directly to general philosophical questions of which the warrant for development assistance is one type. Second, since Rawls, at least, social contract theory has been understood as a philosophical strategy for arriving at consensus on policy, even when the parties to the contract have different (and incompatible) notions of the good. As such, the philosophical underpinnings of the Bumpers Amendment can be seen as a claim on public authority that stands in conflict with the claims made in the philosophical litera- ture. The social contract tradition has the promise of illus- trating how a common mandate for development assistance policy might be formed, even though a great deal of dis- agreement over the larger good remains.

A FEW DISCLAIMERS

Some potentially relevant topics have been ignored. Al- though the conflict between self-interest and altruism is, in one sense, central to the issues in the book, it has seemed reasonable to assume that individual human beings are capable of being moved by altruistic considerations, and by a sense of duty. Such an assumption appears to contradict the view that all human actions are self-interested, a view that continues to be influential among some social scientists. In fact, the social science image of the purely self-interested economic man is compatible with the idea that altruism and duty are effective motivators. One can admit that people act to satisfy their preferences so long as preference sets can include altruism and duty. But if one defines self- interested action to mean that anything a person does is self- interested, one has said nothing to constrain the discussion of altruistic or dutiful motivations. At the same time, if one views acts of self-interest and acts of generosity or sacrifice as motivated by different sorts of goals, then clearly most human activity is influenced by a variety of motives, includ- ing praiseworthy ones. Amartya Sen (1987) has written elo- quently on this point.

The implicit assumption here is that economic growth in developing countries is good, and that the goodness of eco- nomic growth does not need a great deal of clarification and defense. The latter half of this assumption is, of course, false. Samir Amin and Denis Goulet are among those who have written persuasively on the down side of economic growth and Riddell devotes at least two hundred pages to its defense. This author has tried to be sensitive to one element

13

of their critique, namely, that impressive aggregate growth indicators often translate into worsening conditions for the poor. Critics of development assistance have used this observation in an argument intended to show that a developed country's aid programs are self-serving; but bimodal growth ultimately cannot be in the interests of developed countries, as the discussion in Chapter 5 maintains. Nevertheless, the "growth is not development" debate is not a primary consideration in this analysis. Within developing countries, one may ask whether development destroys valued ways of life, whether it is equitable, whether it should aim to alleviate relative or absolute poverty, and how it should be constrained by the environment. The answers to these questions could conceivably undercut the assumption that economic growth is, on the whole, good. In addition, the standard of poverty, population growth, and land reform have become familiar topics in institutional analyses of food policy. Because this book stresses the politics of obligating public funds for foreign assistance within the United States, these important issues become relevant primarily to the extent that they complicate the domestic debate. The issue of whether agricultural development assistance is objectively a good idea, totally apart from conflicts of interest, remains. Even cursory literature reviews and summary discussions of development issues have been dispensed with to keep the main theme more narrowly focused.

A final qualification relates to environmental quality. Global limits to growth may also undercut the assumption that economic development in the Third World is good. If so, then the national interests of the developed world may *not* coincide with global development, contrary to the conclusions of the Brundtland report and to the argument in Chapters 5 and 6. Such a suggestion was the forgotten component of Garrett Hardin's writings on food policy and population more than two decades ago. In the intervening years, Hardin's assumptions about "the commons" have been criticized, as has his naive consequentialism, but Hardin's pragmatic assessment of the interests of developed countries

14

has not been directly rebutted. This point is taken up in Chapter 7, but the argument there merely stresses that during the 30-year period since Hardin and others began to issue warnings about food shortages, absolute world food deficits have been almost unheard of, and in most years surplus disposal has been the primary political problem. Although some commentators appear sanguine in making such a reply, a more responsible conclusion is that Hardin's time frame is off. There is no reason to think that the Earth's resources can be expanded indefinitely by cleverness and innovation; too many societies have already succumbed to ecological forces. At the same time, any satisfactory discussion of long-term environmental constraints on present food policy would involve enormously complicated technical information, conjoined with analysis of whether it would be morally and politically feasible, let alone advantageous, for developed countries to adopt a posture of competition with the developing world for finite resources. These are, of course, the primary burdens that the Brundtland Report has enjoined the global political community to take up. Chapter 7 concludes that, for the time being, at least, the availability of food resources suggests a different picture. Although that conclusion might need to be qualified by environmental factors, the technical complexity of food availability makes it impossible to give adequate attention to the problem of deciding how such factors should qualify it in this book.

THE DOUBLE TWIST BOOTLEG

Although I am by training and intellectual proclivity a philosophical theorist, my conclusions about the role and importance of political theory have been substantially reshaped by my work on the Bumpers Amendment. Throughout my research on the topic, I found myself anxious to get on to the case itself, and increasingly impatient with preliminary theoretical discussions that seem far afield from the concerns of those who actually participated in the politics of the Bumpers Amendment. The research that led me to write this book was initially intended to follow a different track. I received an International Affairs Fellowship from the Council on Foreign Relations in 1986 and 1987 to work at the U.S. Agency for International Development in Washington, D.C., and to study a problem in the management of international scientific research. Some background on how this initial research was conceived may provide insight into the perspective of this book, and explain how such a curious combination of disciplinary areas evolved.

Scientists use the term "bootlegging" to describe the practice of writing a grant application to make a research project appear to conform with the guidelines of a special grants program established to pursue other goals. Bootlegging also occurs when a scientist is able to convince a potential funding source to support ongoing research that would have been done anyway. In one example, an environmental scientist managed to get a research program that had been initiated under a solar power project picked up and expanded by the Strategic Defense Initiative. Although there is more than a hint of dishonesty in the term "bootlegging," the practice is not improper, so long as the scientist does not misrepresent the work that will be done.

Agricultural scientists have long regarded AID as an opportunity for bootlegging. The agency has a congressional mandate to enhance the development of poor countries. For most agricultural scientists, international development is not a primary professional goal, although it is increasingly common for individuals who want to help the foreign poor to become agricultural scientists. Most would describe their research goals in terms that would translate into increasing agricultural productivity or, even more narrowly, crop yield. Nevertheless, increasing agricultural productivity is often a promising means to enhance international development, so there is a natural fit between the goals of the agricultural scientist and the AID administrator. This fit has spawned several decades of AID-funded agricultural research. Agricultural scientists are doing nothing improper, then, by bootlegging AID programs; indeed, for AID to have overlooked the opportunity to fund some agricultural research would have been highly improper.

Nevertheless, one expects some tension between goals when bootlegging is going on. As long as the scientific goal is perceived as a means to the social goal, what interests the scientist, and motivates the research, may not be the most efficient means to achieve the social objectives of development. In some areas of developed world public policy, the tension has been resolved as scientists have come to control the policy agenda thoroughly, ensuring that research goals are perceived as having value intrinsically, not just within the context of a scientific research program. Scientific goals then simply *become* social goals. Shared norms regarding the goodness of truth and academic freedom reinforce this notion. As such, scientists and other academic researchers may readily feel few pangs of conscience when the bootlegging of development programs undercuts the humanitarian objectives for which they were originally intended.

The original research plan called for a study of the tension between agricultural research goals and international development goals to find out whether bootlegging was perceived as a serious problem either by scientists or by development professionals within AID. In the course of research, a large file of correspondence was reviewed concerning U.S. agricultural commodity producers' complaints about AID programs for enhancing developing country agriculture. (The substance of this controversy is taken up at length in Chapter 2.) U.S. farmers were asking many questions about the goals and consequences of agricultural development assistance. Many felt that helping foreign farmers grow could only make it more difficult for the U.S. farmer to compete in world grain markets.

The AID officers who were required to respond to these inquiries were, almost without exception, agricultural scientists. Most had doctoral degrees in biological disciplines, though they came to rely increasingly on the advice of agricultural economists. This group of professionals was consulting with many other scientists to construct a defense of

AID's agricultural assistance policy (dubbed in Chapter 4 the True Interests Thesis). At stake was AID's program in support of developing country agriculture, or, more probably, the freedom of U.S. university scientists to transfer information and technology to developing countries in the form of collaborative research. Failure to answer the questions emerging from the U.S. farm community may not have completely crippled AID's mandate to enhance development in poor countries, but it surely would have crimped the fit between the goals of development assistance and the research goals of agricultural scientists. The defense concocted by researchers and bureaucrats was shortened with the help of a media consultant to the slogan "Foreign aid helps, not hurts, U.S. agriculture."

What had, in effect, been going on, was a double twist bootleg. Agricultural scientists had established a strong link between their work and AID's development priorities. Now they had to protect the ground they had gained from a flank attack on the agency by U.S. farmers. The attack was a backhanded tribute to the first bootleg, because it assumed that agricultural science was successfully creating new competitors for the United States among producers in developing countries; but it threatened to undercut public support for the funds that made possible agricultural scientists' participation in development. An interest in what was happening to scientists' perception of development goals as the True Interests Thesis was being constructed ultimately led to the writing of this book.

The argument being assembled on behalf of agricultural development assistance in general and AID programs in particular seemed both repugnant and seductive at the same time. Defending aid on the ground that it helps the United States rather than the recipients is obnoxious, and many at AID who mouthed these lines must have found them distasteful. But the idea of aid has itself become increasingly distasteful as the paternalistic and manipulative color of bilateral relations that emerge from aid relationships has become clear. How much better it would be to have goals that place developed and developing states on a more nearly equal footing. This thinking precipitated a rationale for agricultural assistance that would serve as a basis for several components of U.S. international food policy. This rationale needed to justify U.S. agricultural assistance, but it also needed to soften the stress being placed on development goals by the double twist bootleg of the True Interests Thesis. Whether this book has succeeded can only be judged by its readers.

Chapter 1

The food weapon and the strategic concept of food policy

The phrase "food as a weapon" is generally traced to Earl Butz, secretary of agriculture under Presidents Nixon and Ford, but the concept hardly could have originated with him. When princes defended themselves from marauders by retreating into the fortress castles of the medieval era, the siege – starving them out – was one of the attacker's tactical options. Butz's idea was that the United States might starve another nation into submission, not with a military blockade, but simply by refusing to sell or give them grain. Secretary Butz left a legacy of aphorisms that have come to haunt U.S. agricultural policy in the intervening years. His suggestion that the United States should regard food as a weapon in the conduct of bilateral foreign policy relations with the developing world is conceptually linked to his injunctions to "get big or get out" and to plant "fencerow to fencerow." These precepts are linked by a vision of U.S. agriculture dominating undersupplied world grain markets well into the future. U.S. farmers could get rich while helping stave off worldwide hunger and famine, and the U.S. government would find a new source of power in world relations.

Butz was not alone in believing that food scarcity would preoccupy international diplomacy during the final quarter of the twentieth century. Food policy literature of the mid-to-late 1970s is full of dire predictions of undersupply and warnings of famine (Singer, 1972; ERS, 1974; Hardin, 1974; IFPRI, 1976). Events of the 1980s, however, appear to have

falsified much of the basis for linking a reevaluation of the political meaning of food with a call for increased farm production. World markets became glutted with both food and oil. Foreign sales of U.S. farm products became a vulnerable target, rather than a weapon, in a trade war with other industrialized nations (ERS, 1985; White and Hanrahan, 1986). The phrase "food as a weapon" has been heard less frequently in foreign policy debates following this turn of events; nevertheless it is relevant to ponder the implications of this metaphor, even while its pragmatic credibility appears at lowest ebb. Although current predictions call for continued oversupply through the foreseeable future, climatic disturbances and population growth have the potential to reverse this situation both suddenly and in the long run. Even a temporary world food shortage could restore the appearance of credibility to the food weapon. Furthermore, the food weapon metaphor is not without implications for food and agricultural assistance policy, even while excess production languishes on the docks and in the silos of the American grainary. The FY 1987 budget of the United States allocates nearly 70 percent of economic assistance funds to three countries: Israel, Egypt, and Pakistan. Other sections of the foreign assistance budget reflect similar priorities. Conversely, the United States has ended or curtailed assistance to countries such as Nicaragua, Ethiopia, and Zimbabwe. In each case, action has been justified by a general policy of tailoring U.S. Agency for International Development (AID) policy to geopolitical imperatives, of using aid (including food and technical agricultural assistance) both as a reward for favors and as retaliation for offenses against the United States (Osterlund, 1986). The food weapon metaphor is very much alive in AID programming.

THE MORAL BASIS OF AID AND TRADE

U.S. foreign aid has always been allocated according to a blend of diplomatic and humanitarian motives. The primary

motive for trade, however, is neither diplomatic nor human-itarian, but profit. Trade agreements are intended to define the constraints on international markets. Even when food is sold at subsidy, assistance transfers need not take place within the mechanism of world food markets. The humani-tarian aims of aid appear to stand in contrast to the self-interested aims of trade. What is more, security and eco-nomic assistance are routinely allocated according to the "behavior modifying" aims of foreign policy (Shaughnessy, 1977). Food and agricultural aid are in the same package of foreign assistance programs as foreign sales of military weapons and economic aid tied to treaties and agreements, including those that authorize U.S. military bases on foreign soil. The simple legislative packaging of AID programs, no doubt, encourages analysis in terms of security goals and military objectives. There are, therefore, prima facie reasons for thinking that aid and trade sanctions must be treated as separate issues, governed by distinct moral imperatives. The simple division of aid and trade, however, neglects impor-tant differences in the nature and purpose of foreign assis-tance. It is, therefore, useful to examine, in turn, the moral basis of trade and of those forms of foreign assistance in which food and agricultural development policy play a sig-nificant role.

International politics is thought to center primarily on the construction and maintenance of alliances and national boundaries, supported by tradition, public will, and military power. Trade would then be allocated to the monetary or economic goals of a nation. The distinction between political and economic goals is vague and uncertain even in the best circumstances; nevertheless, it has served as a basis for ob-jecting to sanctions or embargoes when trade relations are altered not to maximize profit, but for other, often contrary, reasons. The distinction more properly stated is between diplomatic or security objectives and economic or monetary objectives, as economic goals are also political goals. Any at-tempt to make a sharp distinction between political and eco-

nomic motives isolates the goals of profit maximization and balance of payments from the matrix of competing claims that, at any given time, determine the national interest of a sovereign state; but such a result is absurd. Interesting philosophical issues arise when national interest appears to conflict with the profit-maximizing goals of citizens or with humanitarian imperatives, but the fascinating character of such conflicts should not be allowed to overshadow the more typical case in which these goals are consonant. Encouragement of trade is, in normal circumstances, a national political goal, one of the traditional aims on which a social contract is thought to be founded.

Foreign aid can be rendered in four forms: emergency, development, economic, or security (military) assistance. Of these, only emergency aid and development assistance are directly relevant to food policy. Economic and security assistance are rendered under a government's mandate to preserve and protect the safety of its citizens. They consist of monetary and military support to governments deemed friendly to that purpose. Economic and security assistance are paradigm examples of foreign policy motivated by diplomacy and military imperatives. The unambiguous character of their mandate perennially influences the more tentative goals of emergency relief and development assistance.

Emergency aid is frequently a direct gift, or deep subsidy, of food for the short-term relief of famine and malnutrition. The intent is to save lives and reduce suffering. Generally, emergency assistance has not been used as a bargaining chip in a larger foreign policy gambit, at least not when genuine need has been established. The 1984 famine in Ethiopia is a case in point. Reagan administration officials at first resisted aid programs on the ground that the Marxist government of Ethiopia had created, or at least exacerbated, the hunger and that it was its responsibility to redress the policy problems before aid could become effective. When public awareness of the famine began to mount, the Reagan administration reversed its position on aid, leading some to question whether the United States had, indeed, attempted to use food aid as a weapon against the government of Ethiopia. As hindsight has shown, the situation was far more complex. Many lives were saved by the relief effort that ensued, but the Reagan administration's original view of the Ethiopian government was not unfounded. Media attention on the famine probably influenced the regime in Addis Ababa to be more cooperative with the international relief effort than it might have been. To the extent that world attention did moderate policies in Ethiopia, the change in U.S. policy may have been as much a response to an improvement in the prospects for effective humanitarian assistance as to the growing public outcry. In any case, once the issue became sharply defined in terms of saving lives and relieving misery, support that might have existed for conditioning aid on political reform in Ethiopia evaporated. There is, therefore, precedent for separating the humanitarian basis of emergency assistance not only from trade considerations but from diplomatic imperatives as well.

Development assistance includes gifts, long-term concessional sales of food, and also technical and financial support intended to strengthen economies by increasing employment, building productive capacity, and improving human capacity through health and education. Although it is generally accepted that governments use power appropriately to render emergency short-term relief, the moral basis for long-term development assistance has been more controversial (Walzer, 1981). Peter Singer's 1972 paper "Famine, Affluence, and Morality" set the terms for philosophical discussion of this controversy at whether development assistance is supported by an optional duty of charity or demanded by justice. Although the details of this debate are relevant to conclusions that follow, the alternatives of charity and justice do not exhaust the moral ground on which development assistance might be offered. An alternative account of development assistance would ground it securely in the national interest imperatives that have served as the moral basis for the encouragement of trade.

A final caveat, however, might be noted both by way of clarification and by way of excuse for not enjoining the recent philosophical debate more directly. The position developed throughout the book is couched within the terms of mainstream capitalist, some would say conservative, thought. The legitimacy or desirability of international relations built in large measure on trade is not questioned. The argument will, no doubt, fail to impress radical critics who have brought the legitimacy of capitalist international political economy into question (Amin, 1976; George, 1984). The aim of this analysis, however, is to establish an alternative philosophical basis for food policy that avoids two obsessions that have plagued capitalist food and development policy. One is the overidentification of national interest goals with those of military security. The other is to see the issue as a conflict between property rights and distributive justice. The view that will be sketched here, therefore, seeks to define a philosophical position consistent with the general aims of capitalist liberalism while avoiding the pitfalls of Hobbesian or libertarian conservatism. The approach leaves important philosophical options and objectives unmet, but there is only so much one can attempt in a single project.

AID AND TRADE: THE LINK

Despite the lack of fit between trade issues and some more visible forms of humanitarian emergency relief, links between economic development (the goal of food and agricultural aid) and international trade provide ample basis for resisting pressure to view these policies under separate rubrics. Humanitarian aid does figure in agricultural trade policy. Food shipments donated under the Food for Peace (PL 480) program have provided a convenient mechanism for reducing U.S. agricultural surplus, while keeping excess production off world markets. Stabilization of U.S. grain reserves was one of the original motives for enacting PL 480. Food for Peace programs have, however, been criticized for

25

their impact on domestic markets of recipient nations. Local markets in developing countries can be flooded with cheap, high-quality imported grain devastating poor local farmers (Shuman, 1977). Food aid, therefore, affects trade policy for both donor and recipient nation. These mutual effects provide a preliminary reason for evaluating foreign assistance within the context of trade policy rather than security assistance.

Although the motivation for development assistance has traditionally been humanitarian, theories of agricultural commodity trade and of economic development support the two-stage thesis that (1) expansion of demand for U.S. agricultural exports is dependent on economic growth in nonindustrialized, low-income countries and (2) the most likely route to economic growth in most such countries is through development of the agricultural sector. These theoretical tenets provide the conceptual basis for the Linking Thesis (*LT*), which states that foreign agricultural development assistance stimulates not only economic growth for recipient nations but also trade prospects of developed nations (Mellor, 1972; Rossmiller and Tutwiler, 1987). In addition to its theoretical basis, *LT* is supported by a growing body of empirical studies on the correlation between development and agricultural trade patterns (Kellogg et al., 1986; Christiansen, Robert E., 1987; Christiansen, C. et al., 1987; Bachman and Paulino, 1979).

The first component of *LT* is implied by a basic postulate in agricultural economics. The demand for agricultural products, and particularly food, is virtually inelastic, and consumption of agricultural products is therefore only moderately sensitive to price. The assumption here is that people will buy what food they need but obtain little additional benefit from having more than they need. As such, a drop in food prices means that a greater share of the consumer's income will go toward nonfood items; even when consumers do expand their food budget as their wealth increases, the extra expenditure is traced to convenience features, such as frozen pizza, or service, such as eating at a restaurant. One important exception to this general rule, however, occurs when consumers make a dietary shift from greater consumption of basic grains, such as wheat and rice, toward consumption of meat, poultry, and dairy products. These foods are obtained by feeding animals a comparatively greater portion of feed grains, such as maize or soybeans, than would be consumed by a human eating a diet of basic grains. Such a shift in diet, therefore, does lead to an increased demand for agricultural products, and it also involves a change in the type of products demanded. Aside from changing dietary preference, the only major market growth in agricultural products comes from an increase in the number of consumers.

As it happens, the developing world holds promise for increased demand from both potential sources. Diets in the developing world rely heavily on basic grains, but as incomes increase many consumers are expected to consume more animal proteins. This will create a demand for animal feeds that far exceeds current demands for basic grains. In addition, the number of consumers in the developing world will increase as these countries become more industrialized. People currently involved in subsistence agriculture, or those too poor to provide themselves with adequate diets, even in basic grains, will become consumers of agricultural products as they obtain cash income from industrial employment or perhaps even from the commercial sale of such nonfood commodities as cotton or tobacco. General economic growth in the developing world is, therefore, one of the few sources for expansion of agricultural exports.

But how can economic growth be achieved in the developing world? Writing in *The Wall Street Journal*, Randall B. Purcell (1987) answers,

> Contrary to conventional wisdom, the best way to achieve this is through the development of local agriculture in the developing countries themselves. Because most Third World workers are employed in agriculture, the development of this

sector achieves a more even distribution of income than does the development of other sectors. And in the early and middle stage of economic development, as people have more money, the first thing they spend it on is increasing and diversifying their consumption of food.

Theories of economic development from the 1950s recognized the importance of industrialization in general economic growth and for this reason stressed the formation of manufacturing capabilities in developing countries. This "conventional wisdom" referred to by Purcell has been significantly revised as development economists have improved their understanding of agriculture. Investment in capital-intensive manufacturing industries created severe political problems in many developing economies. Wealth tended to accrue to small elites, while industrial workers, and the urban poor lured to cities by false expectation of industrial growth, expended a high percentage of their income on basic necessities. Agricultural sectors still organized for plantation production of commodities for export and subsistence production of commodities for personal use were unable to meet the food needs of the new urban proletariat (Todaro, 1985).

Some of these problems might be avoided by revising the assumption that agriculture is unimportant for general economic development. A carefully chosen investment in agriculture should, as Purcell notes, spread capital (and, therefore, return on capital) across many more people in the developing economy than does a single large investment in industrial manufacturing. The multiplier effect of increasing incomes throughout the economy is greater when more incomes are increased, even if by smaller amounts. Furthermore, increases in rural income are less likely to be expended on imported luxury items, thereby easing pressures on foreign exchange. Finally, the increased production of food and improved efficiency of farming should release labor for industrialization, creating demand for purchased food while increasing the supply of basic foods available on commercial markets. Agricultural development does not replace industrial development in such a scenario, but it *is* seen as being of coequal importance in contributing to overall economic growth (Mellor and Johnston, 1984; Baum and Talbert, 1985). This revision of development theory completes *LT* by showing how growth in world markets is linked with exactly the sort of foreign assistance rendered by AID.

TRADE WARS AND REAL WARS

Food trade and aid are inextricably fundamental components of the U.S. bilateral relationship with other nations, their governments, and their peoples. In some cases, the phrase "food as a weapon" is used euphemistically to refer to the way that aid or trade policy can be linked to other aspects of the bilateral relationship, such as emigration, capital investment, or cultural exchange. For example, even in a food surplus, food export policy might be used as a tool to express pleasure or displeasure at another country's actions, perhaps by dumping surplus food in a deliberate attempt to spoil that country's market. Food is here a weapon only in the broadest sense, whereby *any* component of a bilateral relationship might be construed as a weapon for influencing other components. Such an interpretation equates all political imperatives relevant to food policy with the phrase "food as a weapon." Although there are indeed ethical questions to be raised about the diplomatic use of food policy, they are different from and more subtle than those raised when food trade is seriously posed as an option for achieving diplomatic and security objectives traditionally sought with military power.

The parlance "trade war" is such a commonplace that one can easily overlook the obvious difference between trade war and war itself. Trade war describes the series of tit for tat actions by two or more nations to adjust tariffs, quotas, subsidies, and any number of other economic levers available to governments in the attempt to secure advantages in international trade. That such actions are possible presupposes

functioning bilateral or multilateral institutions and procedures for international exchange, as well as some admittedly
controversial concepts of fairness for such transactions. Real
wars, that is, wars in which the military forces of two or
more nations perpetrate sustained campaigns of violence
against one another, and frequently against civilian property
and populations as well, have generally been fought (particularly in the twentieth century) under conditions in which
such shared conventions have broken down almost entirely.
That is not to say that real wars are never fought within
some framework of shared conventions, nor to suggest that
some tactics useful in trade disagreements, such as the embargo, might not also find application in warfare. Nevertheless, there is an obvious sense in which the term "trade
war," when it describes the ploys and counterploys of international exchange, makes highly metaphorical use of the
word "war."

Within this purely metaphorical sense of war, the various
economic sanctions and policies at a government's disposal
might also be described as weapons. Food is then a weapon
in the sense that a government may enact tariffs or subsidies
on agricultural products as part of a general plan to affect
foreign exchange or in retaliation for similar actions by a foreign competitor. Trade wars can affect individuals by protecting them against foreign competition, but they can also raise
the prices paid by consumers and, in extreme cases, deny
them access to basic necessities. The use of food policy in
trade actions is, therefore, not without moral significance;
the issues are the standard ones of economic justice. Nevertheless, the phrase "food weapon" employed in the context
of trade disagreements is clearly parasitic on the general
metaphor of warfare in the expression "trade war."

Butz's intent in coining the phrase "food as a weapon" is
not clear. He contrasted it to the "oil weapon" of the OPEC
states, which suggests that he may have been speaking
within the general context of bilateral relations, though oil,
like food, is not without strategic significance. Nevertheless,

subsequent authors have clearly intended that food trade be analyzed on a par with tanks and missiles, as a component of the U.S. arsenal (Ponte, 1982; George, 1977). Under this interpretation, the food weapon raises ethical issues because the use of any weapon raises ethical issues. A weapon is an instrument for destroying an enemy who is bent on subjugating you. There are, of course, other uses, but they are disanalogous to the food weapon's proposed use and consequently irrelevant to the issue at hand. The plausibility of a food weapon, therefore, turns on a strong analogy to military weapons, which are of two kinds; tactical and strategic. To make a moral evaluation of the food weapon, the strength and exact import of this analogy must be assessed.

FOOD AS A TACTICAL WEAPON

The first point to be established concerns the possible analogy between food and the traditional tools of war, referred to here as tactical weapons. Tactical weapons are those used in combat: bayonets, barbed wire, bombs, bombers, pistols, machine guns, punji sticks, napalm, and torpedoes. The traditional moral criteria for the use of tactical weapons have included injunctions against inflicting needless suffering and against unnecessary destruction of nonmilitary personnel and personal property. As such, two characteristics become important in determining the moral acceptability of tactical weapons; destructive power and the deliverability of that power.

Destructive power refers to the weapon's capacity to render enemies harmless by killing, injuring, or, in some other way, incapacitating them once a target has been struck. Assuming the destructive force of the weapon can be delivered, how likely is the weapon to be effective? In this connection, the cruelty of a particular weapon becomes pertinent. Weapons that incapacitate an enemy without undue pain and suffering are, ceteris paribus, morally preferable. Weapons that have success in destroying enemies are tactically preferable. These are not necessarily exclusive categories.

Deliverability refers to the ability of a soldier to strike the target. How likely is the target, and only the target, to receive the destructive power of the weapon? The primary moral consideration is indicated by the qualification. A weapon capable of being precisely aimed at military targets is morally preferable to one that exposes innocent people and their property to the risk of destruction. Tactically speaking, the criterion is accuracy: Will a weapon hit what it is aimed at? Again these considerations can and do conjoin in practice. These are the considerations raised, for example, by Richard J. Krickus in his discussion of the morality of chemical/biological war. Krickus argues for a distinction between chemical and biological weapons based on the fact that chemical agents can be limited to battlefield use, though biological agents cannot be easily controlled. The nature of biological weapons makes discriminate use against military targets impossible. Krickus concludes, "From the viewpoint of the just war doctrine, then, chemical weapons can be justified, but biological weapons cannot" (1979, p. 494).

The analogy between food and conventional tactical weapons depends minimally on an assessment of the proposed food policy in terms of destructive power and deliverability. The primary moral considerations arise in connection with deliverability. Following Krickus, the moral justifiability of a tactical weapon is partially a function of a user's capacity to control and direct its destructive force. Weapons that destroy indiscriminately, that cannot successfully be confined to a field of battle or to military targets are not morally acceptable according to the dictates of just war.

The telling point against the food weapon metaphor arises when purely tactical aspects of deliverability are addressed. Deliverability refers to the weapon's capacity to be aimed at and strike a target with destructive force. A weapon that cannot be aimed is worthless. The problem with food assistance programs, however, has been that gifts of food or the benefits of increased production are poorly distributed, never reaching the intended recipients. Delivering five hundred tons of explosives on target is far easier than delivering five hundred tons of rice. There is little reason to assume that withheld food would be taken from the mouths of the target population; in the absence of contrary evidence, however, one can reasonably assume that the effects of withholding aid will be as poorly distributed as those of assistance programs. Certainly military and political targets will be among the last to experience the debilitating effects of a food weapon. The tactical effectiveness of food is limited by the fact that food aid must be distributed through various market and bureaucratic mechanisms of the targeted country. Economic and political forces are free to influence the trajectory of the weapon (Rothschild, 1976). It is roughly like attacking an enemy with a bomb of significant destructive power, but leaving the final detonation point up to the enemy. An enemy determined to resist attack will simply direct the destructive force of the food weapon away from military and political installations and toward the sector of the population least critical to the preservation of military and political authority and power.

To conclude, food makes a poor tactical weapon, not because it lacks destructive capability, and not because it affects the innocent, but because it cannot be controlled. The point of impact for a food policy initiative is largely determined by factors beyond the control of the agent using the weapon, and, indeed, to a significant degree by factors within the control of the parties the weapon has been directed against. Surely, once poor relations between two nations have escalated to the point of tactical warfare there can be little thought of trade in foodstuffs between the nations; but a wartime breakdown in food trade has more to do with the general bilateral relationship of warring nations than it does with food per se. There can be little point in discussing food as a weapon if there are no strong parallels between the use of weapons and the use of food policy as a leveraging mechanism. The analogy between food leveraging and tactical weapon use breaks down precisely on the point of deliverability. To talk of food as a weapon makes no sense when precise targeting is relevant to effectiveness.

FOOD AS A STRATEGIC WEAPON

If food cannot be successfully compared with tactical weapons, perhaps it may still be compared with strategic weapons. The purpose of a strategic weapon is expressed not in its use but in the threat of its use. Strategic weapons are intended to affect the policies and actions of a potential enemy; if such weapons are used against an enemy, their strategic function has failed. The rationale for increasing the power and effectiveness of nuclear weapons is to preclude their use by making the probable consequences of their use utterly unacceptable. It is crucial here to recognize the distinction between traditional deterrent effects of standing armies and deterrence policy as it informs nuclear strategy. The presence of a powerful, standing army deters acts that might lead to war when a potential enemy is persuaded that the losses from engaging such an army outweigh any gain. The point of nuclear deterrence strategy as conceived by its architects throughout the 1950s and 1960s was to escalate the assumed costs of hostile action far beyond the level at which any consideration of trade-offs would be meaningful. Potential enemies will be deterred from attack when they know that the threat of utter annihilation awaits. As such, strategic weapons are intended to prevent wars, not to be used in war. They are intended to influence a rival's acts so as to make any thought of war impossible.

The idea of food as a policy leverage is clearly commensurate with the basic thrust of the deterrence argument. Talk of food as a weapon arose in Western culture at a time when Americans had grown accustomed to the use of nuclear weapons for deterrence under a policy of mutually assured destruction (MAD). As such, we have become used to the idea that the primary application of a weapon is not use, but disuse, its being held in abeyance against an unwanted turn of events. Given the United States' pre-eminence as a food exporter, why not tie U.S. food policy to the extraction of promises and behavioral conditions? Precisely because it fails tactically, food is not plausible as a weapon of deterrence in the traditional sense, but perhaps it could be compared to MAD. Surely the United States could wreak havoc in the world's food markets if it so decided, so why not turn this power to its benefit? Why not deter other nations from policies it fails to approve just as it deters other nations from attacking with its nuclear arsenal?

Strategic nuclear weapons differ from tactical weapons in that their vast destructive power makes it impossible to draw a distinction between military and nonmilitary targets. The targeting problems associated with tactical application of food trade may, therefore, not appear relevant to strategic concerns. Certainly the fact that harm can be shifted to civilian populations, preserving military strength, is less damaging to strategic considerations. The food weapon would require only two prerequisites to emerge as a strategic option: (1) the United States would have to declare its intent to retaliate against unwanted actions by cutting off aid and trade in food commodities and (2) the threatened nation would have to be convinced that withdrawal of U.S. food would cause a significant, if not massive, disruption of its social order.

There is evidence that the second criterion is not likely to be fulfilled. When the United States cut off agricultural trade with the Soviet Union in 1979 following the invasion of Afghanistan, the Soviets were able to replace lost American grain shipments with contracts from other exporters. The pattern of world grain trade shifted, but the embargo did not substantively affect Soviet access to grain. Indeed, critics of the Carter administration claimed that U.S. farmers had been hurt far more than the Soviets (Clark, 1981; Paarlberg, 1980). The U.S. Department of Agriculture's post hoc evaluation of the embargo concluded that there were no net losers; Soviets found new suppliers, and U.S. farmers found new markets (ERS, 1986). When longshoremen refused to load grain bound for Iran during the hostage crisis, their actions were even more futile (Healy and Batie, 1980). To ensure deterrent effectiveness, the United States would have to ensure that alternative sources of food were unavailable to the enemy and that U.S. food sold to neutral parties would not find its way into enemy hands. In other words, the United States would have to control precisely that which it does not control, the international food distribution system. Short of total control, one might argue, the United States might still be able to cause an opponent some inconvenience. The enemy would have to seek new suppliers possibly charging inflated prices. The enemy government might decide that the nuisance created by a food embargo is not worth the trouble; the policy objective might be achieved. Perhaps, but such petty concerns will not deter a nation from policies that it takes seriously. This limitation in scope is of philosophical importance, because the moral justification of deterrence appeals to the momentous importance of that which is deterred.

If strategic nuclear weapons can be countenanced morally at all, it is only because their extreme effectiveness is thought to deter the realization of a greater harm altogether. Modern deterrence is therefore a strategy for avoiding war among nations capable of mutually assured destruction. Deterrence *may* therefore be justified in light of the extreme consequences of nuclear war. A measure that promotes the avoidance of nuclear war may be morally justifiable even if that measure paradoxically entails the intention to commit the morally indefensible act of nuclear war (Kavka, 1978). Without the conditions of such extreme consequences, deterrence devolves into mere extortion, bullying, and adventurism. But the issues related to food policy are not of such extreme consequence. Failure of U.S. policy in a Third World nation might plausibly be described as a contributing event in a slide toward war, but in and of itself it would hardly be tantamount to the degree of harm required to achieve strategic deterrence. One cannot allow the slippery slope in which any failure of policy is unacceptable; such an argument proves far too much and is too adaptable to changes in mood, style, and opinion. Policy objectives cannot be universally equated with national survival. Failure in policy should not be compared with the threat of annihilation posed by nuclear war.

CABBAGES AND KINGS

The food weapon metaphor arises during an age of deterrence by no coincidence. The strategy of deterrence is predicated on the possession of weapons so devastating that an enemy will not dare to attack so long as there is even the vaguest hint that they might be used. Deterrence hinges on the destructive power of the weapon, but the strategy of deterrence goes beyond destruction of enemy forces. The deterrent capacity of strategic nuclear weapons resides not in their effectiveness against military targets but in their capacity to annihilate an opponent's civilian population. This strategy is, therefore, a euphemism for a kind of extortion that can be morally justified, perhaps, but is a form of deterrence against attack that deviates rather substantially from traditional military norms.

The arrival of strategic nuclear weapons is significant in the evolution of U.S. food policy because nuclear weapons seem to have changed the way that we think about weapons. Nuclear weapons demand thinking the unthinkable or intending to do what must never be done. Nuclear deterrence has allowed U.S. foreign policymakers to become too accustomed to making threats that can never be carried out. In fact, the food weapon metaphor cannot sensibly be grounded in any traditional, that is preatomic, sense of weaponry. Using food as a strategic weapon differs from the conventional siege in tactically crucial respects. Unlike a true strategic weapon, however, food has a piecemeal effect and is impossible to target effectively. As such, it is only meaningful as an empty threat. Extension of the food weapon metaphor is, therefore, bankrupt from both an ethical and literary standpoint. Ethically it come down to bullying, and idle bullying, at that. What is more, it fails metaphorically because, far from revealing a deep similarity of form to standard military weapons, the food weapon attains verisimilitude only by exploiting a flaccid and obscurantist trend in contemporary political discourse. The food weapon is plausible only as a weapon of deterrence, but linking food policy with strategic aims devalues the meaning of "deterrence" by making it equivalent to bluffing in geopolitical poker. Such a result serves neither food policy nor nuclear strategy.

An acceptance of the Linking Thesis and a rejection of any quasimilitary basis for the food weapon metaphor combine to form two basic tenets for understanding the moral imperatives in the political use of food. *LT* establishes the impact of world development on the agricultural trade prospects of donor nations. This link provides a basis for interpreting aid policy consistently with national interest imperatives that have come to govern trade relations. Because development in the Third World is consistent with trade-based national goals, the tensions between political and humanitarian motives should be somewhat abated at the operational level. But this happy confluence of motives can be realized only if military-based national goals are excluded from the set of political motives governing food policy. The rationale for this imperative is as much conceptual as moral. Military weapons provide a backing for policy only within a narrow framework defined in large part by their war-fighting capacity. This framework cannot be extended to bilateral economic relations easily, precisely because the capacity for economic retaliation is so tenuous and laden with ambiguity. As such, potential geopolitical uses of food policy come down either to a morally objectionable form of idle bullying, or to the sort of symbolic gesture typical of diplomacy, intended to communicate umbrage or encouragement but not expected to influence materially the policies of a foreign state. The first alternative must be rejected altogether, and the second, consistent with traditional uses and abuses of trade policy, must be balanced against the broader national goals demanded by the encouragement of trade.

The preceding arguments sketch the basis for a food policy founded philosophically on a government's responsibility to serve national interest, with some of the more poisonous elements of national interest isolated by the negative critique of the food weapon. Some might object that self-interested motives have led to poorly conceived food aid programs in the past; the desire to stabilize domestic food stocks clearly precipitated the Food for Peace program without regard for its impact on recipient peoples. *LT*, however, links development assistance with national interest by demonstrating the importance of increasing income among the poor, the basic goal of development, whatever its motives. National interest is served by strengthening world markets. This strengthening, however, is not obtained, as before, through short-term manipulation of supply but through long-term growth in demand. Only genuine development, with benefits distributed broadly across poor segments of recipient populations, would satisfy the conditions that make aid serve national interest. In doing so, food and development policies are political in that they are justified by basic political mandates of democratic society. The duty to serve the nation by strengthening trade and increasing national income is neither inconsistent with nor implied by international justice or charity. As such *LT* provides an independent and persuasive moral foundation for the political imperatives of food policy. It alsoprovides a prima facie rationale for making foreign development assistance consistent with domestic development goals sought through foreign trade and brings development aid under the aegis of national interest. Although *LT* provides no basis for denying the humanitarian goals of development, its heavy reliance on national interest inevitably introduces a tension that those who have advocated humanitarian arguments for aid may find objectionable. Ultimately the argument for *LT* and for a philosophy of national interest depends on situational factors that limit the applicability of competing alternatives. The case, therefore, requires detailed specification of the contest for debate about the goals of food and development policy. The events precipitating passage of the Bumpers Amendment in 1986 are an excellent example of that context.

Chapter 2

The Bumpers Amendment

In November 1985, Senator Dale Bumpers first offered an amendment intended to prohibit foreign aid activities that would encourage export of agricultural commodities from developing countries. The bill stressed competition for world markets between potential exporters from the developing world and U.S. farmers. The amendment (No. 1129) reads, in part,

> None of the funds to be appropriated to carry out chapter 1 of the Foreign Assistance Act of 1981 may be available for any testing or breeding feasibility study, variety improvement or introduction, consultancy, publication, conference, or training in connection with the growth or production in a foreign country for export if such export would compete in world markets with a similar commodity grown or produced in the United States. (U.S. Senate, 1985)

A similar version, now commonly referred to as the Bumpers Amendment, was reintroduced in May 1986 and has become law.[1] In Bumpers's words, the act is to "prevent American tax dollars from being used to help foreign countries who are trying to take our export markets."[2]

The potential consequences of this law are far reaching. The U.S. Agency for International Development (AID) is required to suspend research and implementation projects that could enable poor foreign farmers to increase commercial production of commodities such as meat, maize, or wheat that are exported from the United States, and also of commodities such as palm oil that are not produced for export in the United States, but may substitute for U.S. commodities. As the law is tied to appropriation of funds, rather than project management, these restrictions also apply to U.S. contributions to multilateral agencies such as the World Bank and the International Agricultural Research Centers (IARCs), famous for the success of the "Green Revolution" in strengthening the developing world's production of wheat and rice. In addition to these direct impacts, the Bumpers Amendment could negatively affect the pace of world economic development, leading, ironically, to declining growth in demand for the very agricultural exports that the legislation was intended to protect (Kellogg et al., 1986; Rossmiller and Tutwiler, 1987).

Finally, the amendment has broad implications for the future of agricultural research. Indeed, all publicly funded scientific research that could affect the productivity and efficiency of foreign nations becomes vulnerable if the basic principle of the Bumpers Amendment is applied to authorizing legislation for agencies such as the National Science Foundation or the National Institutes of Health. In spirit, the law makes international agricultural research subject to a test of national economic loyalty. Scientists could be prevented from experimentation, collaboration, and even travel to foreign countries. Foreign graduate students could be prevented from attending American universities. Such events are not likely to transpire in agricultural research and are even less probable for other areas of science. Their potential, however, indicates the implications of a strong interpretation of Senator Bumpers's argument.

This chapter summarizes the politics that preceded, some would say caused, the Bumpers Amendment. However, no attempt is made to assess the likely consequences of this law. The Bumpers Amendment points toward the philosophical principle that provides the most potent challenge to foreign aid in the form of development assistance. The principle is stated in Senator Bumpers's comment about the appropriate use of tax dollars, but the philosophical beliefs that support it were expressed in the stream of letters, articles, and press statements on behalf of American farmers that preceded passage of the amendment in Congress. Although Bumpers's words reflect a philosophical principle, events leading to passage of the Bumpers Amendment were influenced at least as much by the economic and political circumstances of American agriculture during the period in question as by philosophical interpretations of the social contract. Nevertheless, to assert that philosophical considerations were absent from their motivations entirely would needlessly impugn the character of the participants. Although justification of the Bumpers Amendment depends on a defense, or critique, of principle, the importance of principle in public policy can only be grasped against the backdrop of more conventional political considerations.

PUBLIC RESEARCH FOR FOREIGN FARMERS: THE POLITICAL MILIEU

The Bumpers Amendment was reintroduced in 1986 following a series of attacks on AID science policy that date back to the early 1980s. In 1982, newspaper items critical of AID's Collaborative Research Support Project on peanuts (Beegle, 1982; Anonymous, 1982; Wayne, 1983) precipitated equally critical comments in the *Congressional Record*.[3] Three years later, national newspapers ran items linking trade problems to the success of international agricultural development projects (Sinclair, 1986). An erroneous report pegging U.S. public support for international farm production research at $341,137,588 was picked up by a number of farm publications, and criticism of international agricultural research was rekindled.[4] The general thrust of this criticism was that these programs harmed the already weakened U.S. foreign trade in agricultural commodities, and, therefore, the income of agricultural producers. As such, these programs represented a misuse of public funds.

Public criticism of U.S. development assistance policy can be analyzed in several threads. The common theme in all

43

these lines of attack is simply dissatisfaction with the status quo. In addition to the challenges from farm groups, development assistance policies that had been pursued by institutions such as AID, the World Bank, the Food and Agriculture Organization (FAO) of the United Nations, and other public sector donors were being vehemently attacked by critics on the left. Their criticism was twofold. First, leftists claimed that the developed world was only making developing countries more dependent by extending so-called aid programs.[5] Second, they noted undesirable environmental consequences of attempts to transfer industrial agricultural technologies to developing countries.[6] Critics on the left would not have endorsed the suggestion that AID funding should be curtailed because it harmed the trade interests of U.S. farmers, but neither were they inclined to defend U.S. development assistance programs against new attacks from the right.

Development assistance policy, generally, and AID, in particular, were in a vulnerable position during the 1980s. The Reagan administration proposed a series of budgets that eliminated all language committing U.S. foreign assistance allocations to specific programs, including programs aimed to promote economic development. Some interpreted this as a lack of sympathy for development assistance, though such a conclusion was speculative, as best. Church groups and humanitarian organizations that might have normally been among the strongest supporters of foreign aid appeared to have both less influence and less interest in AID funding as the decade neared midpoint. Criticisms from the left had certainly diminished the luster of foreign aid as a humanitarian activity. The general political environment was, therefore, one in which any organization wishing to demonstrate its political clout might have selected AID as a target.

Malaise had also begun to settle over U.S. farm policy by 1985. After a decade of unprecedented growth and dominance of world markets, the agricultural economy had fallen into a slide that reached crisis proportions by 1983. Farm

bankruptcies dominated the national news, and farmer dissatisfaction with federal policies mushroomed. Most analysts concluded that the farm crisis was precipitated by
macroeconomic policies of the Federal Reserve Board. Policies to stem inflation had caused farmers' interest expenses
to soar. As inflation rates fell, investment in land became
less attractive and many farmers found themselves holding
notes for land that would never produce agricultural commodities at a rate that would justify the purchase price.
Increases in the exchange value of the dollar put U.S. producers at a disadvantage in world markets, lowering farm
profits at just the time that interest costs seemed to be increasing without limit. Although U.S. farm organizations
have successfully influenced farm legislation, the forces affecting farmers in 1985 went far beyond the legislative mandate
of the 1985 Farm bill.

Traditional farm organizations were faced with policy
problems that exceeded their historical command over
Washington's political machinery, and the increasing competitiveness of foreign growers was a key aspect of their
problem. There was, nevertheless, a significant gap between
the problems of U.S. producers and foreign agricultural assistance. The new competitors for U.S. growers were not
beneficiaries of U.S. foreign aid. Most were industrialized
growers in Europe and Australia who were responding to
subsidized production incentives of the sort that U.S. producers had enjoyed for years. Among developing countries,
only the most wealthy, such as Brazil, Taiwan, and Argentina, were emerging as U.S. competitors in world markets,
and not as a result of AID funding. Even given AID's vulnerability and the turmoil in U.S. farm policy, one cannot
easily see why the U.S. farm community would launch into
a spontaneous attack on development assistance to poor
countries. The missing piece in this picture of the politics of
the Bumpers Amendment is the activity of U.S. commodity
organization staff members, and of one group, the American
Soybean Association (ASA), in particular. Before discussing
these activities, however, the general political milieu must be

completed by examining the role of commodity organizations more closely.

U.S. farm politics have come to focus primarily on specific commodity programs for major crops such as wheat, corn, cotton, rice, and soybeans. The principal vehicles for government subsidies to farmers have been administered on a commodity-by-commodity basis. Farmers have organized to concentrate monitoring and lobbying efforts on these commodity programs. Commodity organizations receive financial support from growers of the particular commodity, and the professional staff of the organizations must justify this support by rendering a consistent stream of services to members. These include technical and management advice, as well as monitoring legislative activity and lobbying for members' interests, as policies for loan rates and deficiency payments are set on a commodity-by-commodity basis. The staff are, therefore, personally interested in presenting members with a never-ending string of battles in which lobbying, letter-writing campaigns, or media attention can bend public policy to accord with members' business concerns. As employees of the membership, that is, it is useful to appear busy and effective at whatever it is that the staff has been hired to do (Browne, 1988).

The political milieu of 1985 farm policy must have been frustrating for commodity organizations. If the macroeconomic analysis of the farm crisis was correct, the usual avenue of commodity policy offered little opportunity to reverse the plight of U.S. producers. Instead, the relevant levers of power appeared to be located in the Treasury Department, on the Federal Reserve Board, and to the extent that exchange rates were regarded as foreign policy concerns even in the State Department. These were not the usual bailiwicks of commodity organizations, and they were corridors in which U.S. banking and manufacturing interests might oppose agricultural concerns. Representing U.S. farm interests within the Reagan administration, Secretary of Agriculture John Block had had considerable difficulty in getting Jimmy Carter's Soviet grain embargo lifted against State Department objections, even though the president had made a campaign promise to do so. The macroeconomic policies affecting farm interests did not, therefore, present an opportunity for commodity representatives to make a public display of their influence. The need to be perceived as active on the international trade front, then, and the uncertain prospects for modifying policies to benefit farm producers created a unique situation. Commodity organization staff may have had an incentive to seek out weak targets, even if the victories obtained were merely symbolic.

THE AMERICAN SOYBEAN ASSOCIATION

In just such an environment, the American Soybean Association, producer organization for 30,000 soybean growers mostly in the central and southern United States, devoted its June 1985 newsletter to the topic "ASA Leaders Draft Resolution Aimed at Government Export Policies." The newsletter to ASA membership reported, "Citing the U.S. government's lack of commitment to an aggressive export policy as the root cause of the current farm crisis, ASA farmer leaders recently proposed a resolution calling for an end to administration policies that adversely affect exports." Among the nine initiatives listed, three addressed development assistance:

3. Eliminate grants and technical assistance which directly or indirectly assists foreign nations expand the production of competing commodities.
4. Vote against loans by the World Bank and other multinational financial insitutions which expand the production or export of competing commodities by foreign countries.
5. Redirect research funding from federal monies currently aimed at assisting foreign competitors to research aimed at boosting U.S. agricultural productivity, lowering costs of production, and boosting overall U.S. agricultural competitiveness. (*ASA Newsletter*, June 1, 1985)

A subsequent newsletter included the erroneous account of AID support to foreign farmers cited earlier and criticized

U.S. approval of a World Bank loan to Brazil to improve railroads. ASA leaders feared that improved railroads would help Brazilian producers "get their farm products to export markets faster" (*ASA Newletter*, August 1, 1985).

In the newsletters, soybean producers were requested to write members of congress in support of ASA initiatives, and many did. AID staff did a land-office business from late 1985 through 1986 responding to enquiries from congressional representatives and the president, who had received letters complaining about AID assistance to foreign producers. Trade magazines for farmers picked up the theme of development assistance harming U.S. farm interests, and several featured editorials, including one by ASA officer John Baize. ASA President Kenneth Baden was invited to speak or participate in a series of forums on aid and trade, including ones at AID and the Council on Foreign Relations. When the Bumpers Amendment was adopted in June 1986, ASA leaders could justifiably claim that their initiative had elicited a response from government.

Although the Bumpers Amendment was ASA's most visible success, a related intiative was more important to its members. AID's major soybean initiative was a Cooperative Research Support Program (CRSP, pronounced "crisp") based at the University of Illinois. CRSPs are major research programs organized around a single commodity that help support collaborative research between U.S. university scientists and agricultural research institutions in the developing world. The soybean CRSP is INTSOY. For decades soybean scientists have been developing new soybean varieties that can be produced in warmer climates. Soybean research in the United States had extended the range of soybean production from upper midwestern states, such as Nebraska and Illinois, to southeastern states, from Arkansas to Georgia. Internationally, this has meant soybean varieties adapted to the climates and soil conditions of Argentina and Brazil. INTSOY could be regarded as a threat to U.S. soybean producers because it gave scientists in developing countries easy access to varieties of soybeans and techniques that had already extended the range of soybean cultivation to the American South.

ASA leaders wanted INTSOY to terminate all research on soybean production, and to focus its research program on marketing and utilization of soybeans. Although ASA leaders had no objection to research that may help increase the demand for soybeans in the developing world, they felt doubly justified in their demand. Not only were U.S. tax dollars being used to implement the technology transfer they saw as harmful through AID's funding of INTSOY, but the INTSOY program diverted activities at U.S. agricultural universities away from the traditional land-grant mission of supporting U.S. agriculture. After a series of private meetings with ASA officials and members, INTSOY and AID converted the program into a soybean utilization program. AID scientists had independently concluded that the developing world had no legitimate need for soybean production research, and the INTSOY project would have been terminated in 1985, if ASA had not intervened. AID did not, however, want to appear to have canceled the INTSOY project under pressure from ASA. Meanwhile, INTSOY staff used the confrontation to propose a new round of funding for research on soybean utilization, a project that ASA would support, that would allow AID to save face, and that would continue the flow of funds to the University of Illinois. The conclusion that AID, the University of Illinois, and INTSOY succumbed to pressure from ASA should, therefore, be resisted. Whatever did happen was certainly more complex, and the conversion of INTSOY to utilization research was welcomed, under the circumstances, by all major players.

The INTSOY episode is a fascinating case study in science and administrative politics, but it was a minor event in the context of ASA's broader policy concerns. The impact of the INTSOY episode may have been greater than that of the Bumpers Amendment, however; there is little evidence of major programmatic change in AID's assistance efforts since June 1986. The Bumpers Amendment gave ASA a visible victory that elevated its officials to an unprecedented level of

visibility outside agricultural circles. In terms of broader policy concerns, the amendment firmly asserts a principle that
favors U.S. producers over foreign producers, without regard to needs and quality of life. The INTSOY episode demonstrates that ASA was active in the politics of the Bumpers
Amendment across a broad range of political fronts. Indeed,
ASA's public initiative against AID may have been intended
to provide leverage in the more private initiative against
INTSOY, though no ASA official has admitted as much. The
politics of the INTSOY episode do not appear to have been
influenced by philosophical concerns; rather, everyone
seems to have been satisfied to get the best of a bad bargain.
INTSOY is not irrelevant to the larger philosophical issues,
however. Much of the soybean producer's feeling of justification in diverting INTSOY's programs arose from the belief
that public universities had a contractual obligation to serve
U.S. farmers.

THE BUMPERS AMENDMENT AS
A MATTER OF PRINCIPLE

In 1986, Dale Bumpers, a liberal Democratic senator from Arkansas, represented a region where soybean production is
important and where soybean growers were among the most
vocal and active respondents to ASA mailings and news articles. It is possible, therefore, to regard his support of ASA
initiatives as a calculated response to constituent interests.
Many members of congress received letters, however, and
many were willing to support the amendment proposed by
Senator Bumpers. Bumpers's primary arguments in support
of the amendment are more carefully worded versions of the
case presented in ASA mailings. Bumpers cites the decline
in the dollar value of U.S. agricultural exports from 1981 to
1986, noting that 40 percent of U.S. farm production was being harvested for export. He then states,

> Yet, the Agency for International Development has awarded
> grants for research and development of export crops from for-

eign countries with whom we directly compete for agricultural products. Certainly, the U.S. needs to provide strong
support to less developed nations for food security and subsistence agriculture. But the U.S. should not provide assistance for countries to better their export capability and
undercut the ability of U.S. farmers to compete effectively.
(Quoted in Johnson, 1987)

Like ASA, Bumpers cites the case of Brazil and alludes to the
INTSOY program. He first notes the growth in Brazilian soybean production, then states,

The Agency for International Development, however,
awarded a $6 million grant to a midwestern university to aid
the development of better tropical soybean varieties. The research was applied in Brazil, Paraguay, and Argentina, all of
which directly compete with U.S. farmers in the global agricultural market.

Given the barrage of letters sent by angry farmers, this argument was sufficient to ensure passage of the amendment.
The only reluctance, one shared by Bumpers, came from
those who feared that the law might affect development assistance aimed at helping the poor peasant classes in the developing world. Senators assured themselves that the truly
needy tend not to be in countries that export the major grain
commodities grown by U.S. farmers, and, in any case, poor
subsistence farmers contribute almost nothing to the store of
commodities traded on world markets. The presence of
senators' remarks in reports on the Bumpers Amendment
strengthens AID's position to interpret congressional intent
for a liberal reading of the law that permits a variety of development assistance programs. What is more, the final version (PL 99–349) stipulates explicitly that "this section shall
not prohibit: (1) activities designed to increase food security
in developing countries where such activities will not have a
significant impact on the export of agricultural commodities
of the United States; or (2) research activities intended primarily to benefit U.S. farmers." The first clause implies the
validity of U.S. efforts to help developing countries increase

agricultural productivity to meet the food needs of their own population, and the second clause effectively permits U.S. public sector scientists to work without restriction in developing countries, because anything that enhances their expertise can be rationalized as "to the benefit of U.S. farmers."

The text of the Bumpers Amendment, Bumpers's remarks, and these two qualifications provide a basis for the philosophical principle that would justify the law. Having determined such a principle, one could compare it to alternative principles, such as the Linking Thesis, that might indicate different legislation. The balance of this chapter is devoted to three theses that might justify the Bumpers Amendment:

The Representationalist Thesis: Public officials should appease interests that have the power to remove them from their posts of authority.

The Humanitarian Thesis: Public officials should aim to maximize the benefits accruing from public expenditures, or use funds to benefit the most needy.

The Social Contract Thesis: Government is a contract among citizens. Public officials should not compromise vital interests of citizens in order to provide benefits to noncitizens.

Philosophers would doubtless protest that although the Representationalist Thesis might describe the motivation of public officials, it cannot justify the Bumpers Amendment, or any other public action. Nevertheless, if the Representationalist Thesis were regarded as a legitimate principle of public policy, it could be interpreted to justify the actions of Bumpers and his colleagues. There are, furthermore, many instances in which the need to appease powerful opponents suffices as a rationale for public policy. Bumpers's words, and, indeed, ASA newsletters, clearly indicate that the Representationalist Thesis was not put forward as the basis for this policy. ASA could have threatened Bumpers, or crassly stated that future support of the organization was contingent on his offering the bill. They did not, and neither did

Bumpers indicate publicly that he regarded ASA activities as a threat. That is not to say that future political contests were absent from the minds of the protagonists, but merely to stress that none of them wanted naked power to be advanced as the primary reason for passing this legislation. Machiavellian considerations may have been causally efficacious; the principle advanced by the protagonists may have been their fig leaf. Even so, a principle-as-fig-leaf must have the capacity to impart some rationale for policy that stands apart from the Representationalist Thesis. That rationale is what is of interest here.

Philosophers will also object to the Humanitarian Thesis, running together as it does utilitarian and Rawlsian approaches to social theory. Crucial in this context, however, is an approach to policy that stipulates impartiality with regard to the interests of U.S. farmers and farmers of the developing world. Given the disparity of wealth between the United States and developing countries, transfer programs would be justified either by a standard utilitarian injunction to do the greatest good for the greatest number (Singer, 1972), or by Rawls's (1972) more pointed Difference Principle, which requires just policy to benefit the worst-off group. Many economists and moral philosophers who might disagree on fundamental interpretations of policy would share the assumption that in weighing benefit and harm, the full range of consequences to all parties must be taken into account without bias toward any group. Such a principle seems to be at work in the first clause restricting the intent of the Bumpers Amendment, and in Bumpers's statement that the United States has a legitimate role in helping subsistence farmers. In the case at hand, the utilitarian maxim and the Difference Principle would almost certainly coincide in favoring a humanitarian policy toward the poor of other lands.

Yet nothing could be more obvious than that the primary arguments in support of the Bumpers Amendment reject the impartiality condition of the Humanitarian Thesis. Indeed, the point of the ASA campaign and of Senator Bumpers's legislative response was to establish the priority of U.S. agricultural trade interests against actions that might return larger or more needed benefits to producers in other lands. Above all else, the Bumpers Amendment places a constraint on policies enacted in accord with the Humanitarian Thesis, and establishes the right of U.S. producers against harm by development assistance policies without regard to the weight of benefits received by noncitizens. The primary thrust of the Bumpers Amendment must, therefore, rest on the Social Contract Thesis, cited earlier, if it is to rest on any of the three principles posed here. In fact, in letters to Congress U.S. farmers persistently complain about use of public funds for projects that help noncitizens at the expense of citizens. Letters, editorials, and other public remarks repeatedly describe tax revenues as a public trust and assert that actions that threaten the earning power of taxpaying citizens violate that trust. That a principle like the Social Contract Thesis is being advanced to justify the Bumpers Amendment, therefore, seems likely.

The Humanitarian Thesis is not, however, abandoned entirely, for remarks in the *Congressional Record* that form the baseline for interpreting the law are clear in limiting its intent. It is not to be construed as an attack on the legitimacy of aid to the poor of the developing world. A harsh reading of the Social Contract Thesis might be thought to invalidate noncitizens' claims as beneficiaries of U.S. policy entirely. Bumpers's remarks and the first qualifying clause contradict such a reading of the law, and, in turn, of its underlying principle. In fact, the Bumpers Amendment places the Humanitarian Thesis and the Social Contract Thesis in tension, without giving clear priority to either. In the language of the law, the clause establishing the legitimacy of aid to promote food security appears as a constraint on the primary clause establishing the priority of U.S. trade interests. As the humanitarian clause constrains the assertion of contractual rights, one might think the corresponding humanitarian principle more fundamental. The political history of the Bumpers Amendment, however, indicates the opposite, that

the trade opportunities of U.S. producers must be acknowledged as a constraint on utilitarian or Rawlsian principles.
The purpose of the ASA campaign was to establish the primacy of this point, and its passage in the Bumpers Amendment would appear to be a congressional endorsement.

The passage of the Bumpers Amendment makes a fascinating case study of the relation between interest group politics, food policy, and the philosophical justification of public
policies. Policy analysts trained in political science emphasize interest group interactions, but although private incentive, power, and reward may offer attractive reasons for
explaining and predicting policy outcomes, policies are generally advanced with a rationale that stipulates a different set
of reasons for thinking the policy justified. These justifying
reasons are usually philosophical in that they appeal to principles of ethics and political philosophy, or in that they indicate why an ethical or political principle normally thought
to govern policy is inapplicable.

Although the Bumpers Amendment appears on one level
to be an unexceptional instance of interest group politics, the
rhetoric used to muster popular opposition to AID and then
to express legislative intent appeals to a social contract tradition that traces its roots to Hobbes, and has been associated with democratic political theory since Locke. That
Bumpers-type legislation could have been even proposed,
let alone passed, without such an appeal to principle seems
impossible. Although one would be naive to think that justifying principles are the primary causal factors in U.S. politics, one would be equally naive to think that vested
interests could succeed without finding some rationale to
justify the policies they want by democratic traditions or the
public good. A statement of general standards for assessing
such justifications is one task of political philosophy, and an
assessment of the particular justifications offered for the
Bumpers Amendment is the next task here.

Chapter 3

Does helping foreign industries violate a basic principle of government?

The politics that precipitated the law limiting U.S. development assistance to competitors of U.S. agriculture mix private interest with philosophical principle. The principle appeals to the social contract tradition of political thought, but the argument that would establish such an appeal is absent from the public record. There is little point in bemoaning the lack of rigor and attention to detail in American political rhetoric. Most advocates of the Bumpers Amendment undoubtedly thought that they had made their case clearly enough, and eventual passage of the law afforded them some practical satisfaction. Philosophical justification has always presumed a higher standard, however. Critique of the case for the Bumpers Amendment must be preceded by a careful statement of the argument in its behalf.

POLITICAL PRINCIPLE AND PRIVATE INTEREST

In Chapter 2, the argument for the Bumpers Amendment is broken down into two distinct themes. The first implies an interest argument, asserting that U.S. foreign agricultural assistance programs are in conflict with the interests of U.S. farmers, and appealing to the Representationalist Thesis as its justifying philosophical principle. The second is a principled argument making the same factual claim, but appealing to a version of social contract theory to show that the use of public funds to aid foreign producers at the expense of U.S. citizens is an inappropriate application of the

56

budgetary authority of the U.S. Agency for International Development (AID). The second theme is represented explicitly in most statements of criticism, though some individuals undoubtedly gave little thought to considerations beyond their own interests. In responding to the pro-Bumpers argument, however, AID staff, as well as most analysts, assumed that the interest argument was the one that needed to be defeated. Indeed, if the principled argument was being offered merely as a cloak for private interest, this response would have been appropriate; but producer groups have declined the opportunity to propose analogous interest arguments when an ethical principle cannot be so readily enlisted to support them.

Citizens of a democracy should express their opinions, both in print and through personal communication, to lawmakers and government officials regarding the impact of government actions and programs on their personal or commercial interests. For government officials in a democracy to consider their constituents' individual interests in forming public policy is not only reasonable but necessary. Public policy is in many instances an attempt to balance individuals' competing interests against one another. The principle that assures all citizens of the right to have their interests considered as this balance is struck is fundamental to democracy in a republic. Philosophical political theory may underestimate the importance of competing private interests as legitimate players in public life, but seeing policy as a simple competition of interests is sometimes crucial to an informed understanding of the standard commodity politics of U.S. agriculture (Browne, 1988).

Political theorists who wish to give ethical and philosophical considerations significant weight in the justification of policy would do well to acknowledge explicitly the substantial realm of policy questions in which competing private interests are recognized as having legitimate claims. This picture of the policy process entails that government actions will sometimes *not* be in the interest of some individuals. If a private interest may legitimately be claimed, on occasion the competition among individual interests will be irreconcilable. There is, therefore, no *general* correlation between policies that conflict with individual interests and those that are illegitimate in that they violate principles of ethics and justice. One cannot draw conclusions about the immorality or illegitimacy of a policy merely from premises that state an incompatibility between the policy and individual interests. A claim asserting that the policy is unjust, or otherwise morally unacceptable, implies that the policy violates one or more of the moral standards that govern the use of state power. The simple claim that a given policy conflicts with individual interests does not have such an implication, as there may be other interests at stake. These might be regarded by everyone as at least equal to, if not more important than, thwarted interests. Many individuals, for example, would not regard filing an income tax return in their personal interest, yet the necessity and legitimacy of the federal power of taxation are accepted by all but a few.

The basic distinction between a simple interest argument and a principled argument can be illustrated by contrasting the case at hand, use of public funds to support research for foreign producers, with the more common case in which public funds are spent for research on commodities that compete with one another, either on a commodity-by-commodity or region-by-region basis, within the domestic agricultural economy. Sugar, for example, is produced from beets in some areas of the United States and from cane in others. Furthermore, high fructose corn sweetener substitutes for sugar in many applications. A sugar beet producer can claim with some accuracy that government funds for research and extension activities in sugar cane, or even corn, help producers of these products and, therefore, reduce the competitive advantages that a beet producer might otherwise enjoy. The beet producer might demand to be compensated, through funds expended for research and extension on sugar beets, for example, when such actions are taken. None of this, however, could be construed as a moral claim that government acts illegitimately when it helps cane producers in the Southeast, but rightly and with justice when it helps beet producers in the Great Northwest. Even the most ardently partisan supporter of the beet industry could utter such a patently ridiculous claim only in jest.

The corresponding claim that the government acts rightly and with justice when it helps U.S. producers of commodities such as soybeans, corn, or cotton, but wrongly and illegitimately when it helps foreign commercial growers of the same products, can be and is uttered with all seriousness. Producers who criticize AID express an interest argument, to be sure, for they claim that support of foreign growers is contrary to the interests of American farmers; but they also make a logically and philosophically distinct moral claim. Although the Colorado beet grower who criticizes cane programs in Louisiana is placated by a policy that provides commensurate support for beets, the Illinois soybean grower would not be at all satisfied to learn that the government spends far more to support development of the Illinois soybean industry than it does to support the soybean industry of Brazil or Argentina. Such a response misses the point.

The criticism of AID agricultural assistance programs implicit in the Bumpers Amendment goes beyond an interest argument, and mere compensation of U.S. farmers for the harm done to their interests would be a wholly inappropriate response. The criticism of foreign agricultural assistance at least claims that such use of the public treasury exceeds AID's legislative mandate and can plausibly be interpreted as the even stronger claim that such use of budgetary authority violates basic principles of the just use of government power. Chapter 3 shows how mandate and principle converge for aid and trade. Chapter 4 takes up interest arguments with the aim of showing how economic theory has been applied in an illegitimate, ill-advised, and fallacious appeal to farmers' interests.

59

HUMANITARIAN AID AS A
GOVERNMENT RESPONSIBILITY

As noted previously in the discussion of the Humanitarian Thesis, at least two political principles frequently cited for justifying public policies appear to support the strong claim for foreign industrial assistance or agricultural development. Neither utilitarian theory nor rights theory appears to support the principle of giving priority to domestic producers, largely because both presume an impartiality criterion that is antithetical to the way that citizens' interests are favored by the law. The discussion of the Humanitarian Thesis was intended to bring into focus the politics of the Senate response to ASA attacks on AID. That response recognized the philosophical legitimacy of U.S. farmers' concerns as it endorsed a continuing role for humanitarian policies. In the present context, the task is to construct a principled argument that justifies policies intended to improve competitiveness. To understand what such an argument must accomplish, we can examine why the philosophical theories so far associated with the Humanitarian Thesis are inadequate.

Utilitarian moral theory finds an action or policy morally justified when it promises to maximize utility for the aggregate of all parties affected as a consequence of the action or policy. Students of moral theory will find many deficiencies in this definition, but convenient simplifications and the neglect of more detailed exposition are necessary evils in the present context.[1] Only one feature of utilitarian moral theory is crucial to the immediate issue. Justification is claimed on the grounds that the consequences of a right action or policy are the optimal ones for all affected parties. The optimum may be defined in alternative ways, including some that are inconsistent with a classical utilitarian's emphasis on maximizing utility.[2] Vilfredo Pareto's constraint on maximization enjoined policymakers to consider only options that made no one worse off, but a policy analyst trained in economics might appeal to the Principle of Pareto

Improvement, for example, which under the Kaldor-Hicks interpretation would justify a policy in which winners would reap benefits sufficient to compensate losers. This principle does not, on the face of it, require maximizing utility, but it would appear to justify development assistance. Although measurement of the relative benefits and losses from U.S. foreign assistance would be an empirical matter, one can reasonably surmise that the broad improvements accruing to citizens of poor countries, both through improved production and increased foreign exchange, would outpace total economic losses to more diversified producers in developed countries. Peter Singer's well-known application of utilitarian theory to famine relief, discussed at length in Chapter 6, provides a lucid account of why utilitarian moral theory should be expected to favor a policy of giving aid to the poor.

Utilitarianism is not committed to the poor, however. Infrastructure in poor countries may prevent capital from finding its most efficient uses there. Bernard Boxill (1987) has made a convincing argument to show that the "brain drain" of intelligent and well-educated people from less developed countries to the West may be justified by utilitarian considerations. His example is a highly skilled physician who can save many lives working in a Western hospital, where sterile conditions, technology, and well-trained staff support his efforts. The same doctor may do little better than a minimally trained medic while attempting to work under the difficult conditions that prevail in some developing countries. Boxill argues that application of a utilitarian decision rule would justify such a doctor's migration to a developed country, where a physician's skills can be put to best use.

Boxill's argument underlines the importance of empirical considerations – determining just what the consequences of policy will be – in applying utilitarian moral theory. If one could show that development assistance is an inefficient use of national resources, one might advance a utilitarian argument against programs to enhance foreign productivity in industries where U.S. producers compete. Critics of foreign aid have based their attack on its perceived ineffectiveness in the past (Fletcher, 1977; Eberstadt, 1980; Newman, 1982), and there can be little doubt that some foreign aid programs, at least, have disappointed everyone who might have been tempted to justify them on utilitarian grounds. Such arguments parallel Boxill's medical example in that they attempt to show that more people benefit when the humanitarian impulse to give aid is resisted. They do not, however, address the type of claim made by ASA and U.S. farmers. The ASA complaint never depended on the view that AID programs should be curtailed because the money could be put to better, more efficient use, nor is this kind of reasoning reflected in the Congressional Record. At best, utilitarian arguments would seem to entail that sometimes aid money might be better spent in other ways, such as developing U.S. producers' penetration of foreign markets. They will not establish a reason to prefer U.S. producers' interests over those of developing countries. Indeed, in proposing a utilitarian principle of law 200 years ago, Jeremy Bentham intended to combat just this sort of policy preference.

Rawls's theory of justice presents a more difficult case than utilitarian theory. Rawls is explicitly committed to an impartial approach to social policy, and a series of subtle and technical philosophical concepts is introduced to establish the impartiality justice requires. In one reading of Rawls, the theory of justice lays the groundwork for critique of constitutional values, institutions, and, indeed, culture. This interpretation has been most thoroughly expounded by Thomas Pogge (1989), and is taken up in Chapter 6. Others have read Rawls as primarily interested in supporting egalitarian principles for redistribution of wealth. The key idea in this context is the Difference Principle, which states that public resources should be committed to improving the welfare of the least well off group. On the face of it, the Difference Principle, like the utilitarian maxim, would appear blind to national citizenship of parties affected by the policy. One can reasonably expect that individuals placed in a situation – behind a veil of ignorance, to use Rawls's expression – in which they must choose between two future worlds, without knowing the country in which they will live or their role in that world, will pick a future in which the poor of poor countries will be better off. To do so is to minimize the misery associated with the worst case. Rawls uses similar, though more carefully developed, reasoning to justify his claim that the Difference Principle must be included in any rational theory of justice.

Applying the Difference Principle to the problems of foreign assistance inevitably raises the question whether the society under consideration is a national or world society. Should we understand the requirements of justice in world society by imagining individuals choosing one world, rather than another; or should we imagine the situation that is closer to the politics of our own world, in which representatives of already formed societies negotiate the conditions of justice for the world order? The subtleties of this question make an application of Rawls's theory to the present issue tenuous, at best. It is not clear, for example, that individuals contracting behind the veil of ignorance would even agree to sanction a system of nation-states, McClennen (1986), for one, argues that, given the risks associated with nuclear weapons, a rational chooser would prefer a world government. If the result of internationalizing Rawls is a complete rejection of the current world system of states, however, the theory becomes largely irrelevant to the question at hand, for there must be nation-states if there are to foreign assistance actions. At one point, Rawls suggests that societies, rather than individuals, contract in the global situation (Rawls, 1972, Section 58). This restriction appears to be motivated primarily by a desire to avoid issues that Rawls was unprepared to discuss (Pogge, 1989). As such, Rawlsians have not felt constrained by the master's approach to the structure of international contracts. Nagel (1977), Runge (1977), Beitz (1979), and Pogge (1989) have used analogies to the Difference Principle, not unlike the abbreviated version given here, to defend far more extensive assistance than currently exists. (More details of these arguments are taken up in Chapter 6.) The point here is that the Difference Principle suggests a prima facie rationale for humanitarian aid. Application of the Difference Principle in a global context is another matter.

THE SCOPE OF THE SOCIAL CONTRACT

Rawls's theory of justice, therefore, presents technical problems in determining the scope of political morality, but the Difference Principle supports a commitment of state resources to improve the lot of the poor. This result is orthogonal to utilitarian theory, which unambiguously applies to everyone, but makes no special commitment to the poor. The ambiguity in Rawls's theory provides a window of opportunity to advocates of the Social Contract Thesis, however, for if the possibility of being among the foreign poor is omitted from the bargaining situation that links the Difference Principle to rational choice, one can argue that a purely self-interested chooser might find little appeal in a program that utilizes tax dollars to provide third-party benefits. Those who are not part of the contract have no standing and no claim on the conscience of those who are. The Difference Principle would be rationally chosen within the confines of the contract, but would it be rational to extend the principle to third parties? Pogge sees this problem clearly, and that is one reason why he insists on establishing the bargaining situation on a global basis.

This reading of Rawls's theory of justice overstates the case for a competitiveness argument, however. It suggests that although impartial rationality supports a society in which all members choose to be bound by the Difference Principle, we may be, indeed, should be partial toward our own group and reject opportunities to apply the Difference Principle to the foreign poor. Many people would, no doubt, endorse this sentiment, but the Social Contract Thesis sketched in Chapter 2 does not express partiality in how we extend our concern for the poor. The Social Contract Thesis makes the more modest claim that public officials should not compromise vital interests of citizens to provide benefits to noncitizens. It does not exclude the foreign poor from consideration entirely. The politics that precipitated the Bumpers Amendment even acknowledged that aid to the foreign poor is legitimate and morally justified. The injustice seen by U.S. farmers in AID development assistance for agriculture was confined to programs that helped farmers in developing countries produce for export; there was no objection to international assistance programs, so long as they did not have the perverse effect of accelerating domestic farm failures. In short, the Social Contract Thesis does not follow simply from narrowing the scope of Rawls's theory of justice. The strict reading of Rawls's theory entails either total impartiality or total partiality with respect to interests, depending on whether the interested party is in or out of the contract. The Social Contract Thesis's partiality to the interests of residents entails that nonresidents are less favored, not that their interests fail to count at all.

Although detailed analysis of utilitarian and Rawlsian moral theories is found in Chapter 6, a cursory treatment shows how these approaches to social ethics provide little foundation for policies that favor home interests of sovereign states, as opposed to those of foreign nationals. The burden, therefore, of exposing the general philosophical rationale that makes such policies morally defensible is a heavy one. In the absence of an argument that connects policy to principle, the weight of principled argument rests in favor of the Humanitarian Thesis. The ideals of impartiality and rationality do not unambiguously entail a policy of aggressive aid to the foreign poor, but they certainly do not provide much support for the Social Contract Thesis implicit in the political reasoning that led to the Bumpers Amendment, either. The stress on just society in recent liberal thought does not bestow national boundaries with much moral significance. No defensible application of utilitarian and Rawlsian principles fails to extend the scope of society far beyond the authority of national governments.

Unilaterally extending the scope of morality beyond national boundaries entails that ethical criteria for international relations become contingent on the total outcome of basic distributions of wealth, power, and social service without regard to national or cultural identity. Foreign policy has never been conducted on such a cosmopolitan basis. That Hans Morgenthau and George Kennan called for realism, rather than ethics, as a guide to foreign policy is not surprising. Unilateral cosmopolitanism is, to the diplomat, almost a reductio ad absurdum to the claim that ethical norms should be applied to foreign policies. The burden, is therefore, a double one. If there is no principled argument to support competitiveness policies, moral theory weighs in with the judgment that favoring domestic producers is ethically indefensible. This conclusion may spell doom not for competitiveness, however, but for moral theory if realism prevails.

THE SOCIAL CONTRACT THESIS: HOBBESIAN AND LOCKEAN READINGS

A more plausible basis for the sentiment implicit in the advancement of competitiveness policies can be found, however, in other forms of social contract theory. In the thought of Hobbes or Locke, for example, contracting parties are clearly making arrangements for national societies, with the resulting sovereign nations remaining in a state of nature relative to one another. The state of nature here means simply that no rules of justice bind a sovereign state in its foreign affairs. States will certainly enter treaties with one another, but no overarching (moral or legal) authority can require them to enter or, indeed, live up to a treaty. A primary duty of the national state is to shield its citizens from the uncertainties of the state of nature, and this duty does not extend to persons outside social contract. A national government has no contractual duties to people of other lands, though whether they ought to or may act to provide them with benefits for other reasons remains open. That a government is not obliged to aid the world's poor does not entail that it could never be permitted to do so.

The key implication of Hobbesian or Lockean versions of social contract for foreign relations follows from the way that the state of nature is used to establish the context for political argument. The state of nature has always been a controversial notion. Rousseau criticized the state of nature proposed by Hobbes and Locke for its naive anthropology in which presocial natives were presumed to have the mental habits, including a predilection for property, of the English gentry. Hume ridiculed the idea of a presocial situation, arguing that the norms of rationality had to have been coevolutionary with society and culture. That anyone would have ever thought of the state of nature as more than a literary device seems incredible today.

Before a political theorist can get to the primary subject matter, the reader must have some way to distinguish a principled argument for a form of political society from statements that merely recount the extant forces that shape the society. The readiest rhetorical solution is to propose a utopia to serve as an ideal, an archetype, for the good society. Utopian political thought, however, cannot recognize the validity of practical imperatives. Some political institutions can only be defended in the light of the nonideal character of the real world; they will never have a place in utopia. A political theorist must distinguish what ought to be from what is, but in a way that recognizes realistic constraints on what is politically achievable. Hobbes's and Locke's use of the state of nature is a brilliant approach to this task. They proposed thinking about the sort of society we would voluntarily join, if we were not already bound to the institutions and arrangement of power in our own society.

The state of nature strategy does not ask us to imagine that either we or others will become more pious or make fundamental changes in our loyalties and values. In its quest for realism, Hobbes's version accepts the meanest and least compassionate vision of human nature as reality. However human nature is conceptualized, state of nature arguments allow the political theorist to propose both consent and rationality as foundational principles for the resulting contract. The contract is supported by consent because the contract specifies what we would choose in an unforced situation; it is supported by rationality in that the choosers are presumed to possess no more, or less, than the rational capacity to select the best means for pursuing their interests. The goals of principled argument are achieved by placing the discussion in the subjunctive mood, while utopianism is constrained by assuming that individuals have just the character and interests that they have in reality.

One might think the state of nature ambiguous in the same way that Rawls's theory of justice fails to specify whether to include those who wind up as foreigners in the original position. It is not. In Rawls's theory of justice, the work of the state of nature is done by two conceptual inventions, the original position and the veil of ignorance. But the state of nature theory does not have the scope problems associated with Rawls's theory of justice. Rawls's argument requires that the decision to accept the terms of a social contract be universally valid; all rational people must be willing to accept the principles of justice. Hobbes and Locke certainly thought that a rational person would want to be associated with some civil society, but there is no reason to think that rationality would require everyone to insist on belonging to the same one. For reasons of geography and culture people would naturally congregate in civil societies, each forming a social contract with different terms. If geographical and cultural forces lead to a multiplicity of states, then foreign relations will be among the problems that the resulting society must resolve.

The same point might be put in yet another way. No foreigners are in the original position. Only rational choosers are, and all are present. They choose principles of justice, which become the foundation for constitutional choices, which in turn are the foundation for a civil society. Rawls does not address whether rational choosers, having chosen principles of justice, might then choose to form many civil societies, rather than one. Most readers have assumed that the parties in the original position do not differ from the parties that make constitutional choices, or that a constitutional convention differs from the original position, only in being a representative body, rather than a committee of the whole. Such assumptions probably make occupants of the original position seem far more robust than they are, and puzzles about international relations are probably a reflection of that basic confusion. Hobbes and Locke, by contrast, do seem to have recognizably realistic individuals occupying the state of nature, and such individuals might plausibly associate into several states. Such a possibility even seems probable in Rousseau's or Hume's approach to the social contract.

The relevant features of early social contract theory are rehabilitated by Robert Nozick's contract argument in *Anarchy, State and Utopia* (1974), where individuals form voluntary protective associations that gradually evolve into what we would recognize as the state. In Nozick's version, the state of nature is a bargaining situation in which an individual's preferences dictate whether refusing state-supported benefits that would require a sacrifice of liberty or wealth is rational. If people cannot justly be made to pay for services or benefits that they do not want, state power is severely constrained, particularly in comparison with Rawls's Difference Principle, which stipulates that social policies should aim to improve welfare for the worst-off group. The problem of redistributing wealth is a preeminent point of contention between libertarian and egalitarian social theory. The libertarian prohibition of redistributive policies provides easy ground for rejecting foreign assistance unilaterally, but it presents egalitarians with excellent reasons for preferring the original position and the veil of ignorance to the state of nature.

This debate does not transect the problem of competitiveness and foreign aid. No party to the political debate on the Bumpers Amendment objected to foreign assistance based on the unilateral application of libertarian theory. The point of discussing state of nature theories is not to compare libertarian and liberal approaches to distributive justice. State of nature theories provide a far more plausible account of why a just but nonutopian world might have a plurality of states, and, in turn, what kind of norms would apply to international relations. Nozick's work is, in this respect, consistent with, but no advance on, the thought of Hobbes and Locke. If the voluntary basis of associations formed in the state of nature is understood merely as the philosophical foundation for a narrowly libertarian objection to all transfers of wealth, the state of nature argument is as inapplicable to competitiveness problems as Rawls's use of the original position and for the same reason. Policies to support competitiveness do not depend on outlawing all redistribution. The libertarian argument overstates the case.

Traditional social contract theory, however, does more than set the stage for debate between libertarian and egalitarian notions of justice. It establishes a basis for national identity and a foundation for evaluating government actions in the international sphere. States are the result of associations that are never imagined to have universal applicability. The principles on which these associations are formed do establish norms for use of state power, however, and these norms are not restricted to domestic affairs. As foreign assistance actions are intergovernmental and intended to benefit people who are not party to the contract, the legitimacy of foreign aid is measured less by its effect on the intended beneficiaries than by the internal standards of justice for the donor nation. The foreign poor have no standing as parties to the contract; they are third parties whose interests may be affected by the collective action of the contractees. The government created by the contract does not answer to them but neither is it unilaterally prohibited from acting on their behalf. There are many possible solutions to the problem of justifying foreign aid. Hobbes and Locke offer accounts of the contract that suggest, but do not logically entail, different ways of joining foreign relations to the internal principles of justice.

For Hobbes, the state of nature is a place of unbridled competition and warfare; moral notions beyond an ethic of simple self-preservation simply do not apply. For Locke, individuals are morally bound by the law of reason and by the duty to respect the natural rights of others, even in the state of nature. Morality for Hobbes is purely conventional, having no extension beyond the contract; one purpose of the contract is to establish the basis of morality. For Locke, the contract fulfills a different role. Restrictions on individual action have moral force even in the state of nature, at least prior to the breakdown of civility that leads to a state of war; the problem is that every individual has equal authority to interpret and enforce the moral law, an open invitation to conflict.

Though realists often find Hobbes's portrayal of human relations compelling, Locke is more realistic on this question. In describing the state of nature as a place with no morality at all, Hobbesians ask us to imagine a situation in which everyone is at all times motivated by a single-minded concern with self-advancement; but surely this is an unrealistic portrayal of human motivation. To modify Lincoln, some of the people are self-interested all of the time, and all of the people are self-interested some of the time, but it's just not the case that all of the people are self-interested all of the time. In Locke's vision of the state of nature, people want to follow the dictates of morality, but unexceptional differences of opinion, lapses in judgment, or lack of willpower will inevitably provoke quarrels. Without a civil authority to resolve quarrels, hostilities mount and the situation deteriorates into something that no one wants, the war of all against all.

Hobbes's account of human nature is, therefore, unrealistic in overstating the dominance of self-interest. Nevertheless, the enduring influence of Hobbes's philosophy justifies considering how the resulting social contract might characterize foreign relations. Clearly no pre-contractual moral obligations to the foreign poor or to their governments exist, though it is possible to create such obligations through treaty. The internal duty of sovereign power is to justify its citizens' voluntary surrender of sovereignty by returning benefits, especially security benefits, that exceed those they would have attained for themselves in the state of nature. Because Hobbesian morality is conventional, perhaps citizens of the Leviathan will regard aid to the foreign poor favorably. If this should be the case, nothing in Hobbes's theory would preclude assistance policies, even when they harm the interests of some. The more natural inference is that the state will conduct its foreign policy to maximize benefits to its domestic constituency, constrained by its domestic obligation to protect the life, liberty, and property of citizens. Foreign nationals have no direct standing, and although the prudent government will avoid entanglements with foreign states that threaten to impose costs on its citizens, costless attempts of advancing native interests abroad would appear to be easily sanctioned.

This general line of reasoning also overstates what is required to justify opposition to aid for foreign producers. In the Bumpers case, farmers are not even requesting the U.S. government to act on behalf of their interests in foreign policy; they are requesting that actions contrary to their interests be terminated. Farmers' belief that foreign agricultural development assistance harms their commercial interests is ground enough to oppose foreign aid outright, because there is no obvious reason to think that parties to the contract benefit from it at all. The final judgment can only be made after one has determined whether this belief is true. Another possibility is that while one domestic interest is harmed, another benefits. Any of several contingencies could be decisive for the evaluation of foreign assistance policies. Three principles constrain the choice, however: (1) only the interests of citizens count; (2) government should follow public opinion; (3) no basic principles are violated by aid. These principles combine to make questions of aid policy contingent on perceived interests. Despite its parallels to the simple argument based on interests, the Hobbesian argument is a moral argument, rather than one based on interests. The state has a moral duty to respect the interests of citizens. Noncitizens have no moral standing, however, so their interests carry no weight. In short, the sovereign power must do more than simply consider the interests of its constituents; the absence of morally countervailing interests means that the morally justified course is charted unambiguously, and conclusively.

Although the Hobbesian individual is motivated purely by self-interest, the Lockean individual is moved by more diverse impulses. Locke assumed that the individual at least aspires to the life of reason. The citizen may, therefore, be inclined to extend goodwill beyond the strict limits of the national state. Individuals are, therefore, to be praised for helping the foreign poor, and they are certainly permitted to press their government to do so also, through the political process. For example, a majority of citizens might prefer helping the foreign poor to protecting agricultural trade interests. If so, then majority rule could lead to a policy of foreign aid. Such a policy, duly legislated and enacted by the just and agreed-on procedure for determining government actions, would be just, presuming it violates no minority rights.

Under such a scenario, the sectorial interest group would have to prove that individual rights of citizens are violated by foreign development assistance. The most plausible scenario seems to equate the decline in value of a crop as a property right that has been appropriated through government action, but that is a tenuous argument, at best. Producers' expectation of this income is contingent on many factors unrelated to foreign assistance. Foreign competitors might independently gain a comparative advantage, either through a technology breakthrough or through a simple shift in exchange rates. Although such events would lead to loss of expected income more surely than would the official actions of a development agency, one would not classify them as an infringement of property rights. Expectations simply are not property, and the attempt to protect expectations under property rules strains credulity.

The alternative is for domestic producers to work within the political process to enlist support for a law that would protect their interests. This is exactly what the American Soybean Association did. One might say that ASA's position was justified because it survived the test of procedural review and was endorsed by the U.S. Congress; if it had not survived it would not have been justified. In one sense, this is the Lockean answer, though it is an unsatisfying one. It is as if the pursuit for a contractual basis for the Bumpers Amendment has come up empty-handed. The law is no more justified than any logrolling compromise that also wins congressional approval.

A little more can be said, however. The U.S. farm community's position on foreign aid has to evoke a familiar response from most Americans. One can easily produce analogous cases where one would feel the same way. What if your state government closed the college campus in your town and at the same time sent funds to improve a weak college across the state line in another county or region? What if your public utility company raised your rates to help pay off the debt on an abandoned nuclear reactor built by another utility? In certain circumstances, one might accept these events, but they seem blatantly unfair on the face of it. They seem so unfair that one's natural response is to think that such actions would not even be proposed without further explanation. Such situations generally occur when the right hand of a bureaucracy does not know what the left is doing, and recognizing that government has contradicted itself through bureaucratic miscommunication usually only heightens one's native sense of unfairness. Loyalties are at stake here. Citizens make a trust with public organizations, and this type of event seems to violate that trust. The good being done in such cases cannot be at the expense of the vital interests of one of our own citizens.

For Locke, moral sentiments have a basis in natural law. For citizens to shape their civil codes to reflect and enforce the natural law is right and natural. Moral obligations, therefore, have a claim on public policy, but the claim must be endorsed by the political process, except for basic individual rights and liberties. Like Hobbes, Locke says little that applies directly to competitiveness and foreign assistance. His emphasis on legislative power suggests that, though he would regard the moral question differently from Hobbes, Locke would arrive at a similar emphasis on contingent matters regarding public policy. There might, in other words, be some ambiguity over whether moral obligations to one's fellow citizens were overriding with regard to moral duties to the foreign poor. As such, the moral issue would need to be debated. The policy that is finally chosen, however, would be legitimated by the democratic application of legislative power.

For Locke, too, foreign assistance does not violate any basic principle, but the weight of moral obligations to fellow citizens may overwhelm natural duties to aid others (if there are any – Locke is not clear on this), when the interests of fellow citizens may be harmed. At least three overlapping rationales tend to support such a conclusion. First, contract theory stresses the importance of implied consent. That domestic producers are protesting the aid programs that help foreign competition belies the suggestion that they would, in some idealized state of nature, consent to such a use of state power. Second, nationality may be of moral significance. David Miller (1988) has argued that ethical theories must make room for particular duties and rights – duties to parents, colleagues, and fellow citizens. He would take utilitarian and rights theorists to task for proposing universalizing criteria that devalue the importance of singular duties and rights that arise in a context of shared values and historical contingencies. Third, a different form of communitarian argument stresses that universal ethical ideals are reached by expanding the scope of community, ascending in concentric circles from personal loyalties through loyalty to one's compatriots, toward loyalties to the human race, and culminating in loyalty to loyalty (Royce, 1908). This vision of

75

communitarianism would require that fellow citizens be mollified, at least, lest the bonds of loyalty that bind the various levels of community should break.

Of course, replies can be made to any of these three reasons for preferring the interests of fellow citizens to those of the foreign poor. Counterarguments, as well as direct arguments for utilitarian rights based on Rawlsian accounts of government's aims, would be part of the political dialogue that would precede any legislative action in a Lockean civil society. The limited agency created by legislative mandate would be morally and legally bound to act in a manner consistent with that mandate. No *basic* principle of government is at stake in the aid and trade debate. This means that, from the perspective of traditional social contract theory, either side might prevail. Right is on the side of due process.

JUSTIFYING COMPETITIVENESS POLICIES

The utilitarian maxim and the Difference Principle provide principled reasons for thinking that humanitarian aid is a government responsibility. The effectiveness of using utilitarianism and Rawls's theory of justice to rationalize aid is weakened, however, by ambiguities in the scope of government responsibility (the scope of the contract). Including all people equally is almost self-defeating in that it vitiates the very idea of "foreign" policy, at least concerning duties to aid. Traditional state of nature theories, which clearly leave room for a system of civil societies, preserve the idea of foreign relations, so the burden of proof must be met within the context of traditional social contract theory. Within this context, principled reasons for extending aid can be met by principled reasons for preferring the interests of fellow citizens to those of foreigners.

Hobbes and Locke suggest similar strategies for examining the contest between these two sets of reasoning. Hobbes's conventionalism would entail that consensus on one, rather than the other, determines right; which one gets the consensus is entirely contingent. Locke's early reference to natural law theory leaves open the possibility that one set of claims could have moral priority over the other, irrespective of opinion. Although Locke appears to think that the legislature of the civil society should enforce natural law, little in Locke's theory of government provides guidance on which set of reasons is morally overriding. The legislature has authority to override the public will on only two conditions, when citizens' rights and liberties are at stake, and when the continued existence and viability of the civil society is at stake. The tension between aid and trade does not invite application of the first condition. Barring an application of the second condition, legislatures would be bound to execute the will of the majority. The matter, therefore, is decided by public consensus on the relative importance of duties to fellow citizens compared to humanitarian duties to foreigners. This consensus manifestly might go either way, undercutting either side's appeal to basic principles of government.

The American Soybean Association has a case, in other words, and its ability to prevail with that case in a democratic political process justifies its appeal to principles of competitiveness. Advocates of aid might have won, however, in which case the mandate for public action would be different. One strategy for reversing the commitment to competitiveness is, therefore, to reenter the political process and reinitiate debate on the issues. That strategy is amenable to several tactics, including appeals to interests (discussed in Chapter 4) as well as to principle (discussed in Chapter 6). The alternative strategy is to advance the thesis that contractual arguments bear on this dispute, but that they enter at the level of national interest – the continued existence and viability of the society – rather than at the level of citizens' rights and liberties. The full argument for this claim is taken up in Chapter 5, though this may not have seemed a promising path of analysis in the past.

The Hobbesian characterization of international politics is more relevant to the alternative strategy than his ethical conventionalism. Hobbes thought that monarchs remain in a state of nature with respect to one another. States are to each other as individuals in the state of nature; no higher authority on earth can settle disputes among sovereign powers. The only recourse is to force of arms, the war of all against all. Although the Hobbesian picture of the state of nature is unrealistic for individuals, its application to international relations has probably been far more accurate. Indeed, the Westphalian treaty of the eighteenth century can be interpreted as a contract among Leviathans. The Westphalian system established the autonomy of the sovereign, being effectively a contract among monarchs to acknowledge only each other as legitimate allies and opponents. Among monarchs, however, the Westphalian system gave tacit assent to the notion that national interests were defined in terms of expansion and defense of territory. Conflict among states became a norm, and international politics were not unlike Hobbes's characterization of the state of nature. A sovereign's title to the national lands was only as good as that sovereign's ability to defend them with military force. Wars were conducted to increase the sovereign's independence by securing control over crucial resources, and, beyond that, simply to increase wealth (Rosecrance, 1986).

The picture that emerges from Hobbes's portrayal of foreign relations is not significantly tempered by Locke. Though Locke stipulates that aggressors can never justly acquire dominion over the rights of others, he also concedes that ". . .great robbers punish little ones, to keep them in their obedience; but the great ones are rewarded with laurels and triumphs, because they are too big for the weak hands of justice in this world" (Locke, 1690, repr. 1980, p. 91). Locke's attempt to establish conditions of justice for international affairs is confined to a discussion of conquest. As such, both Hobbes and Locke describe national states embroiled in violent and amoral conflicts. The principal importance of national interest, therefore, revolves around the possibility of violent conquest, primarily from without.

The brutal Westphalian picture of the international state of nature must be tempered if it is to be made meaningful for the world of the twentieth century. Modern governments have more strenuous obligations to their citizens than did monarchs, even if they fail to endorse democratic ideals. At a minimum, the gains of territorial expansion must be weighed against the cost to domestic prosperity. National interest has become more complex. Determining the national interest for democratic societies is a problem of some subtlety, the central problem for Chapter 5. Almost all governments concede the importance of quality of domestic life as a component of national interest, and this alone pulls modern states well back from the Hobbesian characterization of international politics. It means that governments are constrained from seeking advantage over each other at least to the extent that such adventurism imposes unacceptable costs on domestic life. That is a major conceptual retreat from Hobbes's state of nature, where international order is established by power against power.

In summary, if the state of nature is accepted as the norm, neither helping foreign industries nor the Bumpers Amendment that prohibits such help violates a basic principle of government. Hobbes's and Locke's theories would relegate the determination of this question to the political process. Within the context of democratic debate pro-AID policies might be supported by appeals to utilitarian or egalitarian moral principles, but they would have to contend with consent-oriented, nationalist, and communitarian arguments that favor the interests of countrymen. If utilitarian or egalitarian principles are taken to state foundations for governmental norms unilaterally, they would imply duties to aid the foreign poor, but such an interpretation is so thoroughly at odds with the practice of international politics that is begs the question raised by competitiveness arguments. Hobbes's picture of foreign relations is more realistic, but Chapter 5 will present reasons for qualifying the characterization of international politics as a state of nature. To the extent that consent-oriented, nationalist, and communitarian arguments carry the day, the case against aid is made. That is the assumption with which Chapter 4 begins.

Chapter 4

International agricultural assistance and the interests of U.S. agriculture

A growing literature discusses the beliefs and perceptions of key actors and interest groups that supported the Bumpers Amendment. The theme that emerges most clearly is a critique of the effect that foreign agricultural assistance is perceived to have on U.S. farm exports. Although an extensive discussion of the economic arguments that have been assembled to form this critique is not germane to the philosophical point under review, these arguments are sometimes offered in direct response to the interest argument proposed in Chapter 3, and are, in turn, relevant to more Hobbesian readings of social contract theory. What is more, these economic arguments represent the predominant response to the Bumpers Amendment and to the sentiments that spurred it along. They provide a convincing case for concluding that the agricultural interests enlisted in support of the law would ultimately be thwarted were it to be enforced. The Linking Thesis (*LT*) (discussed in Chapter 1) is clearly relevant to such an argument. Although this conclusion should clearly provoke curiosity among farm groups, the dominance of economic arguments has the unintended effect of implying that the interest considerations of U.S. agriculture are the crucial test for setting international agriculture assistance policy. This is not, however, the intent of the *LT* argument. Such an implication must be resisted, if a justified development assistance policy is to be found.

The sections that follow in this chapter analyze the economic argument with an eye to its role in the political rhetoric of the Bumpers affair and toward its strengths and weaknesses as a basis for justifying public policy. Although most specialists who constructed this argument were well aware of its relevance to the policy debate, their primary aim was to establish claims of fact, to refine and validate the key elements of economic theory that form the basis for *LT* as well as less defensible self-interest arguments. Nothing that follows provides evidence for revising, rejecting, or accepting the primary empirical claims of the economic argument; the scope of analysis is confined to the informal and normative implications of the argument for those who wish to advocate one approach to development policy rather than another. The implication that the political uses of this argument compromise the empirical validity of its claims or the objectivity of the economists who constructed it is rejected. Science has political and moral implications; it can be instrumental in the justification of a policy or in moral choice. An understanding of these implications is vital to an analysis of development policy, but authors who presume that the interpenetration of political and scientific values invalidates scientific authority or discredits its empirical claims receive no sympathy here. In Chapter 5, some key claims of the economic argument tie national interest and development assistance through further development of the Linking Thesis.

THE TRUE INTERESTS OF U.S. AGRICULTURE

The Linking Thesis stands on a two-part claim that (1) expansion of demand for U.S. agricultural exports is dependent on economic growth in nonindustrialized, low-income countries, and (2) the most likely route to economic growth in most such countries is through development of the agricultural sector. In Chapter 1, *LT* is offered as a way of understanding the interrelations of trade and development, with an eye toward interpreting the link as a basis for justifying the aspects of development policy that target agricultural productivity. Linkage of these two theoretical tenets also provides the conceptual basis for an argument that has been directed to the U.S. farm community, the True Interests Thesis, which is intended to show that foreign agricultural development assistance does not hurt, but helps U.S. agriculture. The basic rationale for each tenet of *LT* is reviewed in Chapter 1 and is essentially unchanged when the two-part claim is used to support the True Interests Thesis. As such, the main burden of this section is to examine how *LT* and the True Interests Thesis differ politically and philosophically. This task requires giving some attention to the political history of each tenet before we turn to the True Interests Thesis.

The first tenet, that expansion of demand for U.S. agricultural exports is dependent on economic growth in nonindustrialized, low-income countries, is a consequence of two more specific tenets, each of which summarizes a good deal of common wisdom in contemporary agricultural economics. The first is a widely shared belief that U.S. agriculture is thoroughly addicted to its export markets; the second is the less explicitly endorsed but generally reasonable presumption that developing countries provide the most promising new source of demand for food in world markets.

As noted in Chapter 1, former Secretary of Agriculture Earl Butz emphasized expansion of U.S. agricultural production capacity in the 1970s. The goal was to "feed the world," though it was never clearly specified whether the world or the U.S. taxpayer was expected to pay the bill. In fact, U.S. production of agricultural commodities has exceeded domestic demand for many years. As early as 1901 journalist and author Frank Norris completed two-thirds of a planned trilogy aimed to show how the greed of Americans attempting to produce, transport, and market grain for export was ultimately redeemed by the salvific power of food in the stomachs of hungry people far from the site of cultivation. Norris's redemptive symbolism may seem overripe for contemporary policy analysts, but the moral underpinnings of free-market food policies are remarkably similar. Markets convert individual greed to social good. The overcapacity of U.S. agricultural production for domestic purposes can be good, rather than evil, if world markets can be opened. Foreign sales allow U.S. producers to build income on volume, rather that profit margin, keeping prices low for U.S. food consumers, and they improve U.S. balance of payments, as well. The main theme of the free-market ideology is familiar enough not to have to belabor it here. However, as noted earlier, the importance of foreign trade is a central tenet in the American Soybean Association's (ASA) attack on the U.S. Agency for International Development (AID). This makes ASA and the neoclassical policy analysts rhetorical allies, at least, in their parallel attempts to shape public policy. To see why, we must sketch part of the domestic farm policy debate.

Foreign sales of U.S. farm commodities are not universally acclaimed in agricultural policy debates. Suspicion of export-oriented farm policy has been a secondary theme of the family farm debate in U.S. agriculture. Critics of U.S. agriculture have constructed a platform that generally includes some version of the following three claims.

1. Policies and technologies that promote or increase agricultural productivity are biased against medium-sized family farms.
2. Current levels of agricultural productivity have hidden costs in the form of resource depletion and environmental degradation.
3. Chemical technologies required to maintain high levels of production pose unacceptable risks for agricultural workers, residents of rural communities, and, finally, food consumers.[1]

By questioning the wisdom of continuing to produce agricultural commodities at current levels, critics establish a basis for questioning the need for export markets. They see the agricultural sector producing largely for U.S. domestic demand, producing less, and preserving family farms, environmental quality, and public health.

This opposing view from critics of U.S. agriculture has received little support from leading experts on agricultural policy. The view is rejected because (1) economists are not convinced that reducing foreign markets for agricultural commodities will bring about the social and environmental results that critics desire; (2) economists rate the critics' vision of agriculture as inefficient in that farm income would have to be supported by subsidies or much higher prices for the U.S. public; and (3) economists prefer to allow the market to establish a balance between supply and demand, and they predict that in a free-market environment, U.S. producers would be competitive for foreign sales. Who is right and who is wrong, and whether policy experts have even met the terms of debate set out by critics will not be discussed here. The family farm debate is mentioned to illustrate the political context in which discussion of agricultural exports took place.

The critics' policy agenda is also rejected by such large commodity organizations as the American Soybean Association. Commodity organizations generally support any increase in the volume of sales for their commodity. Although such organizations may have members who represent the middle-volume producers referred to by critics as family farms, they are financed by contributions keyed to volume of production. The interests of high-volume producers, therefore, loom large in internal politics. Such organizations are unlikely to adopt a political platform that strongly favors the interests of family farms against that of large-scale, high-volume producers. What is more, some commodity organizations, including ASA, have historically aligned themselves with free-market political philosophies and find the politics of the critics ideologically suspect.

Farm policy experts and commodity organizations agree in rejecting the critics' vision of American agriculture. This agreement is politically significant, because it allies originally disinterested objective experts with unabashedly self-interested commodity representatives in opposition to critics attempting to reform agricultural policy. Commitment to the claim that increasing agricultural exports is crucial to the U.S. farm economy becomes a political value, as well as an economic fact. When combined with the assumption that developing countries provide the most promising source for expanded markets, the first tenet of the two-part thesis becomes the basis for a policy goal that can be endorsed by economic experts and commodity representatives alike.

The second component of the two-part thesis attempts to harness these political interests in support of exactly the opposite objective to that sought by ASA in its initiatives against AID. The idea that general economic growth in developing countries can be best achieved by supporting agriculture has been a lifelong theme of agriculturally oriented development economists such as Theodore Schultze, John Mellor, and Bruce Johnston. Firmly committed to neoclassical economics, these development theorists have labored for 20 years in a no-man's-land between capitalist and Marxist ideas about development. Capitalists have held that an expanding economy driven by private investment produces increased income for all. This view has often been taken to provide theoretical support for a policy of rapid industrialization of developing countries and has been used to justify development assistance policies that encourage growth in manufacturing. Marxist critics have claimed that the limited growth in wealth from new industry is captured by elites who do not reinvest their income in productive sectors of the home economy. What is more, manufacturing industries in developing countries become deeply dependent on technology, expertise, and markets in the developed world, so the capitalist strategy provides few benefits for the poor, while entrenching the power of self-interested elites. Anticapitalist development theorists such as Amin (1976) have argued that politics in developing countries become hostage to the economic dependency, forming, in effect, a situation of collusion between Third World elites and capitalists based in the developed North. When Marxists have offered alternative schemes, they have concentrated on national autonomy and worker control.

Mellor and Johnston (1984) have split this debate by essentially accepting the moral thrust of Marxist criticisms, but rejecting entirely their theoretical foundation. They argue that the basic premises of capitalist theory are correct, but that the institutional structure of developing economies cannot support rapid growth in manufacturing. If growth comes in agricultural production, where the majority of the population is based, the well-being of a larger proportion of the population can be advanced, and labor can be freed for the ultimate creation of manufacturing and service sectors in an orderly fashion. Mellor and Johnston's ideas in economic development theory take on the characteristics of a political position, in that agricultural development economists who have read Schultz, Mellor, and Johnston have found themselves in competition with others in the development community for funding of the projects they deem most promising. Theory and evidence from development studies are the primary implements in this competition, but political allies in unexpected places can make all the difference in budgetary priorities.

Although AID staff members must have seen ASA's activities as an attack, agricultural development economists, who as a group were broadly supportive of Mellor and Johnston, must have seen the American farmer's newly found interest in development as an opportunity to deliver the lecture on the importance of agriculture in the economic growth of developing countries to a new and potentially receptive audience. The teachable moment had arrived. The question before them was how to make this long-standing debate in development theory accessible and relevant to American farmers. The True Interests Thesis, that foreign agricultural assistance helps, not hurts, U.S. agriculture, was the answer. In short, agricultural development in the Third World is important for U.S. exports of agricultural commodities because it is a prerequisite for general economic growth, and economic growth in the Third World is, in turn, the best hope for expanding demand for U.S. exports.

The True Interest Thesis was advanced repeatedly between 1986 and 1989. Randall B. Purcell's editorial in the Wall Street Journal has already been cited. In an article that appeared in *Choices*, the American Agricultural Economics Association publication aimed at a broad audience of farmers and policymakers, James P. Houck (1987) writes:

> Spending public money for foreign aid has long been unpopular with lots of Americans. Spending it for agricultural assistance abroad is especially unpopular with U.S. farmers and many agricultural organizations. Their view is that more foreign agricultural development is simply another threat to our already dismal farm export markets. . . . [T]his opposition is misplaced and myopic for a large bloc of poor nations. First consider forty eight nations with annual 1984 per capita incomes less that $1500. . . . An improvement in agricultural productivity [within these 48 countries], whether achieved with foreign assistance or not, is clearly translated into overall national economic growth. . . . Among these 48 nations, a 10 percent increase in per capita income was strongly associated with an average 10 to 11 percent expansion of their agricultural imports. . . . Hence, for the poorest nations on this planet, a strong case can be made that advances in agricultural productivity are associated with *increases* in their imports of cereals and other agricultural products.

Given the apparent soundness of its logic and its growing empirical support, the True Interests argument provides a definitive response to one feature of the criticisms directed at AID. The critical arguments share the assumption that agricultural assistance programs are contrary to the trade interests of American farmers, and this assumption is largely falsified by a closer analysis of the relation between aid and trade.

Mellor has taken several opportunities to sound a similar theme. He began a 1989 article in *Choices* by saying: "U.S. farmers, humanitarians, and the people of developing countries have a particularly strong mutual interest in the expansion of incomes in developing countries and the related growth in international markets" (p. 4). Perhaps the most pointed statement of the view was made in 1986 by G. Edward Schuh, then director of agriculture for the World Bank, for the Washington Post:

It is important to understand where the true interests of U.S. agriculture lie and especially where future U.S. markets are likely to be. . . . These markets are likely to grow most rapidly in the developing countries (including China) . . . [but] only if their economies expand and their living standards rise. . . . Increasing productivity and incomes in agriculture is thus the key to raising per capita incomes in the economy as whole. These higher incomes are the source of a strong demand for agricultural imports.

Whether Houck, Mellor, and Schuh were intending to advance the True Interests Thesis or the Linking Thesis must await some clarification of the difference between the two.

AGRICULTURAL INTERESTS AND THE BUMPERS AMENDMENT

The True Interests Thesis serves as a response to the original ASA statements circulated through newsletters and in agricultural trade publications, but not to the principle advanced in support of the Bumpers Amendment. Although some key points that support the True Interests argument can ultimately be used in a philosophical defense of agricultural assistance, and, thereby, a rebuttal of the philosophical beliefs that support the Bumpers Amendment, the True Interests argument not only fails to address the larger philosophical issue, but does so in a potentially malicious way.

As noted earlier, an interest argument plays an important role in the adversarial component of public policy formation. Competing interests state their case with the realization that all parties have an equal claim to a hearing of their arguments, at least. The philosophical argument against foreign assistance, however, is based on the presumption that foreign nationals have no standing, and that, therefore, the interests of citizens are not to be compromised for their benefit. An interest argument is almost always offered by those whose interests are at stake or by their representatives; only they can negotiate a compromise among competing parties. The philosophical argument might be offered by anyone on

grounds of principle alone. In point of fact, interested parties are most frequently associated with philosophical arguments, and one would expect them to use whatever moral
suasion they might find helpful for their case. Victims of injustice are, furthermore, most likely to be aware of the moral
wrongs they have suffered. Nevertheless, the validity or significance of philosophical argument does not depend on
who has made it.

If there is a valid ethical argument for restricting agricultural research to U.S. shores, then the fact that to do so
is not in the interests of those who have made the case
becomes logically irrelevant. To suggest that they are wrong
in their moral argument because making the argument is
not in their interests is to commit the logical fallacy of circumstantial ad hominem. The True Interests response to
criticisms of AID says nothing about the general moral
principle that underlies the Bumpers Amendment, namely,
that the United States ought to prohibit research that could
help foreign nationals improve their competitiveness in
world markets.

A more formal presentation of the respective arguments
shows how the True Interests Thesis leaves the crucial philosophical claim of the Social Contract Thesis untouched. The
original criticisms of AID policy are represented in the following syllogism.

P1: No publicly funded research that helps foreign nations
improve their ability to compete with domestic producers in world markets is justified by democratic principles
(the Social Contract Thesis).

P2: AID agricultural research assistance helps foreign nationals improve their ability to compete with domestic
producers in world markets.

C3: Therefore, AID agricultural research assistance is not
justified by democratic principles.

The Bumpers Amendment gives the first premise (P1) the
force of law. If justified, it is so because P1 states, or is at
least consistent with, basic principles of democracy, and has

been endorsed through the democratic process. The law implicitly endorses both the empirical claim of the American Soybean Association, here represented in the second premise (*P2*), as well as its political attack on AID, represented in the conclusion (*C3*), but this endorsement is entirely contextual, given the history of the Bumpers Amendment and the events that precipitated it.

The True Interests Thesis aims to show that agricultural development assistance helps U.S. farmers because it contributes to economic development, and, in turn, to a growth in world food markets. It forms the basis for a response to the foregoing argument that might be schematized as follows:

> *P4:* No agricultural research that contributes to growth in world food markets can be said to help foreign nationals compete with U.S. producers in world markets.
>
> *P5:* AID agricultural research assistance contributes to a growth in world food markets.
>
> *C6:* Therefore, AID agricultural research assistance does not help foreign nationals compete with U.S. producers in world markets.

This syllogism responds to the first one by offering complex economic arguments in favor of *P4* and *P5*. The conclusion (*C6*) that follows stands as a direct contradiction to the original empirical premise (*P2*). The True Interests response, therefore, demonstrates that the original conclusion (*C3*) has not been established, and in contradicting *P2* rebuts ASA's empirical claims. But this does nothing to address the primary normative principle of the original assumption made in *P1*, that agricultural research helping foreign nationals compete with U.S. producers violates basic principles of democracy. As it is *P1* that is enshrined by passage of the Bumpers Amendment, the True Interest Thesis represents no response to the Bumpers Amendment.

The logical interplay of these syllogisms may appear arcane, but it has two important policy consequences. First, it leaves the case at hand open. Although farm groups that come to accept the True Interests response may be less likely to press the issue against AID, other arguments using P_1 may be forthcoming. For example, economic growth in developing countries may be a threat to U.S. heavy industry. If agricultural development is a prerequisite to economic growth, as the True Interests argument maintains, AID policies may violate an alleged democratic principle, not because they harm agriculture, but because they harm the auto or steel industry. The underlying moral issue, in short, has not been enjoined by the argument based on the True Interests Thesis, and other versions of the original criticism may well be lurking in the background.

The second point reaches farther into the heart of public policy. Left to stand as it is by the True Interests Thesis, the normative premise P_1 (the Social Contract Thesis) becomes a litmus test for development assistance, at least, and perhaps for other areas of public policy as well. The principle underlying the Bumpers Amendment would appear to be particularly relevant to publicly funded scientific research. Authorization of tax revenue for support of research is, under this rule, undemocratic when it benefits foreign parties at the expense of the national constituency of the funding government. Although development-oriented research, such as that done frequently by agricultural scientists, could still be permitted, it would first need to pass muster through an empirical demonstration of the sort offered in the True Interests Thesis. The Bumpers Amendment is, in this respect, a full-employment act for economists, who will now be needed to certify that the likely consequences of a given research initiative are consistent with the trade interests of U.S. industry. More seriously, the law articulates a constraint on the purposes that can legitimately be advanced to justify expenditure of public funds for scientific research. Any number of factors, including natural resource endowment, labor supply, and cultural heritage might allow foreign producers to capitalize more effectively on U.S. scientists than would U.S. manufacturers. Witness Japan's capture of the electronics industry.

Are U.S. scientists to be universally constrained by a generalized Bumpers-type principle?

But maybe *P1* overgeneralizes the Bumpers Amendment. Perhaps intent is crucial. AID funds research with the intention of helping foreign producers. Perhaps the relevant philosophical principle selects the intent of the research as a criterion for validity, rather than the more open ended criterion of whether it "helps foreign producers." If intent is the issue, the foregoing discussion of concern over the Bumpers Amendment's broad-ranging policy implications is misplaced. On this reading of controversy, the relevant principle prohibits funding researchers who intend to help foreign producers.

This rejoinder puts too fine a point on the issue. The ASA attack on AID was far more blunt, calling for restrictions on research that directly or indirectly aids its competitors. Although often crucial in case law and moral theory, the matter of intent in public policy can never refer, however elliptically, back to the representation of an act in the mind of a single human agent. The intent of a policy is multifaceted, a blend of the goals sought by the multiple supporting interests, and the enduring prescriptions of political philosophy that may have been advanced in arguments to support the policy. If the purpose of research, the allowable range of interests and goals that might be advanced on behalf of public science, is restricted rather than research itself (e.g., a restriction based on procedures or immediate consequences), the policy becomes unwieldy. Scientific research is done to further careers, to advance industry, to make friends, to defeat enemies, to alleviate boredom, to fulfill human potential, to put an end to human misery, to get revenge, to build consensus, to seek truth, to find God, and to prove God's nonexistence. Authorizing legislation inevitably specifies goals or purposes for the public research projects it commissions, but legislation that prohibits certain goals or purposes for science is inevitably vacuous or virtually all-encompassing.

The Bumpers Amendment must be read as a law that prohibits research that immediately enhances the competitiveness of foreign agricultural producers. Such a reading offers opportunities for interpreting key terms, such as "immediate consequence," but also "foreign producer" and "competitiveness," in alternative ways that would substantially influence the administration of the act, to be sure. Administration of the law is not at issue here. The True Interests Thesis allows the normative premise of the original ASA criticism to go unrebutted. The Bumpers Amendment subjects both development assistance and agricultural science to a commercial loyalty test, and the True Interests Thesis offers no reason to reject the Social Contract Thesis, the principle on which the Bumpers Amendment has been advanced. That principle does not select agricultural producers as its essential beneficiaries, though the Bumpers Amendment itself is constrained to agriculture, therefore, there is no prima facie reason not to extend it to endorse a broad range of restrictions on foreign aid and public science projects. Rebuttal and redefinition of the Social Contract Thesis, therefore, still await.

A final, less sweeping point needs to be added as a footnote. Although the True Interests Thesis is persuasive when U.S. agriculture is considered in the aggregate and in the long run, it neglects short-run consequences that may, indeed, be negative for some sectors of the U.S. farm economy. Alain de Janvry and Elizabeth Sadoulet (1986) note that effects on U.S. export markets may even be negative in the short run. Paarlberg (1986) notes that although increased agricultural productivity has led to an increase in agricultural imports for some often-cited developing countries, counterexamples abound. Peterson (1986) points out that arguments citing aggregated results for the entire U.S. farm economy are unlikely to persuade producers of individual commodities, some of whom face stiff competition from growers in climatically well suited developing countries. Houck limits his endorsement of the view that increasing agricultural productivity in developing countries will help, rather than harm, U.S. farm export sales to the 48 poorest countries and specifically excepts Brazil and Argentina (Houck, 1987). As these are two leading exporters of soybeans, the ASA membership might well question the relevance of the True Interests Thesis to the specific problem that instigated the Bumpers Amendment. The short-run/long-run, country-by-country qualification of the True Interests Thesis is of particular importance, given the political context in which the ASA argument was made. If directly assisting competitors of U.S. producers is wrong, it is so because the interests of specific producers are harmed. Just because this will lead to long-term improvement in foreign markets does not make it right. The producers who are temporarily harmed today may not be the producers who will benefit tomorrow. Given the high rate of farm failures during the years preceding the Bumpers debates in 1985 and 1986, farmers would appear to have prima facie justification for rejecting arguments that conceal individual farm failures by aggregate growth in U.S. agriculture. The highly aggregated nature of the True Interests Thesis leaves plenty of room for skeptics in the farm community to doubt that foreign agricultural development will benefit them. U.S. agriculture as a whole may benefit, but in an era of rapidly evolving farm structure, many individuals may question whether they or their heirs would be involved in U.S. agriculture long enough to reap the rewards.

In conclusion, although the True Interests Thesis casts doubt on the assumption that foreign agricultural assistance harms U.S. farmers' trade prospects, it lays no foundation for an argument against the Bumpers Amendment. Mellor has made a persuasive case for the view that pursuit of humanitarian and scientific goals by agricultural researchers in the developing world is not incompatible with the interests of U.S. farmers, but the situation in which these goals coincide may be temporary and will almost certainly not pertain in all cases. If the normative premise expressed in the Social Contract Thesis is allowed to stand, the criteria for identifying valid policy priorities are profoundly altered in favor of purely commercial goals. Perhaps this conclusion is forced on us, but the Linking Thesis provides an alternative way of interpreting the two theoretical tenets that form the basis of the True Interests Thesis.

AGRICULTURAL INTERESTS AND THE LINKING THESIS

The difference between *LT* and the True Interests Thesis is subtle but crucial. As stated in Chapter 1, *LT* is based on the presumption that encouragement of trade is generally and noncontroversially mandated by government's pursuit of national interest and also notes humanitarian objectives for development assistance. *LT* allows agricultural development assistance to be captured under mandate of national interest, because it, like the True Interests Thesis, shows why agricultural development assistance programs might reasonably be interpreted as encouragement of agricultural / trade. The True Interests Thesis, however, aims not at national interest, but at the commercial interests of U.S. agricultural producers. Under *LT* and its general principle supporting encouragement of trade, there is no group of individuals whose commercial interests are advanced as a criterion for valid policy. Although the duty to encourage trade must ultimately benefit some individuals, *LT* does not select particular individuals in time or space to serve as the test. Government might encourage trade in a way that fails to benefit present-day agricultural producers, and indeed, might even harm them.

More abstractly, *LT* and the True Interests Thesis exchange terms of generality and specificity. *LT* identifies the enhancement of trade as a general category of legitimate national interest and notes that agricultural development assistance is a specific strategy that is consistent with it. The True Interests Thesis identifies U.S. agricultural producers' commercial interests as the end and then constructs a hypothetical imperative that justifies development assistance and *could* be used to rationalize all manner of policies as a means to this end.

The consonance of commercial interests and development goals justify policies that seek to enhance the agricultural productivity of the developing world. It is one thing however, to note and rejoice in such coincidences (*LT*), and another thing entirely to make development assistance or science policy decisions depend on them (the True Interests Thesis). The True Interests Thesis places a special interest group in the position of public policy beneficiary; but democratic public policies must show that pursuit of special interests is also pursuit of the public interest. *LT* advances a conventional standard of public or national interest as the policy goal and justifies policies that both enhance trade and help poor countries by showing that these policies serve that goal.

There is also a rhetorical difference between *LT* and the True Interests Thesis that is of philosophical significance. The True Interests Thesis is directed to the U.S. farm community, including producers and others whose interests are closely tied to farm exports. This is a large and not exclusively rural group that includes many traders, farm state members of Congress, and business leaders who read the *Wall Street Journal* or the *Washington Post*. The True Interests Thesis is a pointed attempt to get a group of people who are aligned against foreign agricultural assistance, or are, at least disinterested, to support it actively. Like most principled arguments, *LT* is directed to no one in particular. It attempts to appeal to all citizens. It appeals to nonspecific interests, which should, if well grounded, be the interests of rational people in a free and prosperous society.

Political rhetoric can seek to achieve more than one purpose. Advocates of policy change can be vague about the audience that they hope to reach. The passages cited earlier may represent the True Interests Thesis, and they may represent *LT*, but most likely they represent both. Observing that the writings of Purcell, Mellor, Houck, and Schuh are vague about the intended audience is not to indict any author of pandering to special interests. The political and rhetorical differences between the principled argument that all thinking people should respect, even if it is ultimately rejected, and the narrow appeal to special interests mirror their differences of logic and principle that distinguish them as philosophical theses. Attention to the political circumstances of debate reveals potent elements of the link between philosophical justification of a policy and use of philosophical language to form consensus and compromise. Individualistic, interest-based rhetoric may undercut the formation of the shared belief that impersonal philosophical justification is relevant and possible. To the extent that this is so, philosophical justification and philosophical rhetoric come together, and choosing rhetoric takes on unexpected philosophical implications.

In this connection, nothing said on behalf of *LT* counts against the primary normative principle of the Bumpers Amendment, the Social Contract Thesis (*P1*). As the True Interests Thesis allows the Social Contract Thesis to stand, so does *LT*; as a counterargument to the Bumpers Amendment, it does no better. But the True Interests Thesis makes use of the Social Contract Thesis and the sentiments that led to the Bumpers Amendment in a way that *LT* does not. The True Interests Thesis must be conjoined with the Social Contract Thesis, the idea that government is contractually obligated to pursue, and to refrain from harming, the individualized economic interests of its citizens, to form an endorsement of agricultural development assistance. *LT* merely shows that agricultural development assistance is one means of pursuing national interest in the enhancement of trade. If the trade component of national interest must, in turn, be clarified and justified by a principle like the Social Contract Thesis, the distinction between *LT* and the True Interests Thesis becomes little more than semantics. The burden of proof is an interpretation of national interests in agricultural trade that, at a minimum, establishes a policy foundation distinct from the Social Contract Thesis and, to be decisive, provides a basis for rejecting it and, therefore, the rationale for the Bumpers Amendment entirely.

Chapter 5

The trading state
and the social contract

Since Hobbes (1651), social contract theories have presumed that individuals unbound by obligations and constraints of government would, or rationally should, abandon some personal liberties in exchange for certain guarantees and benefits that can be secured only by enforceable schemes of mutual cooperation. The philosophical basis for competitiveness sentiments can be found in the implicit themes of the social contract argument. Contract theorists make the implicit assumption that benefits accrue primarily to contracting parties. Rational self-interest is the primary motivation for entering the social contract, so the benefits of entering the contract must outweigh the costs for each individual. One can imagine situations in which external effects of the contract benefit third parties, but the Bumpers case involves intentional action to benefit foreigners at the expense of citizens. Although the state's responsibility to protect economic interests from foreign threats is uncertain, the social contract cannot plausibly be understood to permit state intervention on behalf of foreign competitors unless significant state interests are at stake.

The plausibility of social contract arguments in political theory comes from their analogy to standard personal contracts in which parties consent to be bound by terms and conditions. The presumption is that parties so agree because they perceive a mutual benefit in making the contract. There may, to be sure, be cases where parties contract for services that will benefit others indirectly, as when the services one contracts from a house painter so beautify the neighborhood that others reap aesthetic benefits, or even increased property values. There may also be cases in which others benefit directly as a result of altruistic intentions, as when one contracts the same house painter to render services to a local charity. Cogent exceptions for the point under review would be Third World agricultural development as an indirect benefit, or if it were altruistically desired by the parties being required to sacrifice to achieve it. The arguments made for a Bumpers-type law indicate that neither of these conditions obtain. The model of mutual benefit to contracting parties demands that altruistic motives be explicitly and voluntarily expressed by the parties.

Furthermore, one of the most basic guarantees assures parties to the contract that the newly created state power will secure their person and property against any foreign threat. This guarantee can be interpreted to entail, at a minimum, that state power may not be actively used to place them at a competitive disadvantage to foreigners. One can even reasonably expect that state power will be used to gain advantage over noncitizens, although many versions of contract theory would not support such claims. Hobbes and Locke write as if the individual's pecuniary interests are entirely confined to the domestic economy, and even Nozick neglects foreign trade. That the state's duty to protect citizens' interests extends into the economic realm is not, therefore, unequivocally clear. The duty to protect citizens from external threats would constrain states from abetting foreign attempts to capture expected income, at a minimum. Even when this constraint is modestly interpreted to mean that states should be neutral with regard to economic competitors, without regard to their country of origin, neutrality would, on the face of it, be all that is required to support the pro-Bumpers philosophical argument.

This is not to say, however, that government might not favor a foreign competitor if some vital national interest were at stake. If, for example, national security demands that the mineral production of some foreign state remain or become economically viable, perhaps to secure a continuing source of supply, one might encounter situations where government initiatives to support this foreign industry would be justified, even if they harmed U.S. producers in some non-fundamental way. As such, a general argument might be raised against policies or actions justified on the basis of competitiveness. This type of argument stresses national interest, as opposed to sectorial interests of U.S. farmers. If the Linking Thesis (*LT*) is sound, it provides an entree to an interpretation of national interest that can serve as a counter-weight to the criticisms directed at the U.S. Agency for International Development (AID). The critical arguments share the assumption that agricultural assistance programs are contrary to the trade interests of American farmers and depend on the Social Contract Thesis to show why home interests should be favored over foreign ones. If national interests were at stake, however, they would override sectorial claims.

If sound, *LT* shows that the sectorial interests of U.S. agriculture are served in the long run by assistance to poor foreign agricultural producers. Why, one might ask, is there a need to formulate *LT* in terms of national, rather than sectorial, interests? There are two reasons. The analysis of the True Interests Thesis in Chapter 4 shows why many individual producers may still feel strongly motivated to press the American Soybean Association's (ASA) interests in letters and petitions mailed to congressional leaders. Even if the broad factual claims of the True Interests argument are correct, the short-term interests of some farmers will not be advanced by foreign assistance. More important, the True Interests Thesis fails to make a principled response to the litany of reasons for tying the Bumpers Amendment to foundational presumptions of social contract theory. Certainly, U.S. farmers will have little personal stake in opposing foreign aid through a Bumpers-type law once they are convinced that foreign aid serves their interest. As a principled political claim, however, the case is different. If it is wrong for government to help foreign competitors, just because U.S. citizens indirectly benefit does not make it right. Indeed, there are almost always *some* domestic beneficiaries from any act helping foreign competitors. The injunction against this sort of activity is stated on principle and is not mitigated because some people who thought they might be hurt are helped. An argument overturning that principled philosophical case must attack it either at the level of the founding principles (the strategy rejected in Chapter 3), or by showing that some overriding social good is more important. Simply showing that the people who offered the argument may have harmed themselves by having done so counts for nothing; the True Interests Thesis is a circumstantial ad hominem. Who made the argument does not matter, only that it has logical force.

The distinction between the True Interests Thesis and the philosophical argument made available by *LT* can be considered in terms of an important philosophical distinction between presumptive and discretionary goods. The main point, addressed in the second section that follows, is to show that the main philosophical claims behind ASA criticisms of AID involve presumptive goods, while the True Interests Thesis presumes that the issue is merely a dispute over discretionary goods. This distinction points the way for the application of *LT* in a sketch of the strong argument for development assistance.

PRESUMPTIVE AND DISCRETIONARY GOODS

The dual nature of the U.S. farm community's case against international agricultural development can be clarified by noting how social and political philosophies typically distinguish between those services and duties that a government is permitted to provide only when there is an effective political demand for them, and those that a government is required to provide whether demand is effective or not. The benefits citizens enjoy from government services are of two kinds. Discretionary goods are benefits that are provided solely because they are desired and supported by a majority of citizens. If tastes or opinions change, the government would not only be justified in discontinuing its support of discretionary goods, but would be mandated by public opinion to do so. Presumptive goods, on the other hand, are benefits, services, or guarantees that necessarily must be provided for just continuance of the state. If a government fails to provide presumptive goods, it may not only weaken itself, but its legitimacy may also be called into question. A distinction between discretionary and presumptive goods or duties is implicit in the theories of traditionalists such as Locke. In Chapters IX and XI of the *Second Treatise* Locke recognizes that government has both ends and self-generated requirements that are prerequisites to the existence of a just state, but in Chapter XIV he notes that governments may provide services for the public good that are not required by duties of justice. The distinction, but not the terminology, has become standard in political theory at least since John Rawls (1971) based much of his argument in *A Theory of Justice* on the distribution of what he called "primary goods." Among the frequent examples of discretionary goods are parks, roads, museums, and public arts projects. National defense and protection of basic rights to life and liberty are standard examples of presumptive goods.

The line between a discretionary good and a presumptive good is neither unambiguous nor noncontroversial. Although some examples cited earlier may seem easily classified, many government actions might be described by advocates as securing presumptive goods, and decried by critics as providing only discretionary, and, indeed, unwanted, goods. The classic debate has been over welfare benefits. Liberals have seen the redistribution of wealth to secure minimums of welfare and opportunity to all citizens as a presumptive good, one required both to stabilize society and to guarantee the human rights necessary for the legitimation of government (Nagel, 1977; Levin, 1981).

Conservatives and libertarians have disputed the presumptive character of welfare benefits, arguing that the state is founded instead on minimal protection of security, liberty, and property claims of individuals, and that active state welfare programs would be justified only to the extent that individuals support them through voluntary contributions (Nozick, 1974). As such, the conservative view not only makes welfare benefits discretionary, in founding them on the willingness of citizens to contribute, but also finds the unilateral use of tax dollars to support welfare programs a coercive violation of property rights, and, therefore, a governmental failure to provide a presumptive good (Klosko, 1987).

This classic disagreement over discretionary and presumptive goods as applied to welfare rights is relevant to food policy in general, because nutrition is among the most basic survival needs of human beings. The familiar rationale for including a food entitlement among presumptive goods is discussed in Chapter 6, but at present the notion of presumptive goods will be put to different purposes. Although government may provide many discretionary goods to its citizens who want and support them, when the provision of a discretionary good conflicts with government's ability to secure presumptive goods, presumptive goods must prevail. Government's obligation to provide presumptive goods "trumps" any responsibility to supply discretionary goods, because presumptive goods are essential; without them there is no just state. They prevail without regard to the preferences or opinions of the majority, and, indeed provide the philosophical basis for protection of minorities against the tyranny of a majority view. This is not to say that presumptive goods are always decisive in determining policy, as two or more presumptive goods may not be simultaneously attainable. In such a case, one is forced back to fundamental philosophical goals in the establishment and legitimation of the state in an attempt to set priorities or fashion a compromise.

PRESUMPTIVE GOODS AND THE TRUE
INTERESTS THESIS

Two deficiencies of the True Interests Thesis have already
been noted. An empirical deficiency is found in its highly aggregated and time-dependent portrayal of benefits to U.S.
agriculture. Critics of the argument question whether particular individuals could reasonably be expected to receive
any benefits alleged to flow from development assistance, at
least within the time frame in which they would be of most
value to them. Second, in portraying the outcomes of AID's
development programs in terms of discretionary goods to
benefit U.S. producers, the True Interests argument fails to
address the fundamental philosophical objection, namely,
that these programs aim to supply competitive benefits to
foreign nationals. The second deficiency is clarified by the
distinction between discretionary and presumptive goods.

Advocates of the True Interests Thesis direct an argument
to the U.S. farm community using evidence to show that the
initial presumption of conflict between U.S. producers' trade
interests and AID's development assistance policies is false.
In fact, the True Interests Thesis states, U.S. farmers should
join in support of these policies; it is in their commercial interests to do so. In making this type of claim, the True Interests Thesis treats AID development goals as if they were
an attempt to secure discretionary goods, which are justified
simply because Americans want them and are willing to
support them. The attempt to build political support for
these goals implies that they are appropriate actions for AID
only to the extent that they are endorsed by American citizens in the political process.

The principled philosophical argument against agricultural development assistance claimed that aid policies were
in conflict with a state's duty to confine its support of commercial enterprises to those undertaken by citizens. For this
argument, AID's actions are beyond the scope of governmental activities sanctioned by the implicit terms of a social
contract, at a minimum, and are most probably in conflict

with the presumed purposes of state power. Respecting this constraint is, therefore, portrayed as a presumptive duty for government. As such, that the farm community might be shifted from the column of those opposing a discretionary good to those supporting it carries little philosophical weight. The number of people supporting the discretionary good against the presumptive one is irrelevant; the presumptive good "trumps" all discretionary considerations.

Though the distinction between the True Interests Thesis and *LT* is subtle, it is sufficient to mitigate both deficiencies in the True Interests Thesis, and open the way to apply *LT* in arguing that foreign agricultural assistance is beneficial to national interests, and to the U.S. economy as a whole. If one emphasizes U.S. trade interests, rather than using the True Interests Thesis in an appeal to individual farm producers, the argument might be restructured to show how these development activities help the government secure a presumptive good, rather than a discretionary one.

The distinction between presumptive and discretionary goods also indicates the strategy for a philosophically adequate response to AID's critics. Such an argument must not place much importance on the discretionary benefits that AID's policies might return to U.S. citizens. These benefits will never override the more basic claims made in the ASA argument. Instead, a reply to the philosophical version of the ASA argument must demonstrate that AID's efforts at international agricultural development attempt to secure presumptive goods, whose provision the U.S. government is, as a matter of justice or national interest, required to pursue. A full account of how such a claim might be established is beyond the realm of this discussion. The argument requires that key empirical issues be settled. Although one can describe the research that might contribute to a settlement of these questions, the more purely philosophical considerations that can be brought to bear in the present context are admittedly indecisive. As such, the following remarks are a sketch of such an argument, although important gaps are acknowledged. This argument returns to a theme introduced in Chapter 1, that U.S. food policy has been muddled by the military preoccupations of U.S. foreign affairs. In addition, several topics are pinpointed that are in particular need of multidisciplinary research if the issues raised by the Bumpers Amendment are to be resolved.

TRADE WARS AND REAL WARS: A REPRISE

Two books of the mid-1980s attempt to show how military dominance of U.S. foreign policy failed to serve the national interest. Paul Kennedy's *The Rise and Fall of the Great Powers* reviews research on the impact of military spending on the domestic economies of the United States and the Soviet Union and concludes that both nations have suffered in comparison to nations that stressed economic development after World War II. Kennedy argues that the great powers blithely assumed that Cold War rivalries over high technology weapons and territorial hegemony were the dominant problems of the half-century. Meanwhile, the rest of the world set sail on a globally unprecedented economic expansion. The command economies of the military sector of both superpowers grew more slowly and less efficiently than the demand economies of manufacturing and service sectors in the rest of the world. The superpowers have been left behind, and the historical tides may have gone out for good (Kennedy, 1987; see also McNeil, 1982). In *The Rise of the Trading State*, Richard Rosecrance argues that the balance of geopolitical power and prestige shifted in the nineteenth century, particularly in the last 25 years, from those nations with dominant military strength to those with the most cultivated and extensive trade networks. Rosecrance's thesis is that international trade has come to share the foreign policy stage with territorial expansion and military force. National interest cannot be defined exclusively or even primarily in terms of armed might and military alliances. Increasingly, the military capability of a nation must be balanced against its capacity to enter into mutually beneficial trade relations with other countries. Both parameters affect national interest, and one cannot tell which will be more decisive for the future of the nation (Rosecrance, 1986).

If Kennedy and Rosecrance are right, healthy, nondomineering trade relations cultivated with developing countries may play a greater role in U.S. national interest over the long run than do the more celebrated and discussed supply of arms and military support. If helping the agricultural sector of developing countries grow is instrumental to their participation in a global economy, foreign assistance may be an important component of a foreign policy that seeks to link the U.S. economy with the rest of the world, rather than trying to dominate it by force. If national interest hangs, in an important way, on these economic and cultural relations, there is good reason to think that a presumptive good is being sought by these development goals, rather than a discretionary one. Closer examination of the connections between food, trade, and military power is, therefore, necessary.

As noted briefly in Chapter 3, the Hobbesian picture of international relations looms large in the literature on foreign affairs. This picture is rooted in the social contract tradition, being essentially the negative background assumption (the state of nature) that allows the positive configuration of civil society to emerge within the domestic sphere. In *Leviathan*, however, the sovereign powers of the world remain in a state of nature with respect to one another. This situation leads of necessity to a perennial testing of strength and will among nations, to an international politics in which warfare is entirely consistent with any other means by which rulers of nations seek advantage over one another. Rosecrance suggests that this picture of foreign relations was institutionalized by the Peace of Westphalia in 1648. This treaty removed the pretense of authority vested in the Holy Roman Empire and created a European continent populated by independent and autonomous states, each with a sovereign at the head (pp. 83–84).

The Westphalian system of states institutionalized several features of social contract theory. In the first place, it tended to provide a closer fit between political authority and the economic structure of European society, though the fit was uneven, and varied drastically from one state to the next. The head of state in Westphalian Europe presided over a political entity that more closely matched the peasant/tradesman/merchant economic organization of seventeenth-century Europe than did the Holy Roman Empire, which the Peace of Westphalia displaced. It was possible, in other words, for nation-states to emerge and for the borders of political power to more closely resemble the sort of associations that might have emerged through voluntary affiliation. Whatever loyalties emerged from community ties were further strengthened because Westphalian heads of state were bound to their people primarily by a duty to provide protection from assault by bandits and marauding armies. The common person could, therefore, expect something from the state, though sovereigns delivered on security commitments in uneven fashion. Whatever the effectiveness of Westphalian states in protecting their peoples, the expectation of security provided the pretense, at least, that the commoner's loyalty to the sovereign was repayment for protection of life and limb. This loyalty was, perhaps, less than a contract in many European monarchies, but it established a form of political organization that was far more congenial to contractual theories of legitimacy than the thoroughly ambiguous mix of religious duty and brute force that it replaced. The Westphalian monarchies and principalities were, therefore, more like contractually based civil societies in two respects: The boundaries of political authority corresponded, however roughly, to natural borders of social and economic organization, and the sovereign and subjects were bound to a bargain in which loyalty was given in exchange for security against invading forces.

These two factors had important implications for the foreign relations of Westphalian states. First, as the economies of these states were closed, trade beyond borders was not crucial to economic stability. To be sure, the importance of trade was increasing, but not until the nineteenth century did the fortunes of the common person begin to depend on imports of raw materials, and exports of manufactured goods (Mintz, 1985). Trade was the motivation for the voyages of exploration throughout the sixteenth century, but early European trade centered on luxury goods, supporting a form of consumption by the ruling classes that could be sacrificed without the onset of starvation or the collapse of the general economy. Desire for such luxury goods, however, provided rulers with an incentive to seek forms of wealth that could not be obtained within the domestic economies over which they held power. For Westphalian rulers, conquest of new territories was a means of securing wealth and resources beyond their current grasp, but as the economies on which their power was based were closed, disruption of the international economy during periods of conquest did not impose significant costs. To possess commodities from foreign lands was important enough to persuade a monarch to fight, but trade in such commodities was not so important that its disruption negatively affected national economies (Jones, 1981; Rosenberg and Birdzell, 1986). The second factor, national loyalties given in exchange for protection from invading armies, reinforced the tendency of Westphalian heads of state to behave as if they were in a state of nature. Their duty to their subjects was one of protection. They were most likely to be called on to fulfill this duty when their own personal interests were being assaulted by a neighboring sovereign. Therefore, even sovereigns not motivated to attempt conquest had to be prepared to test wills and military strength. They could be assured of the loyalty of their subjects in making a military response. Heads of state had personal interest in conquest, and these interests were not seriously constrained by domestic considerations.

The political economy extant in Hobbes's Europe, therefore, lends an aura of robustness to the social contract argument advanced in *Leviathan*, and particularly to its characterization of the relations among sovereign powers. Humanity may have never experienced the state of nature, as Hume opined years later, but the state of nature was a fair characterization of international politics in Hobbes's day and for at least a century afterward. The lesson is one that places territory and military power at the forefront of international relations and justifies foreign policy largely in terms of its ability to secure the citizen against attacks on body and property. Where foreign policy is concerned, national interest is defined in terms of territorial expansion and military power. Even Locke and Rousseau found little occasion to revise this aspect of the Hobbesian social contract, and contemporary theorists have addressed it with mixed results. It has served as a rationale for realism in foreign affairs and has implicitly justified a U.S. foreign policy cast in military terms since World War II.

Kennedy and Rosecrance, however, attack precisely this picture of international relations. To assess the validity of that attack in this context is impractical, but some crucial contrasts between the sixteenth and twentieth centuries are worth noting. First, the fit between political authority and economic structure is altogether different today. When political boundaries failed to match sixteenth-century economic units, the political boundaries were far more likely to be too big, whereas today they are too small. Sixteenth-century Europe was evolving from a form of economic organization in which the full range of food and manufactures for the common person would have been produced within a few miles of any domicile, to one in which key natural resources were transported longer distances, sometimes across borders, but more frequently still within the territory of a single state. Larger European countries, such as France or Spain, incorporated a number of economically separable regions into a larger unit and clearly gained advantages from doing so. In the modern world, the economies of even the largest states, many far larger than sixteenth-century France or Spain, interpenetrate those of other states extensively and in fundamental ways (Lee and Reid, 1991). Nowhere is this contrast more striking than in the agricultural economy.

Second, the twentieth century differs from the sixteenth century in the relative importance of military conquest as a theme in foreign relations. Westphalian rulers could regard conquest as an expedition into the wilderness, that is, the state of nature, where one's right to wealth and territory was largely a function of one's ability to wrest it from its natural state, or from human competitors. Twentieth-century wars have increasingly required ideological rationalizations, even when ownership of territory and natural resources is clearly a point of controversy, as in the Gulf War of 1991. Although making too much of this distinction would be a mistake, it, nevertheless, underscores that international relations in the twentieth century fail to conform to the terms laid out in state of nature theories. There are rules and institutions for foreign affairs today, where state of nature theories describe none. Doubtless there were rules for foreign relations in Westphalian Europe, but Hobbes's picture does not preclude the possibility of international etiquette. The rules are more serious now that the global economy is a reality.

Finally, corporate organization of business activity was nonexistent in Westphalian Europe. The modern business corporation was anticipated by nationally sponsored trading companies such as the British East India Company, chartered in 1660, but these organizations conducted their activities under royal charters. Acting on the authority and under the protection of the regent, these companies conformed closely to a state of nature model of international exchange. Rosenberg and Birdzell (1986) trace the rise of the modern corporation to legal reforms that began only in 1720, and that are largely confined to the nineteenth century (pp. 195–202). Even until recently, both U.S. and foreign multinational corporations tended to develop new products for home markets, relying on export sales as secondary markets. Since the 1970s, however, corporate organization has gone farther, manufacturing and marketing products in several national markets. The intense competition in international markets and the speed with which technical innovations are adopted on a global scale have created a situation in which corporate national identities have been further obscured by transnational corporate alliances and by the emergence of overlapping and truly global markets for both disposable goods and human services (Lee and Reid, 1991, p. 24).

One could continue in this vein indefinitely, but the point can be put succinctly. Although Hobbesian state of nature theory provides an adequate metaphor for characterizing the terms of military, and perhaps even economic, competition between the states of Westphalian Europe, it is woefully inadequate for the present day. National interest was, perhaps, adequately described in military terms for sixteenth-century European states, but no longer. The language of warfare is therefore a highly imperfect source of metaphors for analyzing the moral and political imperatives of international trade in the twentieth century. This broad point must be acknowledged, but specific attention to the globalization of the food and agricultural system is worthwhile.

THE AGRICULTURAL SECTOR AND THE RISE OF THE TRADING STATE

How can the significance of international trade in the world food economy be evaluated? One way is simply to look at volume. In 1984 and 1985, developed countries, not including centrally planned economies, had net exports of 127 million metric tons of cereals. The Soviet Union alone had net imports of 54 million metric tons (USDA, 1987). One need not contrast current levels of trade in food to those of the sixteenth century to see dramatic increases. Comparison over a 20-year period is sufficient. Per capita cereal imports for developing countries alone doubled between 1961 and 1981, and food aid (e.g., donations of food) declined by 50 percent on a per capita basis over the same period. In total volume, cereal imports by developing countries increased from 30 million metric tons in 1961 to 97 million metric tons in 1981

(Huddleston, 1987). Clearly, a large amount of food is crossing international borders.

The Bumpers Amendment is better testimony to the internationalization of the food economy than these numbers. American farmers in the 1980s faced declining income, despite constant domestic food prices throughout those years and the decline of inflation to its lowest point in two decades. Why? Fluctuations in exchange rates increased the cost of U.S. grain to foreign buyers. Growers in Europe and Australia expanded production in response to changes in their own domestic farm policy. Mounting Third World debt led some developing countries to import less food, and arguably worsened the credit problems of American farmers, as rural banks began to feel the squeeze (Schuh, 1987). The decade of high prices that preceded the farm crisis of the 1980s had also been tied to international trade. The success of the Organization of Petroleum Exporting Countries (OPEC) gave oil-producing states the opportunity to increase food purchases. Oil profits also found their way into many U.S. banks, fueling the surge of expansion and farm debt during the 1970s. In 1972, the Soviet Union completed the first in a series of grain purchases, expanding international demand and creating huge profits for grain traders (Morgan, 1979). As noted in Chapter 1, Earl Butz's aphoristic injunctions to "plant fencerow to fencerow," to "get big or get out," and to "use food as a weapon," were predicated on a vision of international opportunities.

Earl Butz, Dale Bumpers, ASA, AID, and the economists who forged the True Interests Thesis all share the assumption that the economic well-being of the U.S. farm community, indeed, the well-being of all U.S. residents, is a proper and legitimate concern of the U.S. government. This commonplace assumption is, however, an important point of contrast to the seventeenth century, when heads of state had no sense of responsibility for unemployment, for prices, for interest rates, for inflation, or for access to credit. The economy was not a government responsibility, and although a generous monarch might take pity on the poor, any feeling of obligation to help them would have arisen from the disparity in personal wealth, rather than from the idea that a growing economy was part of the contract. Put another way, a sovereign's obligations were completely discharged by fulfilling the security commitment. The idea that the sovereign should make the society work in any productive or distributive sense was just not part of the bargain.

Incorporating such responsibilities into the bargain has been the work of political theorists much closer to our own time. The utilitarian maxim and Rawls's difference principle are artifacts of democracy, not monarchy. The absence of this responsibility in Westphalian states meant that seventeenth-century sovereigns could freely conduct territorial campaigns without serious regard for their effect on the domestic economy. They not only had the power to do so, as Louis XIV demonstrated both amply and with panache, but they had the warrant, for the peasant economy was not their responsibility. This situation did not last beyond the eighteenth century, and the appropriate balance between geopolitical initiatives and the costs they impose on the domestic economy has continued to tip in favor of peaceful economic growth for 200 years.

The state of nature, therefore, may have been a fitting geopolitical image for a world of independent states, headed by monarchs whose primary obligation to commonfolk was one of defense. That such leaders fixed on territorial expansion and military conquest was not surprising. Westphalian states could understand national interest in Hobbesian terms. This picture of the international realm has become less descriptively accurate over the last 350 years. Even nondemocratic governments in the modern world must attempt to secure the economic health of their domestic economy, and the interpenetration of state economies makes this difficult as long as governments regard each other as combatants, real or potential. Today's states literally own pieces of one another, and their welfare is mutually interlocked. The state of nature no longer characterizes relations among nations, and its portrayal of national interest is no longer adequate.

NATIONAL INTERESTS IN NORTH/SOUTH BILATERAL RELATIONS

Kennedy and Rosecrance argue that the world has shifted from a place in which national interests could plausibly be interpreted in terms of territorial expansion and war to one in which world economic growth and stability are often more important. Governments that conceptualize foreign policy solely in terms of defense place their nation at a disadvantage to trading states that seek to build on comparative advantages and expand their domestic economy through foreign investment and exchange. In social contract terms, governments that base policy decisions on a Hobbesian picture of foreign relations leave themselves open to exploitation by nations that perceive national interest in terms of production and exchange. The rise of the trading state does not vitiate the role of national interest in foreign relations. National interest remains prominent and is not replaced by moralistic notions of human rights or global community. The reform consists in the reinterpretation of national interest.

Rosecrance's models for trading states are precisely those one would expect: contemporary West Germany, France, Japan, Taiwan, as well as nineteenth-century Great Britain for a time. These nations adopted policies that stress growth of trade over military strength, and owe their significant advantages in contemporary world politics primarily to that strategy. They are not in a state of nature with respect to one another, or with respect to any of their trading partners. Their strength and welfare are tied not to their ability to defeat other nations in war, but to their ability to trade with them on terms that are at least not disadvantageous and are often mutually advantageous. Trading states have invested in the productive economies of other nations, particularly the United States, and thereby share an interest in their growth and prosperity, rather than their weakness and defeat.

How the revised notion of national interest would apply to the bilateral relations of developed and developing countries remains to be seen. There are at least two possibilities. A pure extension of the military/territorial model would portray developing nations as potential prey for developed countries. The basic territorial objective of developed countries would be construed as closely akin to colonial domination, but this objective would be radically modified by the bilateral territorial tension between superpowers, poised to oppose each other's expansion efforts and backed by nuclear arsenals. Under this constraint, the military/territorial model is revised. Developing countries become military client states of the superpowers and are free to pursue territorial objectives of their own, perhaps as proxies for the superpowers. The alternative extreme extends the trading model into relations between developed and developing countries. Here there is little political difference between developed and developing states, because trade relations are premised on comparative advantages in any case. If trade negotiations are fair, international politics will converge on mechanisms that allow both parties to the exchange to feel satisfied that national interests are served. This is not to imply that fairness in bilateral trade relations between developed and developing economies will be easy to define or to implement; countries with large industrial economies have opportunities to impose terms on developing countries that they would not accept if their resources were larger. Furthermore, some mixture of military/territorial and trading state images is more likely to dominate the thinking of foreign policy officials in both developed and developing countries. As such, portrayal of these images as alternatives is contrived and artificial. Nevertheless, the broad contrast between a military/territorial relationship and a trading relationship provides a meaningful basis for returning to the discussion of national interest.

Developed countries have the opportunity to perceive their interests in terms of finding new trade relationships with developing countries, and in expecting to benefit from future growth and diversification of their economy. The tropical location of most developing nations suggests that opportunities for trading advantage in agriculture are great. Most developed countries lie in temperate regions that, when soil and water conditions permit, are more adaptable to production of feed grains. Tropical climates are advantageous for producing many fruits and some vegetables, as well as traditional colonial crops, such as coffee, tea, and sugar. Other advantages will surely emerge as developing countries shift to a division of labor that is more amenable to industrial manufacturing. Finding such mutual advantages will sometimes require difficult adjustments for developed countries. U.S. sugar producers have been shielded from comparative advantage for several decades, for example. If the trading state model comes to define a developed nation's sense of national interest, in some instances adjustments will inevitably have to be made in the domestic economy. To expect one group of producers to bear those costs without compensation would be unfair, but to sacrifice key national interests to appease private ones would be foolish and imprudent.

Although a developed country may perceive its national interests in terms of trade, a bilateral relationship requires that this perception be reciprocated by the less developed state. Trade with developed countries must be perceived as in the developing countries' interest, too. Some trade relationships clearly should be resisted. The most uncontroversial cases will involve trade in products that are inappropriate to the institutional structure of the developing country. Literacy and language competency are part of a society's institutional structure, for example, and trade in products that require literacy or competency in a given language could be harmful where such institutional capacities do not exist. Chemicals and drugs are among the most obvious products that fit into this category, as instructions in

117

English on proper use are of no use to someone who is illiterate or reads only Spanish or Swahili. The notion of bilateral relations built on trade does not, therefore, mean wide-open, unregulated trade. Each nation must have the opportunity to decide what forms of trade are truly in its interest, and those decisions must be respected by the more powerful party.

The alternative is the Hobbesian state of nature, but with the twist that superpowers holding nuclear arsenals fight their battles by proxy, and that expansionist developing countries achieve their objectives by walking a tightrope between ideological opponents. In some parts of the world this image is hard to resist. Civil wars in Ethiopia, Angola, and the Sudan pit populations with military/territorial objectives against one another on the subnational level. Policies that ignore the conflictual basis of foreign relations are hard to imagine in such instances. Relations with internally divided states pose difficulties that compromise the applicability of the trading state model, but not its attractiveness. In their case, a developed country's ability to realize broad-based interests are so thoroughly compromised that the narrowed set of military/territorial concerns becomes dominant by default.

Some developing country governments might opt for a military/territorial approach to policy, even if superpowers such as the United States and the Soviet Union give them opportunities to establish more peaceful relations. Any normative judgment that national interest should be conceived in trading terms is, therefore, subject to qualification when bilateral cooperation appears impossible. There is a general qualification to any endorsement of the image of the trading state. To think that a developed country such as the United States should formulate foreign policy on such terms is only reasonable if the move is expected to be reciprocated. Meanwhile, a developing country is limited in its ability to pursue the self-image of the trading state so long as superpowers continue to base policy decisions on a military/territorial model of the world. There is, in other words, an assurance problem here, as determining what one should do depends on being sure that the other party will reciprocate. The normative issue, therefore, turns on predictions regarding future North/South relations.

Rosecrance is ambivalent. He provides a series of reasons for rejecting the idea that North and South are irrevocably poised in a combative posture, at least for the short run. Here he describes a window of opportunity for moving to relationships built on trade. But he seems to endorse the idea that developing countries may need to undergo a process of institutional maturation in which territorial and ideological objectives dominate trade interests. If this is the case, the internal problems of developing countries will tend to force bilateral relations into a military/territorial mode, no matter what developed countries do. At this point *LT* becomes relevant to the general types of foreign policy considerations introduced by Kennedy and Rosecrance, for it aims to show how carefully planned development assistance can increase the probability of success for trade-based bilateral relations over the long run.

AID AND TRADE: THE LINK REPRISED

In one sense, the True Interests Thesis places too much attention on the United States relative to the countries that receive aid. The Linking Thesis relies on the same empirical claims, but it stresses that agricultural development in poor countries is crucial to the diversification and growth of their economies. General economic growth, particularly in currently underdeveloped nations, is in the U.S. national interest, not the cash payoff to individual Americans. The Linking Thesis shows why agricultural development assistance is consistent with that general vision. The completion of the argument, therefore, depends on seeing how growth in the world's poorer countries is in U.S. interests, and in seeing how *LT* links development assistance to growth. The resulting evolution in normative international political theory continues to accept national interest as a dominant goal, but modifies the notion of national interest to rest on a non-militaristic conception of international order.

There is little point in belaboring the reasons for thinking that economic growth in poor countries is in U.S. interests. This is not a new idea, but was part of the intellectual basis for creating the U.S. Agency for International Development. The rationale for creating a foreign aid program modeled on the Marshall Plan but directed toward developing countries was constructed in the 1950s and emerged as a continuing component of U.S. foreign policy during the Kennedy administration. Proponents of foreign aid to developing countries built an elaborate argument in its defense, which accepted the validity of the Humanitarian Thesis, that foreign poor are deserving of U.S. government aid by virtue of their need. However, the poor's need was deemed not enough, usually meaning that humanitarian sentiments were not capable of creating the necessary political support to get a foreign aid bill through Congress (Millikan, 1962). Supporters of foreign aid also attempted to establish two claims: that economic growth in developing countries would be in U.S. interests, and that foreign aid would be economically beneficial to the United States (Rostow, 1986). In then Senator John F. Kennedy's writings, the former of these two claims is advanced as the primary reason for foreign aid (Kennedy, 1957; 1962).

Although U.S. national interest has been continually linked to growth in Third World economies, the earlier rationale for this connection is different from that proposed by the Linking Thesis. *LT* describes how growth in the agricultural sector of developing countries can be expected to expand global demand for the feed grains in which the United States has both a proven track record in world markets and competitive advantages based on soil, climate, and technology. No moral suasion or talk of loyalty to U.S. interests is directed toward these future consumers. They are merely expected to buy grain on the world market at the prevailing market price. The previous stress on economic development in the Third World was conceived against the background of perceived rates of economic growth in the People's Republic of China and the Soviet Union that far exceeded U.S. expectations. Although these growth rates would not be sustained throughout the 1960s, the early success of socialist economies provoked Kennedy and others into the belief that sponsoring growth in developing countries and outdoing the Communists were part of a larger ideological contest. Encouragement of capitalist development was, in this view, part of the test that democracy must pass (Rostow, 1986). *LT*, therefore, makes a simple link between world development and growing world markets, as the previous rationale sees world development as part of the West's ideological struggle with the Communist world.

In point of fact, President Kennedy's rationale for foreign aid placed aid programs squarely in the foreign policy tradition that takes relations among states to be an unbridled competition of interests in which security considerations are constantly dominant. In the decades following World War II, the contest was focused almost exclusively on communist competitors, particularly the Soviet Union, but also China, which were seen as threats in conventional military/territorial terms. Although the argument for foreign aid paid homage to economic growth in developing economies and to U.S. economic interests (two components of *LT*), these themes were intended to support a conclusion that defined U.S. interests in military/territorial terms. Industrialization in the Soviet Union and Mao's Great Leap Forward appeared, in the late 1950s, to be causing unprecedented economic growth. If socialist countries exported these development programs, they would increase their territorial hegemony among unaligned powers. They would secure strategic locations for military bases and would gain allies among developing states that could, in time, become militarily significant. The Soviet Union's emerging relationship with Cuba cemented this perception, and the argument for foreign aid was unalterably fixed on a national security argument (Rostow, 1986).

Kennedy's rationale for aid is, to be sure, a national interest argument, but it is different from the one supported
by *LT*. Just as Earl Butz's plea to use "food as a weapon" entangled food policy with military metaphors in the 1970s,
President Kennedy's rationale for foreign aid entangled humanitarian and economic rationales with national security
rhetoric in the 1960s. To note this parallel is not to impugn
Kennedy's motives or judgment; the military/territorial justification for foreign aid may well be the right one in a world
accurately characterized by Hobbes's state of nature.
Kennedy's critics, however, were well aware of a number of
inconsistencies in the pro-foreign aid argument. Edward C.
Banfield notes a tension, to say the least, between the expectation that recipients of U.S. foreign aid would be loyal to the
United States in strategic matters out of gratitude, and the
expectation that the United States could extract concessions
from foreign governments in exchange for aid dollars, a
practice that would hardly inspire gratitude. Banfield dismisses the notion that a growing economy would necessarily tend toward either democracy or capitalism, meaning that
emphasis on increasing growth in developing countries
could well backfire, as far as U.S. interests were concerned
(Banfield, 1963). However, Banfield's concerns are entirely
irrelevant to the concept of U.S. national interests implicit in
LT. Whether new grain customers are capitalist, socialist, or
communist does not matter; they do not have to like the
United States; they do not even have to buy U.S. grain, so
long as they buy grain from some country in the world market, thereby increasing overall demand. Some nation will
buy U.S. grain, and the more net buyers, the better off all
grain exporting nations, most prominently, the United
States, will be.

LT explains why increasing the agricultural productivity of
developing countries is in the U.S. national interest. The national interest served by *LT* is obvious enough if one pictures
a world of trading states, whose ability to serve their citizens
depends on their active participation in a healthy world
economy. In the food policy of trading states, emergency

food aid, development assistance for agriculture, and international trade are organized to enhance the productivity of individual human beings and promote global relationships of mutually beneficial exchange. This vision of the national interest has, perhaps, been implicit in U.S. foreign policy for 40 years, but it has been entangled in political rhetoric that confuses it with national security objectives at one extreme and moralistic appeals to fulfill humanitarian duties on the other. Such confusion may be a symptom of the hope that a single rationale could undergird all foreign aid programs, but this is a vain hope. *LT* shows why agricultural assistance serves the national interest; it does not form the basis of an argument for all forms of foreign aid. Food policy is only one part of any developed country's aid and trade portfolio, and although analogies may be possible, the argument suggested here must be restricted to the narrow range of policy issues that have been addressed.

WHAT HAS NOT BEEN SHOWN

The national interest in foreign affairs must be disentangled from the military/territorial objectives that have dominated American foreign policy. Food policy has little to do with such objectives; it is, at the least, a thoroughly unreliable instrument for achieving them. The argument here, as well as Chapter 1, proposes *LT* as a strategy for articulating food policy goals that are consistent with the national interests of trading states but distinct from the military security concerns that dominate thinking on the national interest as perceived through the lens of the Hobbesian state of nature. Although that strategy has been expanded into an argument, the argument must still be regarded as hypothetical. Further analysis is needed of the adequacy of Rosecrance's thesis, its broader implications, and the links that might be made between aid, trade, and an enlightened view of national interest. Moreover, the development of *LT* presented here rests on incomplete economic research. More data and more empirical analysis are needed to determine the scope and validity of the claim that international agricultural development helps U.S. agriculture. This research should address not only the broad aggregate relationships mentioned in the popular arguments made by Purcell, Houck, and Mellor, but should also involve country-by-country and commodity-by-commodity studies of impact on three groups: producers, including the rural community, and consumers in developing countries and U.S. producers. In the light of the long-term goals of linking food policy and agricultural development with a broader view of national interest, empirical research on development should also be sensitive to a broad view of the political aims and effects of trade.

Even if empirical and conceptual links could be established, one would still need to show that the presumptive goods secured by aid were philosophically more fundamental than the presumptive constraint on aiding foreign nationals. More specifically on the level of political philosophy, there is a need for research on the philosophical foundations of development policy. The argument presented here would emphasize presumptive and discretionary goods, and where a nation's development assistance policy would fall with respect to the distinction between the two. A popular view of international aid may be as a form of charity, something that a wealthy and developed nation should do, but that is not essential to the fundamental aims of the state. Such a view seems to categorize AID policy as discretionary goods, but if the argument sketched here has any force, that categorization needs to be rethought. Although Rawls's work on primary goods, here called presumptive goods, has generated considerable philosophical discussion, few authors have attempted to integrate them into economic development theory, and even fewer studies have applied the distinction to specific policy problems.

Other philosophers have seen promise in a strategy that stresses the humanitarian basis of food policy but attempts to redefine the Humanitarian Thesis to give its claims greater political strength. This argument also ties food policy to the political idea referred to here as "presumptive goods." As already defined, these are goods that government must make every effort to secure if it is to survive as a legitimate holder of power, and they can be divided into those stipulated in terms of national interest and those required for justice. If agricultural development assistance is to be classified among presumptive goods, it must involve either justice or national interest. The strategy chosen here stresses national interest, but perhaps the goals of development assistance are demanded by justice. Although one has reason to be skeptical of this strategy, it has been pursued in philosophical works by Henry Shue, James W. Nickel, Charles R. Beitz, Thomas Nagel, William Aiken, and Thomas W. Pogge, as well as in such popular books as Frances Moore Lappe and Joseph Collins's *Food First* and Susan George's *How the Other Half Dies*. The argument stressing national interest is, for the most part, compatible with arguments stressing humanitarian notions of justice. But what has been presented so far should not be regarded as a philosophical challenge to this tradition of thought. Chapter 6 takes up some of these arguments, not with the idea of refuting them, but to examine their strengths and weaknesses in the light of recent political rhetoric.

Chapter 6

Humanitarianism, hunger, and moral theory

Philosophical analysis of hunger as a moral issue has roots in antiquity and figures in discussions of ethics and political philosophy throughout the roughly 3,000-year history of recorded philosophical thinking. The twentieth century, however, is a special case. When hunger and food policy became important political issues in the 1970s, the basis for contemplating hunger as a moral issue was reinvented, almost totally. The aim here is not to recover the past, but to examine the moral analysis of food policy that began to emerge about 20 years ago and to assess its relevance to the policy problems that are the primary topic of Chapters 1–5. Because the recent philosophical analysis of food policy arose in conjunction with a broad technical and political debate over the causes of world hunger and the prospects for eliminating hunger worldwide, the last 30 years of popular and philosophical writing on the moral issues in food policy can be referred to as the world hunger literature.

There is one general reason why most world hunger literature is inapplicable to the competitiveness issues raised by the Bumpers Amendment. Most authors that will be discussed here do not consider the political mandate for official aid philosophically important. The creation of organizations like the U.S. Agency for International Development (AID) is not taken up in the existing philosophical literature. The preceding chapters, however, focus almost exclusively on the philosophical problems that arise in attempting to specify and defend AID's mandate. The assumption has been that officers of government agencies have a responsibility to use their resources in ways that are constrained by this mandate, though a mandate must be interpreted more broadly than the enabling legislation that creates an agency and authorizes its budget. If this assumption is maintained, philosophical justification of development assistance policies must include inquiry into the political consensus that creates a mandate for agencies such as AID and, indeed, confine itself to ideas and values determined by that consensus.

In a review of the ethical foundations for aid (1987), Roger Riddell examines how libertarian, utilitarian, Marxist, Rawlsian, and human rights arguments have been and most plausibly would be applied to the evaluation of official development assistance. Although he sketches how utilitarian, Rawlsian, and more conventional rights theories provide grounds for a prima facie justification of aid, he is primarily preoccupied with replying to aid critics. Criticisms are, in Riddell's analysis, of three sorts: libertarian arguments that reject positive political duties altogether; liberal arguments that reject aid on the ground that it does more harm than good; and realist arguments that reject any role for morality in foreign affairs. Riddell's replies to these arguments are insightful, and his extended analysis of the effectiveness of aid is particularly well developed. In this book libertarian views are discussed in Chapter 3, where the principle of noninterference is linked to a pro-Bumpers argument. But one must remember that the Linking Thesis (*LT*) is not libertarian in its foundation, though its emphasis on national interests is, in part, constructed to appease those who hold libertarian and contractualist views. Although criticisms of the effectiveness of aid programs are certainly relevant to the overall evaluation of aid, they are not crucial to the arguments examined in this book. The historical pattern of aid instruments may or may not be effective in securing the goals of development, but the main concern here is the shape and content of the goals, not the means for achieving them. The so-called realists who allegedly deny any role for morality in foreign relations have proved harder to ignore, despite the initial judgment that they had been adequately disposed of by such authors as Beitz and Cohen. Realist themes appear at intervals and are the final topic in the concluding chapter.

Riddell's group of pro-aid theorists (utilitarians, Rawlsians, and rights theorists) provides the overlap between development literature and conventional moral theory. The central elements of these three arguments are reviewed briefly in this chapter. This literature is not really directed to the claim that there is a political obligation to bring aid to the needy of the world's poorest countries. The problem, as Riddell notes, is that official aid is seldom discussed in philosophical literature. Authors in this group tend to dispense with questions regarding the link between personal moral obligation and political action in a few sentences, concentrating their analysis on a moral obligation to help the needy that applies more to individuals than to official agencies. The absence of discussion on political obligations, as distinct from moral ones, is the occasion for Riddell's judgment that no systematic and comprehensive case for official aid exists.

Ethical theorists have failed to justify this omission. Most ethical and political theories identify many moral obligations that governments have no responsibility to enforce or discharge. Liberals and conservatives often differ with regard to areas of morality reserved for individual responsibility, but the pattern of distinguishing between purely moral and purely political obligations is such a constant in Western ethics and political theory that the failure to take up political obligations in the literature on world hunger seems like an oversight. One can impute several strategies for addressing official aid to authors who do not take it up explicitly. One strategy assumes that political obligations for offering aid are fully spelled out in conventional social contract theory. This possibility is taken up in Chapter 3. Each of Riddell's three arguments for aid – utilitarian, Rawlsian, and rights-based – points toward a different strategy in which the fundamental terms of moral obligation are assumed to establish political obligations, as well. Utilitarian and rights theories do this by establishing comprehensive moral imperatives, which, presumably, governments as well as individuals are obliged to follow. Because Rawlsian arguments incorporate contractual language into their account of moral obligation, one can reasonably think of them as extending contractual obligations beyond the range established in conventional social contract theory. The balance of the chapter will show that no one has yet succeeded in applying these strategies to the mandate for official aid.

NONCONTRACTUAL STRATEGIES FOR UNDERSTANDING WORLD HUNGER

Beginning with Peter Singer's landmark article in 1972, an extensive literature has developed on the moral imperatives of policies directed to the relief of starvation. Singer presents a philosophically neutral argument in that one need not share his utilitarian views to find the case for famine relief convincing (1977, pp. 35–36). Singer asks his readers to accept two premises: that suffering and death from starvation are bad, and that when we have the power to prevent evil without sacrificing anything of comparable worth, we should do so. The article is prefaced by a description of famine in East Bengal, and a comparison of British government spending on famine relief with spending on the supersonic Concord aircraft. Singer's article had been preceded in 1971 by Garrett Hardin's "Lifeboat Ethics: The Case Against Helping the Poor." The debate was fully engaged with the publication of anthologies edited by George Lucas and Thomas Ogletree (1976) and by William Aiken and Hugh LaFollette (1977). By the end of the decade dozens of philosophical articles on world hunger had appeared, and duties beyond borders became entrenched in philosophy textbooks on contemporary moral problems. Twenty years after publication of the original articles, Singer and Hardin continue to dominate textbooks.

Despite Singer's attempt at philosophical neutrality, his article attracted attention because his elementary application of the utilitarian maxim demands far more from citizens of developed countries than has traditionally been the case.[1] A person on the brink of starvation suffers far more from lack of food than do wealthy people who defer the satisfaction of higher pleasures to contribute some of their wealth to famine relief. If we are to act in a way that produces the greatest good, and if we are to count the interests of all parties equally, we must support famine relief as a moral duty, and not merely as an act of charity. Singer also argues that utilitarian principles require individuals to petition their governments to participate in famine relief.

Singer's argument is now often counterpoised against the so-called lifeboat ethics of Garrett Hardin and Joseph Fletcher. Hardin wrote a series of articles beginning in the late sixties and throughout the early seventies in which he analyzes moral and management problems associated with explosive growth in human population. In his 1971 article, he attempts to show that food aid and famine relief of the sort advocated by Singer would contribute to rampant population growth in the developing world. Hardin argues that the long-range consequences of hunger relief would cause more death and suffering than simply doing nothing. Fletcher puts the conceptually simple normative premise of Hardin's argument into a philosophically more rigorous format: "Give if it helps, but not if it hurts" (1977; see also Fletcher, 1976).

Philosophically, Hardin and Singer share the same ground. Both accept act utilitarianism as their general ethical principle. According to this philosophy, the morality of an act is evaluated by its likely consequences. The right action produces the greatest good for the greatest number of people. Application of the act utilitarian principle can become complex; interpersonal welfare comparisons and social discounting of distant consequences await those who wish to pursue a more thorough analysis of the Singer/Hardin debate. With respect to these philosophical and methodological questions, whatever goes for Singer surely goes for Hardin, as well. Although evaluating outcome in terms of lives saved and lost oversimplifies hunger issues, comparisons of the greater good accurately capture the spirit of the utilitarian philosophy endorsed by both Singer and Hardin. They differ in their assessment of the consequences, not in philosophy. Both Singer and Hardin are willing to assess the morality of an action by comparing the expected consequences, and both agree that the right action among all alternatives is the one that optimizes outcome.

The ensuing literature on world hunger is notable for its almost total rejection of the act utilitarianism endorsed by Singer, Hardin, and Fletcher. Aside from an important paper by James Rachels (1977) linking hunger to the suffering of animals produced for the consumption of meat, the principal contributions to world hunger literature have stressed nonconsequential accounts of rights and duties.[2] Nonconsequential analysis of the ethics of hunger appeared in 1975 with the publication of Arthur Simon's *Bread for the World*, a book that spawned the relief organization of the same name. Like Hardin, Simon does not explicitly use moral theory in stating the basis for relief. His book includes a discussion of the disparity in income and well-being between the average citizen of the developing world and the average American. He suggests that this disparity establishes a moral duty to aid the world's poor. Simon proposes standards for evaluating assistance policy that would be gauged according to the need of aid recipients, distribution of benefits among the poor, reform of repressive political structures in developing nations, human rights, and a deemphasis on military spending. Absent are criteria that suggest weighing the benefits and harm of giving relief to the victims of hunger. Needs and rights are stressed, suggesting a philosophical argument for aid based on a duty to secure human rights.

Systematic nonconsequential arguments for aid appeared in 1975 with the publication of Onora O'Neill's "Lifeboat Earth," an article that takes Hardin's lifeboat metaphor as its starting point. O'Neill examines whether the act of refusing to give aid should be understood as a form of killing and whether exculpatory circumstances, such as self-defense, would permit killing famine victims. The "triage" theme was analyzed in some depth by papers in *Lifeboat Ethics: The Moral Dilemmas of World Hunger* (Lucas and Ogletree, 1976). Two books that collect original and previously published papers by many authors appeared in 1977: Brown and Shue's *Food Policy: The Responsibility of the United States in Life and Death Choices* and Aiken and LaFollette's *World Hunger and Moral Obligation* expanded the philosophical literature on world hunger dramatically. Although neither work is unilaterally committed to rights-based moral theory, they introduced nonconsequential, neo-Kantian moral theory into the world hunger literature.

The argument based on rights presented a philosophically important contrast to the utilitarian arguments of Hardin and, for many readers, a far more plausible account of the reasons for giving aid than did Singer. The suggestion that the poor of the developing world have a rights claim against developed countries for food and resources is a strong response to Hardin's lifeboat ethics. In this view, morality requires that their rights be ensured, as long as doing so does not violate equally important rights for others. Consequences do not count against this claim, as only after basic, minimal rights have been fully assured do we begin to consider cost, efficiency, and long-term consequences. The rights argument was also more plausible than Singer's utilitarianism in that by requiring us always to do the best thing for the greatest number, Singer set a standard that few could hope to follow. The rights argument gives individuals great discretion over choices that are "within their rights" and requires action only when the rights of others are violated (Van Wyk, 1988).

Discussion of nonconsequential world hunger literature is complicated by two factors. First, important theoretical differences distinguish the views of each contributor to this literature. Significant contributions to the rights-based criticism of Singer and Hardin were made by Arthur (1977), Gorovitz (1977), and Shue (1977), but for more positive attempts to state the terms of rights and obligations, see Aiken (1977, 1982), Bedau (1979), O'Neill (1980, 1986), Nickel

(1987), Shue (1980), Watson (1977), who introduce a variety of philosophical strategies. For example, though most authors stress rights, Onora O'Neill's *Faces of Hunger* (1986) rejects formulations that found duties on human rights, preferring instead an application of deontic logic that makes agency the fundamental moral criterion. The second complicating factor is that arguments for aid based on extending the scope of social contract theory substantially overlap with the neo-Kantian foundations of most rights literature on world hunger. Although rights-based philosophy is a noncontractual argument for giving aid, rights-based arguments may share deeper philosophical foundations with the contract-extending arguments of Charles Beitz and Thomas Nagel. A more telling contrast might be neo-Kantian approaches, including contractual arguments, and utilitarian ones. Sorting out theoretical relationships among all these positions would doubtless try the patience of even the most committed reader. This analysis will, therefore, be confined to a few representative rights-based and contractual positions.

HUNGER AND THE MORALITY
OF HUMAN RIGHTS

Irrespective of the debate between Singer and Hardin, one trait of utilitarian and consequential normative theories has long and widely been regarded as a defect. In utilitarian reasoning, the number of affected parties counts, but in matters affecting the vital interests of individual human beings, numbers should not count. For example, one can easily imagine situations in which providing small benefits to a large number of people "outweighs" causing significant harm to a small number of individuals. The human rights tradition provides philosophical grounds for explaining why trade-offs that are justifiable in terms of the sum of incrementally small units of utility are unjustifiable when they harm vital interests of individuals, even though the aggregate harm may be comparatively small. Although it is not clear that this criticism requires the sacrifice of consequential theory, there is little doubt that the criticism has force within the context of development ethics.[3] Henry Shue (1977), for example, notes that when assistance policy aims at maximizing the increase in productivity of developing economies per aid dollar spent, the needs and interests of the poor may well be left behind. As aiding the poor is a principal component of the mandate for foreign assistance programs, blind utilitarian maximizing of aggregate productivity is inconsistent with the moral basis for foreign aid.

Having made the critical point, however, rights theory must provide some guidance for decision making. A rights theory applicable to policy determination must fulfill at least two requirements. First, it must include an account of what human rights are and how conflicts among legitimate rights claims are to be adjudicated. Second, it must include an account of why this set of rights and rules for adjudication is morally authoritative. These requirements are not unrelated. Although the first requirement can be fulfilled by any well schooled and reasonably clever rights theorist, the sheer multiplicity of rights theories converts the second requirement into the crucial burden of proof for nonconsequential philosophies. Anyone with a healthy skepticism regarding moral theory will want to see the second requirement met before investing much effort into an examination of theoretical structure.

Criticisms of rights theory in the world hunger literature note precisely this point. Mark Blitz (1982) and Rogers Smith (1989) both fault Henry Shue's *Basic Rights: Subsistence, Affluence, and U.S. Foreign Policy* (1980) for failing to justify his philosophically sophisticated application of rights theory to food policy. In Shue's theory, rights claims are interwoven in a web. Possession of one right fails to become meaningful unless others are also guaranteed. The right of free speech means little unless the right to personal security ensures that we will not be beaten whenever we speak. Shue's book shows how rights claims can be adjudicated according to their lexical order. That is, rights can be ordered into a pyramid so that claims made at the level of, say, the right to a college education become meaningful only when prior claims in the lexical order – more fundamental building blocks of the pyramid – have been satisfied. Other rights, such as rights to subsistence and security, require only the minimum network of rights. The right to an education, in this view, winds up as an important but higher level right than rights to personal security, life, or basic liberties.

Shue argues that a society should climb as high on the rights pyramid as it can, but it should never guarantee high-level rights for some when doing so ignores more basic rights for others. Shue's application of rights theory takes food policy and the right to subsistence as its primary policy problem. Shue is able to put the theory in service to the claim that developed countries must not supply their citizens with higher order rights and privileges while noncitizens' basic right to subsistence is neglected. Blitz and Smith appear to accept Shue's theory as an adequate solution to rights theory's first requirement, giving structure to decision making, though Smith calls for more detail. They find that Shue's reply to the second requirement misses altogether, however. Both authors use this alleged deficiency in Shue's theory as an opportunity to promote far narrower, libertarian rights theories of their own.

This criticism is unfair, though Shue invites it by writing that a right is the rational basis for a justified demand. He also writes, "I do not know how to characterize in general and in the abstract what counts as a rational basis or a rational justification" (p. 13). O'Neill (1988a) includes Shue among those philosophers offering constructivist strategies for addressing the second, foundational requirement. Philosophical constructivism offers a way to justify the use of abstract terms that appear to have no natural referent. We think that the claim $2 + 2 = 4$ is true, for example, but since the time of the Greeks, philosophers of mathematics have struggled to understand numbers, equations, and other mathematical relations as referring expressions. To which objects does $2 + 2 = 4$ refer? Kant's answer is that the meaningful use of mathematical expressions is implicit in and presupposed by a certain perspective or "view" of natural phenomena. The philosophical warrant for accepting the claim $2 + 2 = 4$ does not consist in its reference to either natural or ideal entities, but in its role in the construction of a comprehensive and mutually consistent view or account of the natural world. For the perceiving subject to possess a rationally ordered representation or view of reality requires a mental act of imposing order on manifold sense experience. The subject constructs this order by organizing experience into a rational pattern. The objectivity of the subjective perspective from which construction occurs can be specified apart from the arbitrary and peculiar contingencies that characterize the subjectivity of any human being, thinking and perceiving at a given time and place. Construction is an ongoing and dynamic activity, so the warrant for a constructivist claim is not strictly equivalent to a coherence theory of truth. The construction must get us on to the next step, and although constructivist commitments may always need to be revised, we will be reluctant to tear down too much.

This highly metaphorical account of constructivism in mathematics need only provoke an analogous account of how the strategy might be applied in ethics and political philosophy. We find ourselves in a historical situation in which rights claims bear a great deal of weight in our understanding of duty, entitlement, and obligation. Such words as "duty," "entitlement," and "obligation" can only become meaningful when one accepts or adopts a comprehensive view or account of normative phenomena in which these concepts are mutually supporting. A particular structure of rights claims (the lexical ordering of Shue's pyramid) is justified when one shows its capacity (1) to guide action and (2) to achieve a coherent statement of the scope and force of morality. Natural law theory of ages past justified rights claims by postulating an omniscient and all-powerful God as the authority for natural rights. Contemporary rights theory rests on the construction of an idealized moral agent, motivated by a desire to act rightly, capable of understanding that the interests of all persons, rich or poor, are affected by alternative ways of defining right action, but incapable of giving priority to any set of interests.

Readers who wish to know more about recent constructivist arguments should consult Rawls (1980), O'Neill (1986), or Hill (1989). Onora O'Neill gives a concise and convincing account of constructivist strategies applied to rights in "Childrens' Rights and Childrens' Lives" (1988a), though she applies the strategy more directly to international justice in "Ethical Reasoning and Ideological Pluralism" (1988b). Shue's use of the constructivist strategy is implicit, but his 1980 book conforms to the strategy laid out explicitly by Rawls, O'Neill, and Hill. The aim here is to demonstrate why Shue's theory is better grounded than Blitz and Smith thought, and to lay the groundwork for the discussion of how constructivism relates to the myth of scarcity in Chapter 7. All neo-Kantians mentioned here, including Shue, justify moral claims by demonstrating that the moral structure of rights and duties follows logically from a perspective of pure rationality.

EXTENDING THE SOCIAL CONTRACT

Singer's utilitarianism and Shue's theory of subsistence rights offer general accounts of morality, right action, and obligation. If these concepts can be applied to government agencies as well as to individual human beings, then their theories can be interpreted to justify development assistance and hunger relief policies. *If* these theories can be applied to the limited agency of a government organization, one can produce strong moral justification for giving aid. Even if they cannot be unambiguously applied to government agencies, utilitarian and rights concepts can be used to articulate reasons why citizens in a democracy might support foreign aid. Therefore, even if the attempt to apply moral concepts to governmental organizations directly fails, aid policies might still be democratically justified, providing that citizens accept the argument. The policies would be justified not by the moral arguments, but because a majority of citizens want aid policies. This alternative use of utilitarian and rights-based arguments provides weak political justification for aid, an argument with the same claim on democratic procedure as the argument justifying competitiveness.

A stronger claim on democratic procedure would be required to show that aid is owed as a matter of justice. Attempts to justify international redistributive actions by extending the scope of the social contract differ from the arguments offered by Singer and Shue in precisely this respect. They provide a theory of justice that is conceptually and politically separated from the broader claims of moral theory. In other words, extensionist arguments are weaker than the moral justification available in one interpretation of utilitarian and rights theory. Because they are contract arguments, they base justifications on political, rather than moral, considerations. At the same time, social contract theory does provide a theory of justice that is binding on government action, regardless of majority opinion. The extensionist approach does make international redistribution a requirement of justice. In this respect, it is stronger than political justification based on consensus alone.

The contractual argument differs from utilitarianism and rights theory by basing the moral duty to help the poor on obligations incurred through social intercourse, however indirect, with them. It is not as if a moral reason independent of political and economic dealings with the world's poor requires people in the developed world to act; rather these political and economic dealings themselves create an implicit contract, an implicit agreement of mutual benefit and consent. If we use our wealth to coerce them into accepting inequitable terms, or terms to which they would not otherwise consent, the contract is flawed and unjust. Food and development assistance are owed to make the bargain fair. One may still reasonably talk of rights, not of inalienable, metaphysical, or constructivist human rights, but of rights that function as expectations created in the course of social transactions. Such rights are less philosophically binding than human rights, but they do serve the rhetorical purposes of rights, namely, showing why we are obligated to bring aid, why neo-Malthusian arguments are no excuse for failing to bring aid, and why, contra-Singer, we are *not* required to take up the sackcloth and devote our lives to the poor.

Extensionist arguments can be found in papers by C. F. Runge (1977) and Thomas Nagel (1977). The most developed versions are Charles Beitz's *Political Theory and International Relations* (1979) and Thomas Pogge's *Realizing Rawls* (1989). All four build on Rawls's *A Theory of Justice*. The main point is to deny any basis for excluding the foreign poor from the original position, the precontractual negotiation that forms the basis for a broad commitment to provide primary goods. The problem in applying the strategy to foreign policy debates is that, if taken seriously, it so thoroughly vitiates present institutions of international relations that one can hardly understand how the emerging contract could guide them. A certain amount of unrealism is always associated with social contract theory, but unless contractors in an original position would agree to something resembling the current world system of states, and it is not at all clear that they would, the gap between theory and practice becomes impossible to breach.

An extreme example of the problem can be found in a paper by Edward McClennen (1986) in which he takes up questions of military security. McClennen argues that if contractors in the original position know of the possibility of nuclear weapons, they will in accordance with maximin principles minimize the risk of nuclear war. The most obvious way to do this is to opt for world government, thereby rendering the current system of states illegitimate along with those states' capacity to procure nuclear weapons. McClennen's argument puts an interesting twist on the deterrence debate, but it also serves as a reductio ad absurdum with respect to Rawlsian contractarianism in international relations. As the system of states is illegitimate *tout court*, one has little reason to hope that foreign relations can ever be grounded philosophically. Put another way, if there are *no* legitimate foreign relations, international politics is left to the pursuit of domination and power. As in the case of Singer's argument for fairness relief, the moral requirement is so far from practical reality that it vitiates the theoretical approach entirely.

Beitz is aware of this problem, and he responds in his book by suggesting that states contract, rather than individuals. For Beitz, the existence of states is assumed, but their exact borders, and, therefore, their claims to natural resources within their borders, are being negotiated behind the veil of ignorance. As in standard Rawlsian contract theory, this negotiation determines states' claims to primary goods: soil, water, forests, and mineral resources, which are often keys to national wealth. Beitz then follows Rawls in arguing that the standard for a fair distribution of these resources is determined by the distribution that would exist if natural borders were established from behind the veil of ignorance. Beitz's theory of international justice entails a duty to bring aid that is roughly parallel to the welfare rights established by Rawls's Difference Principle. As fair distribution requires equal access to resources, wealthy states have an obligation to redistribute resources under their control in the existing state of affairs.

Beitz's extension of Rawlsian contract theory successfully articulated a prima facie case for redistributive aid, but the mechanism of states behind a veil of ignorance is too cumbersome to withstand application to public policy. Perhaps the greatest single problem is that Beitz's theory establishes redistributive obligations on a state-to-state basis. Although this way of framing international justice avoids McClennen's problem, it stumbles when confronted with the fact that governments in many developing countries receiving food and development aid are singularly notable for imposing injustice on their own people. Although Beitz's theory might have some plausibility in a world of equally just states, the condition of underdevelopment often spawns repression, elitism, and generally unattractive behavior on the part of recipient governments. These themes have been persistently argued by libertarian development theorists such as P. T. Bauer, and Riddell has already analyzed them thoroughly. But if Western governments have an obligation to developing countries, it is to the people of these countries, and it is to promote just government within those countries. That policy must be formulated on a government-to-government basis is a reality of foreign aid, but the idea that duties of redistribution are owed to governments that have demonstrated little concern for morality and justice strains credulity. One can partially rehabilitate Beitz's position by stressing the conventional distinction between states and governments, but doing so only moves the argument back to the domain of pure theory, offering the policy analyst every opportunity to neglect the alleged political obligation whenever it becomes inconvenient.

Beitz's work has been discussed by Riddell (1987) and by Luper-Foy (1988, pp. 1–22) and has been criticized from a libertarian perspective by Mack (1988). The conceptual problems of extending a Rawlsian approach into international relations are formidable. Not the least of them is that Beitz's strategy places negotiations among states in a thoroughly ambiguous position with respect to the negotiations among individuals that would establish the state in the first place. Are states bound by the two principles when undertaking their subsequent negotiations? If so, doesn't that constrain a state that would have either to violate the liberties of its citizens or make transfers that do not benefit its worst-off citizens? A thorough critique of Beitz's version of Rawlsian international relations theory is a major project. The 1983 paper "Cosmopolitan Ideals and National Sentiment," however, appears to retreat from the position developed in *Political Theory and International Relations* and may place Beitz in a position more like Shue's than Rawls's. In this paper, Beitz appears to base his "cosmopolitan ideal" on duties that people in the developed North have to the poor in the less developed South. This is different from a duty established by a redistributive contract among states, and much of what has been said with respect to the views of O'Neill and Shue would apply to this revision of Beitz's position, as well. As such, let us cut short the critique of Beitz to examine the applicability of moral theory to the problems of official aid more directly. Pogge has provided the most thorough development of extensionist strategy; his views are discussed in some detail in the final section of this chapter. But first, let us take up the common flaw of world hunger literature in general.

THE LIMITATIONS OF MORAL THEORY

As already noted, Riddell found fault with world hunger literature for its inattention to the justification for official aid. By official aid, Riddell meant government aid programs, whether administered by intragovernmental organizations, such as AID, or by multilateral organizations, such as the World Bank or the Food and Agriculture Organization (FAO) of the United Nations. An inspection of the literature summarized in the preceding section bears out Riddell's judgment. Peter Singer's treatment of official aid in "Famine, Affluence, and Morality" (1972), for example, is directed at the possibility that "overseas aid should be a government responsibility, and that therefore one ought not to give to privately run charities" (p. 239). Singer goes on to state that governments should be doing more, but his thesis is intended to prove that the responsibility falls on individuals. There is no discussion of where government's responsibility comes from.

Singer's general lack of interest in publicly funded aid can be seen in passages from his 1977 article on famine relief, where he rebuts libertarian criticisms of his earlier position:

[W]hile Nozick would oppose government aid paid for by taxation, he might well accept the Famine Relief Argument insofar as it applies to what individuals ought voluntarily to do. True, Nozick would reject the claim that rich people have an "obligation" to give to the starving, but he could still grant

that giving is something we ought to do, and that though failing to give is not unjust, it is – since justice is not all there is
to morality – morally wrong. (p. 41)

Singer's main objective is to establish a moral argument that
demonstrates why individuals are morally obliged to help
the poor, generally, and the foreign poor, in particular. He
goes on to reject Nozick's theory of justice, perhaps implying that the moral obligation that falls on individuals falls on
governments, as well. Singer along with most authors writing on the moral issues of hunger and development aid
never discusses in any detail how these individualistic moral
obligations translate into government responsibilities.

Utilitarian arguments would establish the moral basis of
foreign aid on the good that it does for recipients, relative to
its cost for providers. Human rights theories establish the
aid recipient's justified moral claim to life, subsistence, and,
perhaps, opportunity, and deduce a correlative moral duty
to provide aid for those capable of doing so. Both approaches
assume an agent capable of bringing aid. To the extent that
government should provide aid, government must have the
power or capacity of bringing aid implicit in the general notion of moral agency. This point is well stated in Onora
O'Neill's *Faces of Hunger*, one of the few sources where an argument for government's duty to provide development assistance is given serious attention.

O'Neill defends the view that governments have a duty to
perform foreign assistance actions, but her view departs
from both the utilitarian and the rights-based arguments
that appear most frequently in world hunger literature.
O'Neill's moral theory is a form of Kantian constructivism in
which agency is the basic moral concept. Rights and goods
are less fundamental constructs that serve as the objects of
moral action. Constructivism has already been discussed as
a general approach to moral issues, and its relevance to development ethics has been examined at some length by Blatz
(1991). In O'Neill's view, an agent cannot, on pain of self-
negating contradiction, intentionally sanction, much less

perform, acts that undercut or violate the possibility of rational agency by others. To do so would be to accept a principle that denies the primacy of rational moral agency, which is to deny the warrant for intentional, goal-seeking action.[4] The argument is relevant to the warrant for government assistance programs, because O'Neill also demonstrates how government bodies fulfill the ontological conditions for agency. In other words, organizations, including government organizations, that can function, that can act, are subject to all the requirements of morality.[5] If individuals have duties to bring aid, so do governments.

O'Neill's arguments establish convincingly that where forms of collective agency, including governments, commercial corporations, and other private organizations, have been brought into existence, they have obligations to follow certain aspects of the moral code. They certainly have duties to desist from actively harming people or from interfering with their private choices, and O'Neill's argument is reasonably convincing as to why organized collective agents should be obliged to perform at least some positive duties, to act on someone's behalf. For example, morality would require multinational companies operating in developing countries to accept some responsibility for providing health and welfare benefits to employees, even though they may not be legally required to do so. The difficulty with O'Neill's position is that some collective agencies would never come into existence if they were required to perform the full range of duties required of O'Neill's moral agents. The organizations supervising and conducting official aid programs are likely to be among them.

Organizations have mandates. Individual human beings form organizations with the explicit purpose of achieving certain ends. Although an organization's mandate can be vague or can grow and change over time, when an organization oversteps the boundaries of its mandate, it may cease to command the assent, the cooperation that makes its mandate possible. An organization can, of course, become so powerful that it can force individuals to cooperate, and this is why political philosophers have questioned the legitimacy of government organizations in the first place. There is a distinction, however, between government at large and the various organizations that arise to perform specific tasks within government. One can admit that individuals have the responsibility to form organizations that can address the problems of world hunger, and even that governments broadly conceived have positive duties to the needy of other countries, but deny that organizations conducting official aid programs should base decisions on the full range of moral imperatives. The mandate, created by due process, that brings a government organization into being may restrict official aid to those activities that have consensual, political support, even when morality seems to require more. If a government or governments create organizations like the World Bank, the Food and Agriculture Organization of the United Nations, or the U.S. Agency for International Development, and they do so by exercising duly authorized powers, the officers of these organizations are bound to administer their activities within the bounds of their legislative mandate. To fail in this duty on the ground that governments have a broader duty to bring aid would be to place themselves not only beyond the authority of legitimate government, but above national and international law.

What is more, the underlying mandate for the existence of these organizations is found within the political culture of the societies that support them. The legal authority bringing them into existence resides in duly elected or appointed officials, but the moral authority for doing so resides in what Rawls calls the overlapping consensus, the decidedly untidy but often effective conglomeration of ideas, values, and beliefs that can be drawn on to support government policies for philosophically contrary reasons. The overlapping consensus rests on the constitution of a society, the norms, institutions, and practices that interact with ideas, beliefs, and values in defining and reproducing the life of the national community. The constitutional mandate for organizations like AID provides the U.S. government with a rationale for conducting development assistance programs, despite a lack of unanimity among U.S. citizens about the moral permissibility or obligation for foreign aid. If the officials charged with administering foreign aid programs depart too radically, or too publicly, from the vague terms of AID's constitutional mandate, the consensus may well come apart. A serious breach of the overlapping consensus would leave Americans with no official development assistance programs, a turn of events that is hardly consistent with the central thrust of O'Neill's philosophical position.

Moral theories that do not analyze the limited, consensual forms of collective agency most likely to carry out aid programs, therefore, do not adequately address a serious philosophical issue. The failure to address the basis of limited organizational agency does not imply that these moral theories are "wrong" in any deep philosophical sense, for arguments at the political level of an overlapping consensus may not even penetrate to the fundamental questions of moral theory. Indeed, ethical arguments on world hunger can be offered as rationally based but essentially rhetorical attempts to influence political behavior or to form ideas, values, and beliefs that are operative at the political level. The arguments would not be intended as a philosophical analysis of the constitutional mandate for development aid but as persuasive gestures, intended to mobilize political action. The philosophical literature is not, however, primarily rhetorical in its intent, though few authors can resist opportunities for persuasion that analysis occasionally provides. Analysis *does* influence ideas, values, and beliefs, even when truth, rather than power, is its primary intention.

Nevertheless, the limited and consensual mandate legitimates, justifies, or otherwise validates the creation of limited, consensual forms of agency within the broader functions of democratic government. Foundational arguments of moral theory may apply to fully rational, autonomous agents, but AID's limited agency is hardly autonomous. Perhaps agencies such as AID are not true moral agents, but political argument over the mandate for agricultural development assistance has tremendous impact on the good that the U.S. government can actually do. The interplay of various interest groups comes into focus at this level of specificity. The broad rationales for giving aid provided by utilitarian and rights-based theories might explain why Americans should form organizations to discharge these duties, but they are too uncompromising in their views of moral obligation to account for the consensus on which they actually do so. Social contract theory has always had the comparative advantage in addressing philosophical questions regarding organized power and the agreements that make power legitimate, and for this reason contract theory is the nearly exclusive focus of this book.

As already noted, the assumption that governments have duties to abide by the same moral obligations and ideals that fall on individual human beings has been criticized by Rogers M. Smith (1989), who finds fault at three junctures. First, Smith claims that the world hunger literature " . . . suggest[s] an unjustified certainty about the requirements of morality that can prevent us from acknowledging the frailties of our view and exploring others" (p. 43). Second, Smith accuses the neo-Kantian authors of much hunger literature of placing too much importance on distributive justice, particularly in relation to pursuit of the good life. Third, Smith writes that "their treatment of morality as principles of justice standing above national senses of purpose prevents these writers from seeing why a nation may legitimately presume that the preservation of its collective existence and interest generally constitutes a valid moral imperative" (p. 44). Smith continues his analysis of the moral basis for foreign assistance by offering a libertarian theory that places most of the moral burden on private voluntary organizations, while mandating U.S. government action for policies that "promote liberty for nonnationals" (p. 54). This limited mandate is constrained by prior negative duties not to infringe on liberties, unless the liberties of American citizens are at stake, and by a prior political duty to "enhance the secure possession and enjoyment of . . . liberties for Americans" (p. 53).

Smith's rejection of the main arguments in world hunger literature is symptomatic of the problem created when one moves too quickly from moral theory to political obligation. That Smith is himself careless in moving from libertarian premises to a policy prescription for development assistance should not obscure the point. Social contract theory presumes that differences of opinion on fundamental moral views do exist, and attempts to adduce reasons for consensual agreement on policy despite these differences. Contract theory is being used here to infer some points of consensus (points that relate back to the contract argument) from the political rhetoric engendered by the Bumpers Amendment. The suggested reform in the interpretation of contract theory should be consistent with the consensual mandate for AID.

Simply dismissing world hunger literature as irrelevant to official aid would be disingenuous, however. Even if arguments from moral theory cannot explain why governments should contribute aid, they articulate general reasons why individuals should support such activities, without regard to whether the aid programs are public or private. World hunger literature explains why many people think that humanitarian aid is important. The values advanced in the literature contribute to an overlapping consensus for foreign assistance. Smith's criticisms explain why other people think that governments should not pursue some important values by demonstrating points where values articulated by neo-Kantian moral theory may fail to overlap sufficiently with libertarian values. Chapters 1 through 5 suggest that humanitarian values might be more relevant to the national interest than to justice. This point aside, the moral argument for direct duties beyond borders is still a serious component of the consensual basis for foreign aid. As such, the main versions of the argument for aid have been reviewed in preparation for a summary argument presented in Chapter 8. Unfortunately, the philosophical literature is also vulnerable to entirely different criticisms, which are taken up in Chapter 7.

THOMAS POGGE'S GLOBALIZATION OF RAWLS

Thomas Pogge's *Realizing Rawls* (1989) is the most extensive and most sophisticated attempt to date to apply social contract theory to questions of global justice and international relations. Pogge discusses previous attempts in some detail and considers many objections against extending Rawlsian arguments to the global situation. The theory of global justice that Pogge defends, which he calls "G," is a more detailed version of McClennen's strategy: Put all individuals from across the globe in the original position and define global justice in the light of the principles that would be selected from such a vantage point. Pogge takes particular pains to show why arguments that appeal to national interests are merely a modus vivendi, having no claim to represent the requirements of justice, and contributing to a substantial portion of the injustice in the world today. As such, Pogge's theory G appears to stand in sharp contrast to the position argued in support of *LT*. The difference between Pogge's view and the argument presented here is considerably less than might be apparent. As G is at first blush so contrary to the views argued in this book, however, the discussion of how moral theory figures in the formation of political consensus can be best closed by reviewing Pogge's development of G.

Unlike Beitz and Nagel, Pogge does not specifically focus on access to the resources necessary for food production in his work on duties beyond borders. Although Pogge includes distributive access to resources on his agenda for global justice, for him the topic is part of a tapestry that also includes military alliances, military and political oppression, the arms race, death squads, and torture. The scope of Pogge's concern with global justice is particularly relevant for his discussion of national interest arguments. In his view, arguments that appeal to a national self-interest in having a stable system of international relations among states contribute a modus vivendi, a compromise agreement among parties reflecting no principles other than being

149

acceptable to contracting parties. The virtue of a modus vivendi for international relations is "that it can work, can prevent all-out war, even among parties who have no faith in
one another and believe they have nothing in common by
way of shared values" (p. 220). The problem is that under a
modus vivendi,

> [V]alues, however deeply held, will have only a marginal im-
> pact upon the participants' conduct and (through this) upon
> the terms of the modus vivendi. Since the parties are fearful
> of one another, each will give precedence to its survival and
> to the long-term security of its values over their short-term in-
> stantiation. No party is likely to impose serious ethical con-
> straints upon its pursuits of power through which alone it can
> hope to *survive* and (ultimately) to *prevail*. (p. 221)

In contrast to a modus vivendi, Pogge advocates a departure from Rawls's discussion of international justice in
which there is a single, global original position. The result is
a theory of justice in which Rawls's two principles establish
criteria for global justice. Pogge's view differs from McClennen's in that individuals behind the veil of ignorance are deciding (with greater consistency to Rawls's use of the
original position) not whether there will be a world government, a possibility Pogge dismisses as "silly" (p. 217), but
rather the content of justice, the ethical principles that are to
guide constitutional conventions, legislative sessions, and
administrative policymakers in deciding the number and
configuration of states. In Pogge's view, this means that each
of us, particularly those entrusted with public decision making, is morally obligated to act in ways that are consistent
with the two principles. This view of the international arena
differs sharply from that of the modus vivendi precisely because the ethical constraints imposed by the two principles
are to be the guiding principles for state action in the international arena. If the two principles point us toward world
government, we are morally obligated to work in that direction. However, the mere existence of a system of states does
not vitiate the force of Pogge's argument in the way that it
does McClennen's.

Indeed, Pogge's most impressive achievement in *Realizing Rawls* is the clarity with which he emphasizes that a theory of justice is to be directed toward the formation of institutions that shape social life. Institutions, in Pogge's sense, are not confined to organizations or even to established rules, but include implicit rules that both give meaning to social life, and that reinforce patterns of conduct through informal sanctions and interpersonal expectations. Pogge's Rawls differs from other political theorists in emphasizing how explicit components of the political order, especially property rights, *engender* patterns of conduct that they do not explicitly stipulate, require, or enforce. Pogge argues persuasively for Rawls and against Nozick that an adequate theory of justice must evaluate conduct that is engendered by law, policy, and governmental practice, as well as conduct that is enforced, protected, or otherwise regulated. Pogge sees this phenomenon as a social analogy to deontological theories in ethics that hold agents responsible for the consequences of their actions but not for the foreseeable consequences of their omissions. As such, we must go well beyond protection from violation of individual liberties in developing a theory of justice, as we know how markets and property rules can engender consequences that are not strictly entailed by the legal structure (pp. 15–62).

The problem with a modus vivendi is that it helps create an assurance problem, where every party to an international agreement has reasons both to keep and to break it, and where everyone also knows that everyone else has the same reasons. The modus vivendi, therefore, engenders a pattern of brinkmanship, in which mutual suspicion pushes self-interested parties to the limit, and occasionally past it. In extending Rawls's two principles to the global level, Pogge develops different motivations for engaging in international relations, reasons that require statesmen to consider the requirements of ethics at a fundamental level. Pogge expects that this framework for global justice will gradually improve global stability. A global theory of justice introduces a powerful justification for favoring the interests of the poor as well. *LT*, by contrast, emphasizes the national interest argument for development assistance, and it assumes a situation of global competitiveness in trade. Although *G* and *LT* will likely support much the same development policies over the short run, *LT*, on the face of it, is everything that Pogge wants to oppose. If *G* justifies the same policies, why isn't it the superior philosophical theory?

The short answer is that, like Singer's utilitarianism, Shue's rights theory, and Beitz's extension of Rawls, *G* does not form the mandate for official development assistance as it is currently conducted by the U.S. Agency for International Development, at least. Nor is it likely for other countries' development agencies or for multinational agencies such as the World Bank, the International Monetary Fund, and the Food and Agriculture Organization to act under the aegis of principles enunciated in Pogge's globalization of Rawls. The current mandate is not Rawlsian, but is at best a blending of ethical imperatives with the kind of thinking that led the American Soybean Association (ASA) to support the Bumpers Amendment successfully. It is a mandate that created official development agencies under severe constraints, some of which limit the extent to which one group, the farmers of the developing world, may benefit at the expense of another, the farmers of the industrialized West.

Pogge considers a series of objections to his view, some of which are similar to the short answer given here. For example,

> [I]t is said on behalf of the advantaged participants in an unjust institutional scheme that they formed "legitimate expectations" guiding their choice of a profession, their decisions to found a family, to save money, and so forth and that it is *unfair* that they should have to change their lives now, after having made consequential decisions on the basis of sincere, albeit false moral beliefs. (p. 261)

Pogge dismisses the view because it is inherently conservative, ensuring against the institutional reforms required by
his theory of global justice. "For it is hardly fair that those
who have been harmed and disadvantaged by unjust institutions should continue to suffer so that those who have
been unjustly advantaged by them will not have their expectations disappointed" (p. 261). He also notes an argument
that cites values such as "our compatriotic fellow feeling or
our deep loyalties and commitments, constitutive attachments and friendships and essential attachments . . . to argue that we may resist progress toward global justice" (p.
262). Pogge rejects this claim, too:

> Even if there were significant moral obstacles to institutional
> reforms (be they entitlements of the more advantaged or fur-
> ther constraints on action), they would not count against the
> Rawlsian *criterion* of global justice. They would merely show
> that it is more difficult to make progress toward satisfying this
> criterion. (p. 262)

This reply suggests the sense in which the aspects of
normative international political theory analyzed by Pogge
are different from those analyzed here. Pogge is concerned
with a theoretical account of global justice, and although he
hopes that his account has practical applications, he is not
going to constrain that account in conformity with existing
mandates. AID officials might have to break the law in order
to apply theory *G*, but that does not count against *G* so much
as it shows why progress toward satisfying *G*'s tenants is difficult. More pointedly, although the two cited objections
might be offered to support the soybean growers' position
on development assistance, or even in justification of the
True Interests Thesis, they do not speak to the concept of national interest that underlies *LT* and the more general view
of the trading state discussed in Chapter 5. The validity of a
rights claim to one's "expectations" is rejected in Chapter 3.
A fellow feeling for one's compatriots was cited there as a
plausible (but not decisive) rationale for the Social Contract

Thesis as it was developed to justify the Bumpers Amendment. Pogge seems to be treating national feeling in much the same way in this passage, and the fact that *LT* was offered as a reply to the Social Contract Thesis should further indicate that *G* and *LT* may be compatible.

This possibility is reinforced by Pogge's reply to Brian Barry's statement criticizing Beitz that a global Difference Principle must be ruled out because it is not mutually beneficial to rich and poor (cited in Pogge, p. 263). Pogge writes that the kind of cooperation required to optimize the socially worst position must not be coerced.

> [A] global order that is just by Rawlsian lights is one under which persons and collectivities are free to shun economic transactions of specific kinds. The populations of more developed countries and regions, in particular, would be free to trade only domestically and with one another and hence can be presumed to benefit from whatever further transactions they would conduct. In this sense one can say, barring externalities, that a national or global basic structure satisfying the Rawlsian criterion is, *by the very construction of this criterion*, mutually beneficial for individuals and collectivities as against a benchmark of noncooperation (though presumably no participants would benefit as much and as disproportionately from their international economic relations as we in the developed West do at present). (p. 264)

This passage points toward cooperation based on mutually advantageous terms of trade, the position advocated explicitly by *LT*.

The most pointed comparison with the view being developed in this book comes when Pogge considers the possibility that "the great international diversity of considered judgments" (p. 269) will make it impossible to arrive at any well founded account of global justice. As a domestic diversity of considered judgments prevents any ethical view discussed here from claiming pride of place as the mandate for official development assistance, this may be the most important argument to examine. Pogge's reply to it is extensive.

But I don't think this problem defeats the idea of globalization, at least when the "search for reasonable grounds for
reaching agreement . . . replaces the search for moral truth,"
and "the practical social task is primary" (Rawls, 1980). To attain this practical goal on the global plane, an agreement need
not specify a particular derivation of or rationale for the criterion of justice; "there can, in fact, be considerable differences in citizens' conceptions of justice provided that these
conceptions lead to similar political judgments. And this is
possible, since different premises can yield the same conclusion. In this case there exists what we may refer to as overlapping rather than strict consensus" (Rawls, 1971, 387–88).
What counts, then, regardless of the considered judgments
and other reasons that may motivate a particular person, is
convergence on the criterion itself. The present objection to
the globalization of Rawls's criterion must then show more
than cultural diversity; it must at least show that agreement
on such a criterion of global justice is out of reach.

I say "at least" because we might envision an even narrower kind of overlapping consensus. Even those who endorse different criteria of justice and a different long-term
vision of a juster world order may still agree about the first
stretch of the road. This is not merely a theoretical possibility.
Many proposals for institutional reforms, politically supported by Third World nations and arguably favored by Rawlsian principles, have been blocked in recent years by
governments of the developed West. Here the fact of cultural
diversity is exploited to complement the tedious appeal to our
collective self-interest (euphemistically, the "national interest") with a *moral* justification for such resistance. Such a justification is perverse. It would allow us to resist institutional
reforms demanded by justice as we ourselves understand it
and to exploit what we ourselves recognize as unjust advantages we enjoy within the current international order, on the
grounds that other cultures do not (fully) share our moral
convictions. (p. 269)

Pogge makes two claims here. One is that agreement on
the criterion is important, but not agreement on the reasons
for accepting the criterion. The second is that diversity
arguments provide morally "perverse" complements to

"tedious" national interest arguments that have blocked significant reform in international affairs.

The second claim contains the most damaging rhetoric.
While I will not defend myself against the possibility of having become tedious, it should be clear that this discussion of
national interest is hardly intended to block reform in international affairs. The link between national interest arguments and what Pogge calls "diversity" arguments is not
accidental, however. Government action often requires mandates, and these political artifacts depend on what Rawls
calls "the overlapping consensus" for substance and sinew.
Although they are rarely pure applications of political theory, they are often compromises that fix on a set of criteria,
just as Pogge endorses doing in the preceding passage.
When everyone agrees that a policy is justified, the mandate
is easy. When someone objects, as the soybean growers did,
there are two important strategies for countering that objection. One is to show that the policy is needed to satisfy the
requirements of justice to individuals, as when we argue
that government has the responsibility to protect individual
rights. The other strategy is to show that action is required
on the basis of national interest, on the common, overriding
need to secure presumptive goods. Pogge would presumably prefer the former strategy, but though he may establish
Rawlsian criteria for international justice, they operate as
values that express the direction for institutional change. He
does not establish a right that can be claimed against U.S.
official development assistance on behalf of farmers in developing countries. As such, the Social Contract Thesis and the
Bumpers Amendment illustrate some difficulties that must
be overcome before G can truly have practical application.
Attention to mandates shows why applying a theory of justice will be difficult and why previous attempts have failed;
it does not imply that it is either impossible or unimportant.
Although Pogge might prefer a rights claim, there is no reason, beyond his distaste for interest arguments, why he
should not accept the alternative, that aid and trade links
should be promoted because it is in our national interest.

Of course, if all interest arguments, including the one presented here, are merely modi vivendi, Pogge might reject *LT* on the grounds that it will engender conduct in the international sphere that is inimical to global justice. However, national interest arguments that originate from a trading state model of the social contract are not unprincipled. Trade in a global economy depends on a thoroughly interwoven set of interdependencies. To support and foster the institutions that support international trade is in the national interest of every state. Convergence of multilateral interests on a set of institutions for trade goes well beyond agreement for the sake of agreement only. Some institutions will foster sustainable growth and development of the world economy, and others will not. All nations share a common interest in a healthy and sustainable arrangement of global institutions. This common interest is the national interest mentioned in *LT*. The argument here, therefore, occupies a middle ground between a theory of justice as Pogge would have it and a modus vivendi. The argument rests on the common interests of nations and their peoples. It does not, for this reason, depend on fully developed criteria for just institutions. Nevertheless, common interests lay the foundation for a principled analysis of global policies, one that presents assurance problems, certainly, but for which the incentives for defection that Pogge outlines in his discussion of the modus vivendi are conspicuously absent.

Indeed, Pogge's vision of international relations seems poisoned by military metaphors in exactly the manner discussed in Chapters 1 and 5. Pogge shares the view presented here that the world is no longer made up of Westphalian nation states, squared off against one another in a global state of nature. Pogge rejects Hobbes's picture and hopes to place a Rawlsian theory of global justice in its place. His theory provides the basis for a deep review of the institutions that undergird the formation of tastes, preferences, and attitudes about political obligation. Hobbes's picture is being replaced in this book by an array of options, each of which offers principled philosophical argument in support of practical policy alternatives. Some arguments focus on specific, legislated mandates, others may be appeals to fellow citizens or to key actors who still have latitude in how they will be disposed toward a policy choice. Others are more explicitly rhetorical, but even these are constrained by limitations of the overlapping consensus on political culture. Pogge's institutional/constitutional arguments are at another level still that raises normative questions about the shape of political culture. By their nature such arguments are less applicable to individual decisions, but they are of obvious importance and relevance, both to political theory and to the future of democratic society. There is no obvious reason why political theorists cannot or should not operate at any and all of these levels, but that theme will be revisited in Chapter 8. The military metaphor – that international politics is a continuation of war by other means – presents political theory in terms of black-and-white choices. A theory based on trade must be more subtle, more flexible, and more accommodating to an array of arguments and applications than even Pogge is prepared to endorse. Although *LT* may not conform to the letter of Pogge's account of global justice, it is consistent with its spirit. It takes up policy at a level of detail that Pogge's theory does not attempt, yet surely it is at this (or a finer) level of detail ethics and philosophy will finally have impact on policy and conduct. Ethics, generally, calls for more attention to the situation of policymaking if it is to be applicable. In this chapter, we have shown how most theory, including Pogge's, fails to address official development policy from the perspective that administrators are required to take by law. Chapter 7 examines another area in which the body of theoretical literature fails to attain verisimilitude.

Chapter 7

Morality and the myth of scarcity

In reviewing the popular literature on hunger and development, one is struck by the repeated use of the term "myth." The word appears prominently in the title of two widely read books by Frances Moore Lappe and Joseph Collins, and is a important term of analysis in books or articles by James Sellers (1976), Thomas T. Poleman (1977), Jean Mayer (1979), Nick Eberstadt (1980), and Gigi M. Berardi (1985). Within the context of a literature that also includes multiple references to "misleading metaphors," and to "false bad news," not to mention seemingly countless titles that promise "the reality," the word "myth" is simply used to denote false or even foolish beliefs. Although food policy authors do not all agree on what is myth and what is fact, they all seem to share the belief that failure to grasp the facts underlies the confusion and disagreement over food policy. This failure is relevant to the philosophical literature on famine and hunger, for philosophically trained authors have exhibited an astonishing ability to display ignorance of easily obtainable information on food availability. As much philosophical writing on food policy is premised on false beliefs about the world food situation, policy analysts have found it easy to ignore.

MORALITY AND MYTHOLOGY

That empirical premises of arguments constructed by academically employed philosophers turn out to be false should

159

not come as a shock, however. If their arguments are important, philosophers writing on world hunger should be able to find methods of presentation that preserve philosophical claims, even in the face of refuted empirical premises. Moreover, the reference to myth in the title of this chapter entails more than a simple equation of myth with false belief. Here, a myth is a belief or system of beliefs that has two essential characteristics. First, such beliefs guide or influence action as working models of the world of which we are cognitively aware. They establish the framework of assumptions about the world that will interact with values or goals to produce intentional action. Although the main ideas of myth are not fully formed, they are, nevertheless, relatively explicit components of our working knowledge. In this myths differ from implicit knowledge, which also provides background for action, but does so without requiring the subject to posit belief in its central tenets. Second, such beliefs have cognitive resiliency; they can be maintained for some time without regard to their factual accuracy. For example, beliefs can possess resiliency because they are rarely subjected to a falsifying test. Belief in life after death is not easily falsified, yet it clearly has the capacity to influence intentional action. More important for the discussion of food policy, beliefs can be difficult to falsify if they tend to be qualified by ceteris paribus, or if they appear in a system of beliefs where one would be more likely to alter other, less deeply held beliefs in the face of adverse experience.

Of course, beliefs might be resilient just because they are true, so the twin criteria of cognitive awareness and resiliency do not distinguish myth from simple true belief. At the same time, true beliefs may be resilient not because they are true but because people find them difficult to test. As such, true beliefs can have exactly the same epistemic warrant as myths; so for convenience, any consciously held, resilient belief that is not tested can be included under myth. This concept of myth, unlike the popular one, does not imply falsity. Difficulty in testing beliefs may arise from many sources, including impracticality and lack of courage or will.

One need not have a full account of the many bases for failing to test beliefs, nor to presume truth *or* falsity for the myths at issue. The following analysis of the myth of scarcity takes up issues of a different sort.

Resilient beliefs – myths – are particulary important for morality and ethics. Normative principles presuppose a general context in which they will be applied. One must have some vision of the case before one can contemplate how a situation ought to be better, or how intentional action can aim at an ideal. Western moral thought has furthermore presumed that normative principles do not change with time and place. Moral values must be applicable in any situation. Moral thought, therefore, needs a general picture of what is the case, and needs to be universally applicable to specific situations falling under that general picture. The need for broad applicability in moral theory limits the relevance of easily tested, local and particular claims. The more enduring components in our beliefs about the world are the most serviceable as foundations for moral thought, so we should not be surprised when we examine morality to find some myth at the roots.

Many authors of recent literature in moral thought have assumed that key moral problems arise in the distribution of scarce resources. When there are not enough valued items to go around, some must do with fewer than they want. If the valued items are necessary for life, doing without may be catastrophic. Moral argument has a twofold role in guiding action to distribute or redistribute scarce resources. First, it must demonstrate why someone who has some of the valued resource should share it. Second, it must defend criteria for fairness in alternative schemes for sharing. John Rawls thought that his argument for a redistributive principle of justice in *A Theory of Justice* is dependent on the assumption of scarcity (Section 22). There is no a priori reason, however, for thinking that distributive issues presuppose the assumption of scarcity. A world in which there is plenty to share, but no inclination to share it, is within comprehension. The assumption of scarcity does, however, put an edge on distributive issues, for it entails that altruism comes at some cost to self-interest. This assumption gives bite to the moral requirements of justice, and furthermore, is highly plausible, and probably accurate, more often than not. It is deeply embedded in a complex system of beliefs about the social world, and its resilience does not require demonstration. On the basis of these points one can identify a myth of scarcity.

The myth of scarcity served not only as the foundation for Rawls's general theory, but for much of the humanitarian discussion of food policy over the last two decades. This discussion has incorporated moral thought in several ways (see Riddell, 1987; Van Wyk, 1988). The philosophical literature on world hunger is reviewed in Chapter 6. In this chapter, we examine how scarcity figures in the moral arguments that have been reviewed and explore some implications of the argument from scarcity that have not been fully appreciated. To some extent, belief in scarcity limits the applicability of moral arguments. A more interesting implication is that the myth of scarcity may reinforce the pernicious power arrangements that authors who write about world hunger have wanted to oppose.

UTILITARIANISM AND THE FORMAL DERIVATION OF SCARCITY

Consequential arguments on famine and food availability were initially offered at a time when a broad spectrum of educated people in Western societies were coming to terms with the possibility of future environmental catastrophe. Hardin and Fletcher were among the authors of many popular works committed to the examination of global environmental disasters. Not surprisingly, the authors of these "Cassandra" books made their arguments by predicting horrible consequences, if current patterns of resource use did not change.[1] The Cassandra literature predicted a future in which resources of every kind would become increasingly scarce. By giving their warning within the context of what would follow from a continuation of current practices, the Cassandras presented utilitarian moral arguments against current practice. If true, their predictions showed that the cost of population growth and increased energy consumption far outweighs any benefits.

Utilitarian theory presents more than one alternative for interpreting the notion of value, of cost and benefit. Sophisticated versions of utilitarianism assume indifference curves for each individual. Sneed (1977) provides an extensive utilitarian analysis of social cost/benefit assessment as it applies to food policy. The indifference curve represents a frontier along which different bundles of goods – more cheeseburgers/less pizza as opposed to fewer cheeseburgers/more pizza – can each be regarded as optimal in that the individual would be equally satisfied with, or indifferent to, a choice among them. Evaluations of cost and benefit are derived from indifference curves in that only actions that entail moving to a new indifference curve are appropriately understood as costs or benefits. Social optima can then be determined by seeing where the indifference curves of individuals intersect. Public policy, or any action for that matter, can be evaluated by determining whether the provision of benefits for one person (moving "outward" from one indifference curve to a "higher" one) entails costs (jumping indifference curves in the opposite direction) for another. Because all individuals are maximizers, everyone wants to move to a higher indifference curve. Except in the limit case where the net wealth of a society is increasing at an infinite rate, these maximizing individuals are placed into competition for resources. (An increase in resources allows the individual to shift outward to a higher indifference curve.) Scarcity therefore becomes a formal component of utilitarian approaches to the theory of value.

Given the formal commitments of the utilitarian framework, the arguments of the Cassandras do nothing more than suggest that the situation may be worse than might have been thought. Beliefs about food scarcity come to dominate the analysis of moral obligation in a direct way. In

Singer's portrayal of world hunger, wealthy individuals in developed countries may be called on to sacrifice certain pleasures to provide food for the hungry. They may be required to reduce overall consumption, as when Singer (1972) suggests donating the money that would be spent to purchase fashionable clothing to a relief organization, or specifically to reduce food consumption, as when Frances Moore Lappe (1971) or James Rachels (1977) suggests that a reduction in meat consumption would make large amounts of grain available for relief of world hunger.[2] Singer applied utilitarian principles in an argument designed to show that the sacrifices of wealthy individuals would be far outweighed by the benefits to the hungry. A world situation of moderate scarcity, in other words, dictates that resources are used in the most valuable way.

For Hardin, population biology showed that the number of individuals in a region would increase to the point of the region's carrying capacity – the point at which limits on the available sources of energy, most particularly food supplies, constrain population growth through the Malthusian controls of death and disease. Following Malthus, the Cassandras spread the view that the overriding moral responsibility for humanity was to stop population growth before Malthusian controls set in on a global basis. The point was not that food resources in a narrow sense were scarce, but that growing consumption of energy in all forms threatened the long-term sustainability of life on Earth. What was morally required was not personal sacrifice to address problems of moderate food scarcity, but societal sacrifice to address global problems of absolute energy scarcity.

In the case of both Singer and Hardin, a formally derived notion of scarcity is fleshed out in ways that lead to radically different estimates of the relative cost of famine relief. For Singer, the cost of famine relief is represented in the wealthy individual's move from an indifference curve that includes fashionable clothes and eating meat to one that does not. For Hardin, the relevant economy has little to do with sacrifice by the rich. The cost of famine relief must be paid by future generations. It is represented in a move from an indifference curve in which future people can enjoy a quality of life roughly comparable to our own, to a curve in which they cannot. In addition to sharing a utilitarian framework, Singer and Hardin share the view that consumption is more valuable to the poor than to the rich, therefore, that reduction in consumption by the rich is justified by the benefits to the poor. But the empirical, not the formal, determination of scarcity decides who is rich and who is poor. For Singer, wealth is money; for Hardin it is access to all resources, and particularly energy. Expending this wealth in the form of food aid reduces access for future generations in a double sense: Nonrenewable resources are consumed, and the future load on resources is increased by the increase in numbers. The present generation's priority in time gives it priority of access. The scarcity of access to resources establishes the basis of value comparison for Hardin, as the scarcity for access to monetary wealth does for Singer.

The contrast between Hardin and Singer makes a great deal of difference in the prescriptions they derive, but in building their prescriptions on a utilitarian foundation, they presume a myth of scarcity. As we have seen, adoption of a belief in scarcity is an explicit component of consequential world hunger literature, but scarcity is a formal consequence of any approach that analyzes action as a choice among alternative bundles of mutually excludable goods. Whenever one action is preferred over another for any reason, a utilitarian will be able to find some good that is being economized to increase consumption of another. Although authors such as Sahlins (1972) have called this a "business-oriented" concept of human nature, when the universe of goods is expanded to include leisure, relief from boredom, altruism, and prestige, among other noncommercial goods, one can reasonably characterize a wide variety of human actions as choices reflecting a preference to exchange one bundle of all available goods for another. The utilitarian characterization of action demands a concept of scarcity because action (choice) only takes place when the agent perceives an opportunity to improve on the current position.

The utilitarian analysis of action implies that any action involves a willingness to exchange one's status quo for another bundle of goods. The status quo is itself changing moment to moment as a result of events beyond an agent's control. We all experience the movement to less preferred positions. Indeed, that is what a utilitarian means by "harm." But harm occurs only when one's current bundle of goods is altered by circumstances beyond one's choice, not by choice. Any willful action by the agent implies a preference for an alternative bundle of goods. Put another way, voluntary choice always reflects a move to an outward indifference curve. That a person acts means that there must have been an array of bundles "out there," each of which was preferred to the status quo, but which has the same value relative to any other. Although some bundles doubtless alter the mix of goods, some differ from the status quo only in having more of one or two goods already present in the status quo bundle. This means that more is always better, at least in the sense that whatever is better – whatever would be chosen – is equivalent to (on the same indifference curve with) some bundle that differs from the current one only in that it has a greater quantity of goods already present in one's current bundle. Neither the number of desirable goods nor quantity of some goods is limited, so the frontier of preferable bundles extends indefinitely. Relative scarcity among these goods is formal requirement of utilitarianism.

THE CONSTRUCTION OF RIGHTS AND THE CIRCUMSTANCES OF JUSTICE

As noted in Chapter 6, most authors writing on world hunger issues have found the language of rights more conducive to their arguments than the language of utility. In Chapter 6, two approaches are examined. One applies moral theory to establish a moral right to food; the other applies social contract theory to establish a political right to food. Both approaches imply that the haves are under moral obligation to redistribute their wealth to secure the subsistence rights of the have nots. O'Neill and Shue provide examples of the first strategy; Beitz and Thomas Nagel provide examples of the second. Both approaches share the assumption that rights are universal, that they are possessed equally by all persons having the capacity for rational deliberation, but O'Neill and Shue base the existence of rights on a form of subjectivity required by the grammar of moral language.

Moral rights theory is heir to the natural rights tradition, which derived its foundations from the all-knowing, purely rational will of God. Natural rights are ordained by God, but God's view of the world remains mysterious to human beings. The theistic rights theorist is in no position to comprehend God's reasons for bestowing rights on His human subjects. Neo-Kantian ethics, and perhaps Kant's ethics as well, attempt to show that the interest of rational beings in preserving personal autonomy prevents them from denying the right of autonomy to every rational being. Any attempt at such a denial is self-contradicting, self-negating, for the personal identity posited in the self collapses when its purely universal, rational underpinnings are removed. Because the construction holds for all rational beings, the philosophical rationale for respecting autonomy captures God's point of view and makes it thoroughly consistent with the purely rational component of human subjectivity and self-identity. Constructivism is not antitheistic, but it is atheistic in that the theory does not depend on the existence of God.

Unlike theistic rights theory, however, neo-Kantian constructivism relies on the myth of scarcity. Construction of an ideal agent aims at objectivity in that it provides a systematic way to eliminate bias and favoritism, but constructivism retains the element of subjectivity essential to the concept of intentional action. In establishing a pattern of human rights, the ideal agent chooses to accept constraints that resolve conflicts of interest by attributing rights in an impartial manner. Unlike the old concept of natural rights, which postulated a well-regulated society operating under divinely inspired natural law, neo-Kantian or constructivist theories of rights are motivated at their very core by the presumption of individual conflict over access to scarce resources. Indeed, the need to resolve problems of scarcity, problems of conflicting claims, is thought to provide the central motivation for the use of moral language in the first place.

Shue's theory of subsistence rights is explicit in its reliance on an alleged fact of scarcity. In *Basic Rights*, Shue writes that the most critical fact about rights to subsistence is that "where subsistence depends upon tight supplies of essential commodities (like food), a change in supply can have, often by way of intermediate price effects, an indirect but predictable and devastating effect on people's ability to survive." This claim is made as part of an argument intended to show that duties to supply essential commodities are on a par with libertarian negative duties not to harm others physically. Both are absolute prerequisites if the full range of liberties and entitlements recognized at higher levels of the pyramid are to become meaningful; both are part of the basic package of rights to life.

O'Neill's strategy is more explicitly constructivist than is Shue's. As noted in Chapter 6, she relies on agency, rather than rights, as the fundamental moral concept. In developing the construction that is to motivate her analysis of hunger, O'Neill differentiates herself from Kant by including the human characteristic of vulnerability to deceit and coercion within her construction of the rational agent's perspective. This characteristic is particularly relevant to hunger and food policy because human dependence on material needs can be readily exploited in deceitful and coercive ways (O'Neill, 1986, pp. 138–142). In applying this neo-Kantian theme to hunger O'Neill writes:

Human beings begin by being physically vulnerable. They are damaged by hunger, disease and cold, and coerced by their prospect. . . . If material needs are not reliably met, the forms of uncoerced and undeceived choosing are a skimpy and formalistic substitute for fundamentally noncoercive and nondeceptive forms of life. A just global economic and political order would then have to be one designed to meet material needs. . . . It would be embodied in economic and political structures which do not institutionalize coercion or deception and so respect rationality and autonomy *in the vulnerable forms in which they are actually found,* rather than in the idealized forms of political and economic theory. (O'Neill, 1986, p. 149)

This conclusion is intended to refute the claim that free markets and nonintrusive governments adequately protect negative liberties, thereby defending the status quo. Whether O'Neill's emphasis on human needs amounts to a commitment to the myth of scarcity is not clear, however. O'Neill avoids explicit mention of scarcity in her construction, perhaps because the conflicting views of experts writing on the development process have made her wary of empirical claims about hunger and development (O'Neill, 1986, pp. 19–26). Furthermore, in appealing to deceit and coercion in her analysis of justice, O'Neill emphasizes moral characteristics that do not depend on the existence of scarcity for moral force. In both these respects, *Faces of Hunger* is less vulnerable to the criticisms that will be raised here than is *Basic Rights*. Nevertheless, the myth of scarcity is not explicitly challenged in O'Neill's analysis, and she uses Singer's work to introduce the basic moral problem (though she soundly rejects his utilitarianism). Belief in scarcity is certainly consistent with O'Neill's analysis of needs. *Faces of Hunger* marks an important step beyond the world hunger literature of the 1970s, but in relying on that literature to frame the issues, O'Neill fails to examine how the belief in scarcity becomes part of the institutional framework that she hopes to reform.

Analyses of justice that extend Rawls's construction of the original position differ from the views of Shue and O'Neill in that contractual obligations, rather than rights or agency, are the basis for analyzing claims of the poor against the rich.

As discussed in Chapter 6, the strategy of extending the scope of the contract produces conceptual difficulties and counterintuitive results. The point here, however, is not to reexamine the considerable conceptual difficulties that the extensionist strategy entails, but to see how it, too, is committed to scarcity. For this task, one can rely on Nagel's version of the argument. Like neo-Kantian rights theory, Rawlsian theory of justice adopts the strategy of founding the distribution of rights on the perspective of an ideal agent. Unlike the more comprehensive approach described by Hill or O'Neill, Rawls's strategy in *A Theory of Justice* and in "Kantian Constructivism in Moral Theory" is to construct an ideal agent who equally represents the interests of all parties in a bargaining situation. This representative position is constructed by placing all parties to the contract behind a veil of ignorance, where all general facts about social organization and individual psychology are known, but no facts about one's personality, taste, and even values are known.

The relevant outcome of Rawls's constructivism is that contractors in the original position will see that property rules that allow unrestricted accumulation of wealth are inconsistent with a universalized concept of self-interest. Thomas Nagel applied this result to international relations in his 1977 article "Poverty and Food: Why Charity Isn't Enough." Nagel's central claim is "that any system of property, national or international, is an institution with moral characteristics; claims of right or entitlement made under it, claims as to what is ours to use as we wish, carry only as much moral weight as the legitimacy of the institution will bear" (p. 57). The test for legitimacy is the Rawlsian test of the original position. Any system that allows the vast inequities that exist between citizens of the developing world and those of the industrialized West cannot pass that test. An ethically defensible system of transfers for food and other basic needs would either have already achieved a more equitable distribution of wealth, or would have established binding rules under which inequities would be remedied over a period of time. The arguments of Nagel, Beitz, Runge, and Pogge all hinge on Rawls's theory of justice in a similar way.

In Rawls's *A Theory of Justice*, moderate scarcity is advanced as part of what Rawls calls "the circumstances of justice." Only under social circumstances of moderate scarcity, moderate selfishness, and relative equality does justice become an important moral and philosophical concern. Regarding scarcity, questions of justice do not arise, says Rawls, when resources are so rare as to make the practice of justice impossible, nor when they are so plentiful as to make them irrelevant. Rawls attributes this view to Hume, who writes:

> Reverse, in any considerable circumstance, the condition of men; produce extreme abundance or extreme necessity; implant in the human breast perfect moderation and humanity, or perfect rapaciousness and malice – by rendering justice totally *useless*, you thereby totally destroy its essence and suspend its obligation upon mankind. (Hume, 1751, pp. 23–24)

Brian Barry (1978) describes this doctrine as "insidious" and attacks the rationale for presuming moderate selfishness and relative equality as prerequisites for justice. He argues that justice is applicable even in situations of extreme scarcity. Even Barry, however, accepts the notion that justice might not be meaningful in a "Golden Age," characterized by abundance. But Rawls needs Hume's doctrine because those in the original position require some general facts that define the conditions under which principles of justice become meaningful. A world without scarcity might well be a world in which the language of rights would be as meaningless for a contracting agent as for a purely rational, neo-Kantian, for example.

MORALITY AND THE MYTH OF SCARCITY

The world hunger literature of the 1970s primarily deals with malnourished people and the moral basis of their claim to an adequate food supply, not with the production of food in the developing world. It almost never addresses agricultural research to aid in agricultural development. The relationship between food policy and agricultural production is a key issue in some analyses of the food crisis of the 1970s (see Lappe and Collins, 1979; Pimentel and Pimentel, 1979; Field and Wallerstein, 1977), and Singer, at least, shows some sensitivity to the negative impact that food aid might have on a nation's indigenous ability to feed its people. Nevertheless, analysis of food policy as it affects economic growth does not play a key role in moral arguments on the world hunger issue. Furthermore, no attention is given to international trade. In 1975, no one recognized that massive expansion in the global capacity to expand food production had been well under way for two decades. Little sensitivity was shown to the impact that U.S. food policies might have on U.S. producers. Even comparatively recent articles (such as Van Wyk, 1988) appear to accept that the world food situation is as Singer described it in 1972. Philosophers' blindness to these empirical considerations can be traced to unwarranted faith in the myth of scarcity.

Is it obvious that the assumption of scarcity is an accurate view of world food availability? From food producers' perspective the dominant problem of the twentieth century has not been scarcity, but surplus. Not that there are no moral problems in times of surplus; even in a world of surplus, many lack the resources to command food that is readily available on open markets. Amartya Sen (1981) persuasively argues that sufficient food was on hand throughout some of the century's most catastrophic famines. There is still a need to argue for altruism, but the opposing view, the "triage" or "lifeboat ethics" position argued by Hardin and others has, temporarily at least, fallen on hard times. D. Gale Johnson's 1984 review of world food availability documents the impact of agricultural science, expansion of cultivated acreage, and increasing use of fertilizer on total world productive capacity. Even Lester Brown (1988) concedes that over the short run, capacity to produce food will outpace demand, when both are computed as aggregate figures. The point has been made decisively for a philosophical audience by George Lucas (1990). Documentation of total world food availability over the last two decades could continue at some length, but the point is beyond dispute.

Why, then, is the presumption of scarcity so prevalent? The answer may simply be that scarcity is so prevalent in all aspects of human endeavor that its recent absence for food availability is an anomaly. Although some reasons to doubt such a claim are introduced in the final section, the immediate concern is to examine whether the resilience of scarcity in moral theory is a function of myth, even if, in the final analysis, the alleged factual claim is true. There are at least three reasons for concluding that the resilience of scarcity is a function of myth rather than fact, at least as the idea applies to world hunger debates. The first is that scarcity lurks just below the surface of the a priori formalist or constructivist assumptions about rationality used to motivate moral inquiry by utilitarians, neo-Kantians, and Rawlsians. The second is that a presumption of scarcity is rhetorically useful for each of the main parties to the world hunger debates. The third is that ceteris paribus and nonfalsifiability have facilitated a commitment to the presumption of scarcity, even with extensive contrary empirical research on food policy, famine, and agricultural production. That moral theorists uniformly presume scarcity is an appeal to myth insofar as these factors account for its resilience, even if, in a broad sense, the presumption of scarcity is accurate.

1. A priori assumptions. As Brian Barry notes in analyzing Hume, the circumstance of moderate scarcity is intended to indicate "an upper and a lower bound on the generosity of nature in supplying men's wants" (Barry, 1978, p. 209). The main point is to describe a circumstance dictated by nature's bounty: carrying capacity, to use Hardin's phrase. To shift the burden of proof from nature's generosity to men's wants is very easy, however. Indeed, the concept of economic rationality presumes that the individual's capacity to want more is unlimited. If this is

173

the correct analysis of human desire, however, any finite amount of natural resources qualifies as scarcity. Infinite wants would give individuals incentives to husband property and power as a means to establish terms of exchange that allow them to trade useless goods for objects of value. The presumption of scarcity comes not to rest on facts about nature's generosity, but on an a priori presumption about human wants.

There are many reasons to doubt that infinite wants really do characterize human nature, particularly when desire for a specific commodity, such as grain, is the focus of analysis. Indeed, Hume himself states that human beings display *moderate* self-interest when characterizing the circumstances of justice and suggests that a society of totally self-seeking individuals would find little use for justice. More important than the empirical accuracy of the assumption regarding human nature is the way that presuming infinite self-interest alters the possibility and, indeed, the relevance of disproving the assertion of universal scarcity. In presuming both scarcity and greed a dialectic is established by which philosophers may appear to be making factual references, but which allows them to shift the debate from an empirical claim about nature to an a priori claim about human acquisitiveness and back again, never having to make refutable claims about either providence or human psychology. When scarcity is challenged, the burden falls on self-interest; when greed is challenged as a universal character trait, the burden may be shifted to scarcity. The dialectic is itself refutable, as one may easily deny both scarcity and unlimited self-interest – but theoreticians must then bear two facts in mind at one time.

2. Rhetorical utility. Each of the three approaches taken in the world hunger literature is concerned with suffering humanity, and with arrangements that would bring food into the mouths of the malnourished. As philosophers, Singer, Shue, and Nagel have much to dispute with one another, but all have offered arguments that ethically support almost the same package of food policies. Opposition to

their view comes from the neo-Malthusians, who argue that limits to growth and the pressures of increasing population mitigate the force of idealistic morality and may require strategies of self-preservation that would be considered insensitive in brighter days. Neo-Malthusian authors such as Hardin do not question the assumption that the ethics of the food crisis of the 1970s revolved around the moral status of impoverished people, and the moralists do not question the assumption that the philosophical problem consisted in defending altruistic principles in the face of increasing scarcity. As questions about whether food is scarce do not arise as contested claims in this debate, none of the parties has any motivation for questioning the assumption of scarcity. Although a well-developed literature contests neo-Malthusians' prediction of extreme scarcity, it is seldom cited in the world hunger literature. Questioning food scarcity has neither been necessary nor useful to defeat the neo-Malthusian claims that philosophers have wished to dispute. As such, the assumption of scarcity endures and becomes a fixed reference point for moral claims on world hunger.

3. Ceteris paribus.   Ceteris paribus qualifications protect dogma by allowing us to reject the implications of disconfirming instances for empirical claims in the light of the belief that some other causal factors account for the anomaly. In the light of the a priori commitments that many seem to hold for a doctrine of scarcity, one would expect that belief in scarcity would be among the last surrendered in the face of unexpected empirical evidence. Along with this general bias in favor of scarcity, ceteris paribus qualifications work in a more subtle fashion in food policy debates. For example, in 1975 economists knew that food aid appearing on markets in developing countries would drive down prices, reducing incentives for farmers, and creating a cycle of hunger (Krishna, 1967). Philosophers, for the most part, ignored this fact, despite its obvious implication that alleviation of scarcity, in local terms at least, can cause serious obstacles to the long-term alleviation of hunger. For moral thought, that

a policy may fall short of its goal may be reason for altering some of its technical provisions, but is not sufficient reason for revising the ethical principles or goals on which it was based. If the obligation to give aid is based on the universal rationale for self-sacrifice, the fact that particular assistance programs do more harm than good is not philosophically that significant. The general ethical principles are still thought to be intact.[3]

Ethical arguments devised in the 1970s attempted to defend broadly altruistic values against the self-defensive attitude supported by lifeboat ethics. This is the debate at the philosophical heart of assistance disputes: Why are the wealthy duty bound to help the poor, particularly given a world of scarce resources in which "the poor will be with us always?" Singer, Shue, and Nagel provide philosophical underpinnings for this duty and a principled response to the arguments of the neo-Malthusians. Given this context, the factual presumptions of the moral argument were not construed in a manner that would likely subject the belief in scarcity to a falsifying test. As long as the failures of food aid are not Malthusian, there is no imperative to revise what has already been said. Failures in food aid associated with abundant food availability could be regarded as anomalies, of interest to food policy analysts, but irrelevant to the broad empirical claims presupposed in the moral evaluation of world hunger.

SHORTAGE VERSUS SURPLUS

Contingent facts about food availability should not be regarded as anomalies, just because they happen to contradict widely shared beliefs about scarcity. In a world of food and resource scarcity, redistribution of food or technical production capacity recognizes the value of that which is redistributed and does not diminish the value of that which remains under the control of the original owners. When persons of wealth fulfill a moral obligation to help the needy, the act reassures them of their stature and worth and, if performed voluntarily, merits a judgment of moral commendation. Furthermore, when there is not enough to satiate needs, there is continuing demand for what is left, even after a portion of the wealthy person's hoard of food and capital has been taxed. The wealth that has been taxed away can be replenished by future production. Although justice is owed to the poor, and the benefit of the redistribution goes to the recipient, the wealthy are accorded a symbolic status that reinforces the value of ownership, even as their possessions are taken away from them.

Suppose, for a moment, that the food that the wealthy have assiduously worked to produce is in abundance. There may still be distributive issues, for some who need may not have. What the rich person gives up in this scenario has no value; there is plenty for those who have the resources to convert their preferences into market demand. There is little dignity in giving up what has no value, even when others will gladly take it, so long as it is free. Simple redistribution of the needed commodity may not even truly benefit the poor, nor satisfy the demands of justice. The supposition is plausible: Redistribution of food *only* creates dependency and reduces the poor's productive capacity. Hardly an act of justice, redistribution can be the creation of an obligation and an exercise of power; it is a modern potlatch. Morality would seem to require redistribution of productive capacity. But under an assumption of abundance, rather than scarcity, expansion of productive capacity only expends the value of the rich person's assets entirely, leaving no hope for future recovery of wealth, and vitiating not only the value of the rich person's possessions, but of ownership itself.

Even if we suppose surplus, in other words, the myth of scarcity will have attraction to the wealthy. The moral meanings of redistribution under a myth of surplus, a widespread belief in the assumptions that have just been outlined, are too depressing for the wealthy to contemplate. The myth of surplus undermines the symbolism of value that supports a wealthy producer's image of self-worth, and exposes the once-prized but now vulnerable fact of ownership to ridicule and pity. Working hard at maintaining a myth of scarcity would be far better, so that declines in price would be regarded as short-term events, soon to be reversed, reinforcing the value of the commodity and its producer. Even if one intends to be selfish, to be seen as a miser who hoards items of value is far better than to be seen as a cheapskate who causes misery to retain control of something that is worthless. The myth of scarcity therefore attains renewed resilience by its service in the interests of the rich.

In calling for distributive justice, moralists who presume the myth of scarcity promote the importance of property. In saying that the poor deserve better, have rights to food, or are owed justice, they use the morality of scarcity to bestow potency on the owners of food and capital. The myth of scarcity may, of course, be right; there may not be enough to go around. What seems more likely is that periods of scarcity wax and wane. Scarcity is not an enduring fact about the world, but a transient one. True enough at times, and worth believing at those times, a belief in scarcity serves the wealthy even when false. It supports a morality that calls for redistribution of their "wealth" even when the value of that wealth resides solely in the widespread perception of its scarcity. Linking morality with scarcity therefore helps maintain a political context in which the poor are kept over the barrel of self-interest, even as the circumstances of scarcity and surplus change.

Although one hopes that the hypothetical suspension of scarcity assumptions persuades those who have adopted moral views founded on scarcity to be less sanguine, one does not want to suggest that there is no truth of the matter. Presumptions of scarcity are sometimes right, but not always. Although the decade between 1975 and 1985 was a particularly inopportune time to be building moral arguments on a presumption of food scarcity, widespread perceptions of food scarcity are probably imminent in 1992. Debunking the claims of the Global 2000 report became a minor intellectual industry in the early 1980s (see Simon, 1980; Simon and Kahn, 1984; Avery, 1985), because doing so was seen as a neoconservative riposte to environmentalism and the attendant calls for regulation. Although even the Global 2000 report did not present much basis for concluding that food would soon be in short supply, the intellectual climate of the early Reagan years created an opportunity for antiscarcity arguments on behalf of the rich. If this analysis is even remotely correct, the more enduring interests of the rich reside in promoting beliefs of scarcity, rather than abundance.

Other more specific interests will promote perceptions of scarcity in the coming decade. They include predictable groups such as international grain trading firms and suppliers of agricultural production inputs. Less obvious but more relevant to the intellectual climate for evaluating food policy are scientific interests. Whatever else it does, the looming dread of impending starvation and ecological catastrophe that emerges from neo-Malthusian scenarios of food scarcity and population growth provides research opportunities for biological, environmental, and agricultural scientists. Even if we are unprepared to *do* anything about global warming, for example, we are quite prepared to study it. As such, scientists have an interest in sponsoring conferences and making pronouncements that support a perception of imminent shortfalls in food production. To note this is not to suggest that scientists will improperly utilize the public trust to promulgate "false bad news," as Julian Simon (1980) suggested. Scientists' advancement of theory and evidence indicating impending food scarcity is doubtless both well meaning and founded on basically sound and objective methods. Such projections of scarcity necessarily presuppose that a great deal of what philosophers want to change about human behavior, about social institutions, and particularly about property rules is unchangeable, however, and that cooperation is out of the question. To rely uncritically on such projections in forming moral arguments is to be unwittingly vulnerable to circularity, at best, and even inconsistency.

The preceding discussion has shown that some undesirable consequences of founding moral views on the myth of scarcity follow without regard to whether the myth represents the facts accurately. A myth of abundance would expose and deconstruct beliefs about ownership and property that emerge from the myth of scarcity, and it might have a liberating effect on oppressed and oppressor alike. It might also encourage wasteful expenditure, lead to genuine scarcity, and create absolute or irreversible forms of dependence on privately held wealth. The rhetorical consequences of abundance, in other words, are as ambiguous as are those of scarcity. What all this entails for general moral theory is unclear. Moral theorists have often written as if the general truth of assertions regarding scarcity were beyond dispute. We need only entertain the possibility of abundance to recognize that this philosophical strategy has ramifications for the legitimation of power. One way to attack the existing distribution of power is to attack the myth of scarcity. But little follows with respect to the metaphysics of morals. Beliefs about scarcity and abundance may be inevitably, even intrinsically, mythic in their capacity to grip human cognition, and this mythic character, in turn, may be a consequence of deep-running epistemological relativism. Nothing that has been said here entails such claims, nor are they informally implied. Similarly, commitment to some form of representational realism *may* be a psychologically and pragmatically necessary prerequisite for both personal and political action, and entertaining the possibility of abundance may even cause the decay of moral will. Even if such hypotheticals are true, their truth would be compatible with what has been said here. Recent thought on the links between philosophical rhetoric and political power has been so eager to leap the inferential chasms between deconstructive analysis of particular themes and sweeping metaphysical generalizations that such disclaimers become necessary. The most that is implied for moral theory is that there may be advantages in qualifying the presumption of scarcity, though the possible strategies for making such a qualification have not been discussed.

The more serious implications have to do with the moral analysis of hunger and of the literature on philosophical foundations for food policy. If scarcity is indeed an uncritical assumption of that literature, this subfield of ethics and policy work is in disarray. Food availability oscillates between scarcity and abundance, but the hungry are with us always. A morality that assumes the main problem to be justifying distribution of scarce resources misses the point; redistributing abundant resources is just as important. The literature on world hunger fails to find a foundation for food policy in times of abundance and may unintentionally contribute conceptual resources to the maintenance of food entitlements that cause hunger. One can sketch how the concepts of consequentialism, constructivist rights theory, and Rawlsian social contract theory might be applied to support redistributive efforts even in times of abundance. One should, for example, be able to argue that one produces more utility by feeding the hungry than by hoarding rotting food, or that subsistence rights establish claims on food, even when there is too much. This suggests that a wedge can be driven between the generalized commitments to scarcity that these theories make in their foundational arguments, and the facts about scarcity and abundance that are cogent in particular cases. As such a foundational theory is not offered here, the burden of proof, the driving of the wedge, falls on others. As presently conceived, the world hunger literature is based on the assumption of the myth of scarcity, and moral theorists have made their stand against hunger largely through inattention to the sand at the foundation. Their belief in food scarcity is not shared by the American farmers who pressed for the Bumpers Amendment, and for this reason their positions reflect no sensitivity to farmers' conviction that they, rather than the foreign poor, are victimized by AID policy. This final point may be put succinctly: There is no overlapping consensus between the Social Contract Thesis that motivated the politics of the Bumpers Amendment and the moral views advocated in the world hunger literature. Although the missing consensus is no reason to reject the philosophical commitments of the literature on hunger in total, it is a gap in the constitutional mandate for food policy that the Linking Thesis can fill.

Chapter 8

The time has come, the walrus said, to speak of many things

A society in which political claims are analyzed solely as expressions of personal interest will ultimately undercut the institutions that support the formation of sound moral character. If philosophers cannot find a way to show respect for moral and political values with which they have fundamental disagreements, political discourse may be overcome entirely by cynicism. If political cynicism is broadcast by policy analysts, news media, and the politicians themselves, what hope is there that a small coterie of political theorists can cultivate the virtues of citizenship in the population at large? In *A Theory of Justice*, Rawls emphasized the need for political philosophers to accept a theoretical language that is consistent with the language of politics. Rawls realized that the need to show respect for opposing views extended beyond personal conduct and, indeed, established the secondary need for political philosophy that made conceptual accommodations with a variety of foundational views. Although sections of *A Theory of Justice* are devoted to clearing the ground for such a political philosophy, the consensual, accommodating theme of that work is in substantial tension with its Kantian themes (Galston, 1982). In subsequent writings Rawls has reemphasized the goal of nonfoundational, consensus-based political philosophy, but Rawls and his critics continue to address the issue in purely theoretical terms. As long as political theorists ignore the rhetoric of politics, the need to respect the terms of consensus in Western politics will remain unmet.

One response to the problem is to examine political rhetoric for expressions of philosophical commitment and criteria of right. Such a strategy presupposes a focus on a self-contained set of political issues or policy problems and will undoubtedly yield different results when different particulars are selected. Nevertheless, the concepts and metaphors of social contract theory can be expected to emerge repeatedly, as they have in analyzing the tension between aid and trade. Contract theory is important because many government offices are required to act in the name of the people. They are agents for the public, and their action implies collective intentionality. Government action is not rationally autonomous. It is a form of limited agency, constrained by its terms of authorization. To the extent that the authority to act on behalf of the public rests on implied consent and tacit agreement, contract theory emerges as a natural expression of the mandate for public choice.

Contract theory is not without conceptual and theoretical limitations. One is the cumbersome character of any attempt to extend contractual concepts to foreign relations. Contract theory helps us understand how we authorize government action, and how our diversity limits what can be done in our name. It does not tell us who "we" are. The lack of specifications for collective identity in contract theory may appear to invite expansion and to reshape the parties to the contract, but to the extent that contract ideals are implicit in public policies and political rhetoric, the legitimacy of expansion and reshaping is severely constrained by history and by political culture. Since Hobbes, contract theory has made it difficult to see that duties extend beyond borders. The tension between foreign aid and foreign competitiveness is symptomatic of this enduring problem.

The primary task here is to examine the tension between competitiveness and humanitarian aid to others, and to apply contract theory in a novel solution to the conflict. The argument is summarized and restated below. Close attention to cases might also illuminate two enduring theoretical issues. First is the applicability of contract theory as a normative guide to foreign policy. Second is the role of contract theory as a middle-level theoretical enterprise, aimed not at the philosophical foundations of human society, but at the basis for the limited agency that characterizes government action in a democracy. These three topics will now be taken up in turn.

FOOD POLICY, COMPETITIVENESS, AND THE SOCIAL CONTRACT

The policy topics that have been taken up here deal with the production and distribution of food, both in the industrialized West and in developing countries. Specifically, when the government of a developed country such as the United States must balance the claims of its own food producers against the needs of hungry and impoverished peasants of the world's poorer nations, government agencies charged with forming and administering public policy are faced with tremendous ambiguity in policy goals. The balancing act pits the needs of the poor against the interests of better-off, sometimes rich, producers and traders, but is complicated by the fact that international food policies are bilateral agreements between governments, not actions that address the needs of the hungry directly. The political culture of the United States has not coped well with these complications. An opinion poll conducted by the Overseas Development Council (ODC, 1987) indicates strong public support for humanitarian values, for helping the poor, even at U.S. expense. But even though humanitarian arguments are successful in moving Congress to support short-term disaster relief, they have never sufficed to generate long-term development support that might have some chance of removing the needy from their state of dependence. Foreign aid programs have almost always been rationalized and legitimated in terms of their service to national interests, rather than humanitarian concern. The policy debates, therefore, often involve the balancing not of individual interests, but of national interest and humanitarian goals.

Traditional social contract theory explains why such conflicts occur among rational, well-motivated individuals. In the first instance, contract theory portrays the civil society as an association of individuals, bound to a common path by mutual advantage. A government's primary duty is to the parties of the contract, and contract theory leaves the status of outsiders unspecified and uncertain. To the extent that the contract idea captures the spirit of just and unjust use of power, governments have reasons to take an inhabitant's interests more seriously than those of an outsider. Indeed, it is not clear that the interests of an individual not bound to the civil society by citizenship or residency have any standing at all. As such, though common principles of humanitarian decency might favor the needs of the poor, if the poor are not *our* poor, so to speak, contractual considerations may require that government action remain loyal to the interests of those residing within the boundaries of the civil society.

The principle of favoring one's fellow citizens in matters of policy is also reinforced by the way in which foreign relations have often been conceptualized in the social contract tradition. Thomas Hobbes characterized the relations of autonomous states as that of persistent vulnerability and war, and an extension of the state of nature that formed the conceptual basis of the contract. Later theorists have been largely silent on the question of international relations, leaving, until recently, Hobbes's work on foreign policy to stand as the last word. If foreign relations are conceived as a perennial contest for advantage among nations, a zero-sum game of territorial conquest, there is little role for the altruism that appears to motivate humanitarian concern for the foreign poor. That we deal not with the poor but with their government seals this conclusion, for even if we were inclined to help them as individuals, their government must be watched with caution and suspicion. Aid is possible, of course, and may be advisable. So are bribes, deals, and coercion, and all are to be measured by the criterion of national interest.

Conclusion

Contractual argument is, therefore, conceptually confined within borders implied by the contract metaphor. Its rhetorical commitment to foreign policies of territorial conquest makes national interest predominate over humanitarian concern for outsiders. Although a number of philosophical authors have recently taken up the question of world hunger, only Thomas Pogge has attacked this feature of contract theory head on. Philosophers have, for the most part, been content to inquire whether human rights or consequential considerations entail moral obligations to help the foreign poor. Authors of world hunger literature have failed to come to terms with the national interest argument, largely because it is absent from academic writings on political theory. Even if one concedes that everyone has a moral obligation to help the foreign poor, and even if everyone has a moral obligation to petition their government to help the foreign poor, and even if they do so, government may still be justified in failing to do so, if vital national interests would be compromised. Contract theory gives governments the authority to protect the civil society, not the government, from dissolution and destruction, and so long as a plausible national interest argument can be brought to bear in questions of foreign policy, it "trumps" majority will. National interest arguments do not trump the rights of citizens or residents, those who owe some loyalty to the civil society and have implicitly consented to the contract; but rights claims in world hunger arguments are not attached to citizens, residents, or people who have in any recognizable fashion accepted contractual obligations. Therefore, a seam in social contract theory gives national interests full sway over an increasingly important range of issues. Arguments that ignore this seam are vulnerable to principled counterattacks that set aside pages of detailed philosophical analysis with a single move.

This is, of course, a theoretical implication of the competitiveness arguments discussed in some detail in Chapter 3. Current political theory seems vulnerable to this sort of argument, and not just on matters of food policy.

Contemporary political theory is well defended against abuses of the national interest (or its close relative, the public good) in domestic affairs, but the contractual foundations of that theory restrict application of rights-based constraints or distributive principles to members of the society. Theoretical contract theory, in other words, gives governments great latitude in conducting foreign affairs. It provides little guidance for the goals of foreign policy, nor does it offer a vision or ideals for world society. Beitz addressed the purely distributive component of this problem in a way that does specify broad goals, but national interest would override any obligation to pursue even distributive goals. Pogge has provided the most extensive and powerful road map for globalizing the social contract of any produced to date. However, his willingness to dismiss interest arguments weakens the applicability of his theory. It is as if interests are never legitimate constraints on policies, as if constitutional consensus always overrides interests. Yet insisting on such an uncompromising standard will prevent accomplishing much good, even in the absence of institutional reform. Pogge might deny that a philosophical thesis that does not address the most basic concerns of justice is properly philosophical. Such a reply only underscores that our arguments are aimed at different levels of analysis.

The approach developed in Chapters 1 through 5 takes a different tack. The goal is to examine the notion of national interest, both as it emerges from contractual considerations that lead governments to favor the interests of their own citizens, and from the Hobbesian picture of international politics as an ugly and uncertain test of will. The argument draws on the revisionist approach to national interest arguments advanced by political scientists Paul Kennedy and Richard Rosecrance. It interprets national interest in terms of international economic development, rather than the territorial imperatives of military power. The Linking Thesis (LT), in turn, applies the broad notion of national interest to the specific questions of food policy. An important intermediate task of the analysis is to separate food policy from the military metaphors that have been accumulated during four decades of political debate about national interest and humanitarian concerns.

The core analysis is a detailed discussion of the contractual considerations that have influenced key areas in food and development policy, and the national and sectorial interest arguments employed in policy debates. The key issue is the alleged conflict of interest between the trade goals of U.S. agricultural producers and the aid goals of international agricultural development programs supported by the U.S. Agency for International Development (AID). This conflict reached a climax in the rough interval between 1984 and 1988. The details do not bear repeating, except that producer groups first mounted attacks on aid programs, and defenses of their trade interests, during an era of domestic farm financial crisis and dramatic decline in U.S. share of world grain markets. Under pressure to act, commodity groups and farm state representatives came together in support of the law referred to here as the Bumpers Amendment.

The law effectively instructed AID to desist from actions that would make foreign agriculture more competitive against U.S. farmers. The law immediately raised ethical issues in that it constrained AID's ability to pursue humanitarian goals among peoples who are unarguably among the world's most needy. Farm commodity groups could not have advocated such constraints without a countervailing moral argument of their own. Such an argument was readily available, however, and its appeal was basically contractual. Farmers could not justifiably be forced to support (through tax revenues) activities that not only harmed their interests, but that failed to benefit other parties of the contract. From the farm groups' perspective, there was no give in AID's actions, only take.

After 1986, development specialists went on the attack, giving speeches, publishing articles and editorials, and organizing conferences designed to rebut the arguments of producer groups. Their replies were dictated by the existing terms of debate. Rather than argue simply and directly that aid to developing countries was a moral duty, as authors such as Singer, Shue, Beitz, Nagel, and O'Neill have done, development specialists attempted to rebut the farm groups' claim by showing the give and take in foreign assistance. They attempted to show that U.S. agricultural interests would benefit, over the long term, from agricultural development assistance, because people in developing countries would be future customers for U.S. grain. Their argument is dubbed the *True Interests Thesis* in this analysis, because they hope to show that AID programs benefit the very parties that attacked them.

At this point the analysis must shift to a normative vein. The commodity groups' argument for constraining AID is consistent with a broad range of contractual arguments. Attempts to extend contractual arguments to duties beyond borders stumble over the question who is party to the contract, and the narrow answer to that question, only domestic citizens and residents, establishes the pro-Bumpers case. Attempts to broaden the scope of the contract cease to be meaningful to the case at hand, because if everyone is party to the contract, there are no foreign relations. The pro-Bumpers argument is a weak contract argument, however, in that it does not establish the domestic producers' claim as a matter of right.

The True Interests Thesis does not fare as well under philosophical scrutiny, though it may have been politically effective. Essentially, the True Interests Thesis tells the U.S. farm community not to oppose AID, and to support more agricultural development assistance as a way of increasing their markets. The argument has two problems. It is a circumstantial ad hominem, an argument that does not defeat the claim it is alleged to disprove, but merely defeats an antagonist's motivation for making it. The True Interests Thesis does not disprove the principled argument for the Bumpers Amendment, and, indeed, the Bumpers Amendment is still in force. Second, in leaving that argument untouched *and* in justifying aid policy in terms of its financial rewards for U.S. producers, the True Interests Thesis subjects U.S. foreign assistance policy to a case-by-case test for consistency with the criterion of advancing the financial interests of U.S. producers, not just in agriculture, but across the board.

The Linking Thesis avoids the pitfalls of the True Interests argument by focusing on a public understanding of interest rather than a private one. Agricultural assistance is interpreted as institution building. If practiced wisely, foreign aid can be used to establish a set of practices and shared expectations among its recipients that lays the groundwork for equal participation, collaboration, cooperation, and exchange with citizens of donor countries. Although experience shows that aid programs have often failed to accomplish these goals, this should not count against the philosophical ideal of aid. Rather it shows that aid programs conducted under the aegis of militaristic or paternalistic mandates are as problematic in practice as they are in theory. Any aid program that is truly in U.S. interests must extend the traditional concern of developed countries for the participation and consent of affected parties to the citizens of recipient nations. Persistently treating the poor as helpless victims does little more to advance their autonomy than does treating them as pawns in a military operation or, worse, as chips in geopolitical poker.

Application of contract theory within the domain of foreign relations requires abandonment of the Hobbesian context, which has been suspect for at least a century. Even in Hobbes's time, states became coherent by performing at least two vital functions. Hobbes recognized only the role of territorial defense. The army and navy of the Leviathan represented an obvious form of power, and their deployment in defense of territorial boundaries made the nation's borders appear to be the natural limits of contractual authority. The second role of the state was in the regulation of trade and exchange, a crucial activity to the constitution of sixteenth-century European states unnoticed by political theorists, including Hobbes. Sixteenth-century states helped to structure European society by certifying promissory notes and exchanges of property. Although certification of transactions was primarily a domestic activity in the Leviathan, sixteenth-century states were active in forming customs authorities and trading companies. Trading activities continue to be neglected by contemporary political theorists, although the General Agreement on Tariffs and Trade (GATT) negotiations may well be the most important component of U.S. multilateral foreign policy. Not coincidentally, GATT is a contractual agreement.

Shifting the focus of national interest from territorial defense to facilitation of exchange introduces a new way of interpreting contract theory as it applies to foreign relations. Briefly, it is no longer a zero-sum game in which one nation advances its interests against those of another. Collaboration and cooperation are goals, and not merely because failure to cooperate leads to violence. With respect to food and agriculture, at least, aid and trade can be, mutually consistent, and in the mutual interests of domestic producers and foreign peasants. Other authors have written extensively on this topic, and the debate is fully engaged (Crocker, 1991).

REALISM, CONTRACTS, AND FOREIGN AFFAIRS

Social contract theory provides a basis for establishing, developing, and defending political norms to evaluate, to criticize or defend, public policies. In earlier times, public policies were coextensive with the acts and edicts of the sovereign, who was generally a living, breathing human being. An early burden of contract theory was to show that sovereignty refers, in truth, to the authority on which monarchs and the nobility act, and that when they violate the grounds of that authority, they no longer act in the capacity of sovereign. They become, in effect, enemies of the state. Hobbes, Locke, and Rousseau differ in how they interpret the grounds of sovereign authority, but for all of them social contract theory is aimed at establishing the norms that power must obey if it is to be deemed legitimate. The application of social contract theory to public policy is, therefore, entirely consistent with its historical development.

Throughout its historical development, social contract theory has been explicitly and intrinsically normative. That is, its intent has been to lay down the principles or foundations for evaluating not only specific government policies, but any government's claim to the use of power over its citizens. Contractual arguments, therefore, establish political norms that justify, legitimate, authorize, or otherwise demonstrate the warrant of governments and their policies. They are, in this broad sense, moral arguments, though the term "morality" can be given a much narrower scope. When social contract arguments are used to evaluate a government's foreign policy, as they are here, they imply that morality (again, broadly conceived) is an appropriate test of foreign policy. As such, the contractualist view argued in developing *LT* appears to contradict the prodigious literature on realism in foreign policy committed to the view that morality and foreign policy do not mix.

If social contract theory contradicts realism, perhaps it is a straightforwardly idealistic claim. Foreign policy idealists have argued that moral considerations should guide U.S. foreign policy. The view commits the idealist to the claim that the United States should adopt policies that promote ideals such as international cooperation and human rights, even when it is costly to U.S. national interests. The contractualist argument that supports *LT*, however, offers an interpretation and defense of the claim that national interest considerations should guide U.S. foreign policy. Therefore, in stressing the priority of national interest, *LT* appears to contradict the central claim of both idealism and realism. *LT*'s application of social contract theory to foreign policy therefore appears to occupy untenable ground between realism and idealism on foreign policy. As the burden of the argument so far has been to show that the ground is not only tenable, but the proper perspective for evaluating a range of foreign policy issues, one of two possibilities must prevail. Either the contradictions are purely apparent, in which case

LT is consistent with one of these two general philosophies, or the dichotomy between realism and idealism is a false one, in which case *LT* may imply principles that extend far beyond the food policy issues discussed so far. The latter possibility is more probable.

Marshall Cohen's review of realist arguments (1984) develops the thesis that some key realists, notably Hans Morgenthau and George Kennan, do not truly endorse the view that morality has no place in foreign policy. Cohen claims that a true realism would be committed to an unadulterated pursuit of power and domination over other nations. Policies of domination would require no further justification, but policies that eschew the pursuit of power would have to be justified, probably in terms of their unacceptable costs. A pure realist would never place democratic ideals above opportunities for domination and, therefore, would never refuse cost-effective opportunities for extending national dominance over weaker states simply because the governments in these states happen to support democratic policies. Cohen analyzes the published views of both Morgenthau and Kennan and finds that they make repeated appeals to the principle of opposing totalitarian states, and supporting democratic ones. Cohen concludes his analysis by suggesting that Morgenthau and Kennan do not object to the application of moral principles to foreign policy, but to the application of short sighted or wrong headed moral principles to foreign policy. What they find problematic, Cohen concludes, is a kind of moralizing in which single-minded pursuit of worthy goals undermines the foreign policy community's capacity to take a broad view of international politics. Such a view does not imply that morality has no place in foreign policy, but merely that pinheaded moralizing has no place in foreign policy. (As, Cohen points out, it has no place anywhere.)

Both Morgenthau and Kennan fumed over moralists' opposition to policies that would have promoted reconciliation between East and West, a development that, in their view, was in the long-term interests of democracy, generally, and the United States in particular. Cohen's analysis of their work is convincing, and it suggests that any contradiction between *LT*, proposed as an argument about political norms, and realism, understood as a reaction to the unfortunate impact of moral arguments on selected policy debates, is purely verbal. Realists object not to morality in the broad sense, but to moralizing in a narrow sense that no moral philosopher would endorse. There are, however, darker themes to confront in the work of Kennan, at least. Cohen's reply to realism mitigates the tension between social contract theory and realist literature, but realism must be stated more precisely before one may say that the tension has been resolved.

In its most profound formulations, political realism judges some acts of government to be deeply immoral but necessary. Cohen's analysis of Morgenthau and Kennan does not take up such a view. Cohen's use of the dictum, "Ought implies can" suggests that he thinks necessary acts can never sensibly be deemed immoral. Morality cannot, according to this dictum, require what cannot be done; what must be done cannot be prohibited. To the contrary, however, the realist literature returns frequently to the view that statecraft requires compromises with morality that cannot be rationalized. Only God can forgive these acts. The statesman must shoulder the burden of tragic ironies and must undertake heinous and indefensible policies. History may vindicate the judgment to adopt such a policy, but the personal guilt that falls on leaders who make such judgments is not erased. Rationalizations that make such decisions easier disguise the deep sense of tragedy that has always been characteristic of political history. Reinhold Niebuhr is the most prominent exponent of such a view, but Kennan hints at it, and many realists are clearly attracted to it.

Niebuhr's view is at once seductive and repugnant. Cohen's summary disposal of the key realist claim promotes a too tidy reconciliation between morality and the realist position. Although logically unimpeachable, Cohen's view substitutes perky optimism for the irony, self-doubt, and, ultimately, courage that statesmen bring to foreign policy decisions. Niebuhr's account, by contrast, is more faithful to the tragic character of policy decisions where ways of life may hang in the balance. Furthermore, it restores dignity to the moral views of those who advocated international cooperation and human rights, even while it rejects their conclusions. It is, for these reasons, a philosophy that thoughtful statesmen might well find evocative. But when stripped of Niebuhr's powerful rhetoric, tragic realism (as it might be called) is discomfortingly reminiscent of the posture adopted by Nazis who implemented Hitler's Final Solution. Adolf Eichmann claimed to be appalled and repulsed by the horror of the holocaust, but he did not question its historical or national necessity (Arendt, 1963).

In making his point, Niebuhr is thinking not only of national socialism, but of the racist and nationalist sentiments rallied in the U.S. war effort. His philosophy respects the precariousness of U.S. society's claim to moral vindication in defeating the Axis powers. One cannot quibble with the chastening quality of Niebuhr's thought, particularly in the light of its applicability to the self-congratulation implicit in many moral justifications of the war against fascism. To the extent that moral defenses of allied participation in World War II are so overwrought and immodest as to rationalize American jingoism, racial intolerance, and hatred, the close identification between tragic realism and Eichmann's logic tells a totally different tale. One questions whether the political realists of American foreign policy are able to maintain the edge that gives Niebuhr's views their poignancy. If not, the analogy between Eichmann and realism is blandly sinister, rather than profound.

Such considerations are hardly decisive for a philosophically adequate evaluation of Niebuhr's views, and these deeper issues are ultimately of little relevance to the question at hand. Tragic realism proposes a view of morality that is far from the broad sense in which social contract arguments are said to be moral arguments. Niebuhr's view is that human action precludes the application of morality. The reason is that although the ideologies necessary to organize human behavior may aim at noble purposes, they inevitably incorporate appeals to baser instincts. Inevitably, that is, whenever they are effective. Moral motives are corrupted and perverted by the ideologies necessary for the organization and pursuit of sustained activities such as national defense, particularly in time of war (Niebuhr, 1932). Social contract theory, however, is just such an ideology for organizing and pursuing activities in the name of public interest. Arguments such as *LT*, which link international development assistance to national interest, are precisely what Niebuhr has in mind when he talks about ideologies needed to organize human behavior. *LT* converts a moral and Christian impulse toward altruism into a self-regarding pursuit of national interest. These are the sort of arguments that may be necessary, in Niebuhr's view, but they are also the sort of arguments that preclude a truly moral conduct of foreign policy.

Nevertheless, the contradiction between political realism and the contractual argument linking foreign assistance to national interest is only apparent, whether Cohen's or Niebuhr's arguments are taken to interpret realism. Cohen's account resolves the apparent contradiction by showing how realists such as Morgenthau and Kennan make appeals that are normative, or moral, in the sense that social contract arguments are. Niebuhr's tragic realism preserves the substance of the realist's separation of morality and foreign affairs, but in Niebuhr's view, social contract arguments do not advance truly moral considerations. As such, there is no contradiction between the contractual advancement of national interest and the philosophical claims of tragic realism. Although both these interpretations of the problem relieve the tension that motivates the appearance of contradiction, whether either captures the force of political realism as it has evolved over four decades of foreign policy debate is still questionable.

Robert Holmes offers an insightful analysis of realism in *On War and Morality*. Though he discusses Niebuhr, he identifies two major strands of realist thought, both of which differ from tragic realism. The first is positive realism, the claim that morality and moral arguments do not or cannot substantively influence foreign policy. Here the claim is that moral arguments are simply futile, as diplomats and statesmen are constrained by reasons of state, and cannot allow moral arguments to influence foreign policy. The events precipitating the Bumpers Amendment would appear to refute such a view, as principled arguments were required for the legitimation of this policy, if not for the motivation of soybean growers who supported it. Holmes's positive realists, however, are concerned with war and peace, not foreign aid. The claim that statesmen cannot be moved by moral suasion, therefore, needs merely to be qualified, rather than rejected. The point is that conduct of war, negotiation of treaties, and other security matters place government officials under constraints. The need to preserve and protect national security limits the range of policy choice so narrowly that moral arguments become irrelevant. Positive realism applies to one area of foreign policy, and the social contract arguments associated with the Linking Thesis to another.

Holmes's second form of realism is normative realism – the view that morality should not influence foreign policy. This is the form of realism addressed by Cohen and by Niebuhr: Holmes, however, shows that in the writings of realists such as Charles Osgood, Arthur Schlesinger, and Henry Kissinger, realism takes a far more practical, policy guiding form than the tragic realism of Niebuhr. Holmes's analysis also maintains a distinction between practical norms and moral norms that is overlooked in Cohen's analysis. This distinction is exemplified in an interpretation of normative realism Holmes calls national egoism. This philosophy corresponds to moral egoism for individuals, where the egoist stipulates self-benefit as the only criterion for normative evaluation of acts. National egoism is the view that all foreign policies should be evaluated in the light of their contribution to the nation's power to dominate other nations in military and security affairs. It is an extreme form of normative realism because it equates national interest and military domination, a mistake that can be costly to domestic policies. A foreign policy that sought only a balance of power, for example, would appear to avoid the extreme of national egoism, yet presuppose no constraints, including no moral constraints, beyond the pursuit of national self-interest. Nonetheless, Holmes understands national interests as purely self-regarding, from the standpoint of foreign policy. The parallelism between self- and national interest carries his argument against normative realism. If self-interested action is not based on morality, neither is policy justified by pursuit of national interest.

Holmes's analysis of realism fails to coincide with Cohen's because Cohen finds moral appeals where Holmes finds self-regarding, practical, prudential (therefore, nonmoral) appeals to national interest. This is partly a verbal dispute, as Cohen's use of the term "moral argument" includes any argument appealing to norms, even when those norms may be in need of defense. Even egoistic views count as moral views, although they are not moral views that a thoughtful person would endorse. Holmes, however, suggests national egoism as a paradigm of normative realism, while noting, as does Cohen that any normative realist's claim that morality should be excluded from foreign policy on moral grounds would be paradoxical, if not simply self-defeating. The dispute is not purely verbal, however, for social contract theory has historically been committed to the establishment of social norms through an appeal to individual self-interest. If the political obligations that arise from contractual theory are more than self-interested promises – if justice, for example, consists in fair principles for social cooperation – Holmes's account of normative realism has failed to take into account subtleties in the argument.

Yet within the context of Holmes's inquiry (e.g., war and morality) his characterization of normative realism as a nonmoral theory seems essentially correct. In Holmes's review of realist authors, moral considerations alter military and national security priorities only at the nation's peril. They must give way when weighty issues such as national

survival are on the agenda. Again, Holmes's topic, the validity and relevance of normative realism for the conduct of
war and defense policy, need not be taken up here. As with
positive realism, the more appropriate conclusion is that the
realists are talking about a different kind of foreign policy.
Their claims are overstated, but if reined in, they do not
flatly contradict social contract claims made in support of *LT.*
Whatever its ultimate justifiability, the normative realist position is a meaningful position only when national security,
rather than national interest broadly conceived, is the primary issue.

To conclude, then, the Linking Thesis and the various versions of realism are technically cotenable on every point.
The ethics of aid and trade do not overturn realism, and neither does realism rule out the contract arguments advanced
here. Yet the qualified realism that emerges from the analysis implies a very different concept of national interest. National interest is not equivalent to the security of borders and
shipping lanes, and the protection of national property. National interest includes participation in global institutions
that build community. These institutions include cultural
and scientific ties. They facilitate exchange and are prerequisites for global economic expansion. They may even enhance security, for trade requires and reinforces political
stability. A philosophy of foreign affairs that defines international relations as a "war of all against all" neglects the national interest in the name of pursuing it.

With this theme, we return to the food weapon metaphor
that launched the inquiry. Food is not a weapon; competitiveness is not a military campaign. Winning territorial victories, proving dominance, and deterring attack may be
meaningful policy goals within some areas of foreign policy,
and perhaps national leaders should be realistic in pursuing
them. When these military metaphors come to dominate all
foreign policy, however, national interest suffers. Contractual arguments will, indeed, become pernicious, as Niebuhr
might have thought, if the militarism pervasive in U.S. culture during the twentieth century cannot be overcome. In-

dividual self-interest arguments become pernicious when they are thought to imply that individuals cannot or should not invest care in the development and maintenance of institutions that build shared meanings, shared goals, and community action. In this respect, the arguments of individual and national interest are quite similar.

Contract theory, which rejects the food weapon metaphor, is incompatible with the spirit of realism, although realism can be interpreted in ways that permit the assertion of *LT* without implying any contradiction to realism's central claims. The incompatibility is one of emphasis. Realism takes military conquest as the dominant theme of foreign relations. *LT* takes the image of the trading state to depict a nation's interest in foreign affairs more accurately. Though the application of contractual arguments to aid and trade policy does not require a realist to abandon any propositions advanced by Kennan, Morgenthau, or Niebuhr, the present emphasis on the trading state does suggest a different framework from that assumed by Osgood, Schlesinger, or Kissinger. The suggestion that trade is a better philosophical paradigm for foreign relations than war is far reaching, and cannot be defended exhaustively in this context. Richard Rosecrance addressed some of the relevant issues in *The Rise of the Trading State* (1986).

SOCIAL CONTRACT THEORY AND POLITICAL DEBATE

Political economy has fallen into a division of labor in which the study of how political argumentation does influence opinion and public policy falls to policy analysts and communications specialists, and the study of how political arguments should affect opinions and policies falls to philosophers and political theorists. Although there are methodological and historical reasons for this division, it nevertheless creates a gap between theory and practice that invites avoidable confusion. For one, people never seem to be persuaded to adopt political opinions as a result of the

rational and moral reasons that should determine their beliefs. Moral suasion, in turn, never appears important in
democratic politics, and, correlatively, political debate appears to be not a debate at all, but merely a show where
aligned interest groups puff their breasts at intervals between the secret exercise of raw power. Although observers
of democratic politics are not faced with a shortage of well-
founded opportunities for expressions of cynicism, this car-
icature of interest group politics too conveniently serves the
academic politics of the disciplines. Those who study how
interest groups align to influence policy need not concern
themselves with the appeal to principle, as it is mere rhetoric, a mask for more potent forces. But those who study theory are also relieved of any responsibility to take what is said
in political debates seriously, as it is aimed not at rational deliberation, but to manipulate the ignorant and weak-willed.
Those who study the rhetoric, the media consultants and
communication theorists, need not have any interest in policy: Whether the product is peanut butter or foreign policy,
the process is the same.

A second confusion centers on the role that philosophical
argument would play if it could be brought to bear on policy
decisions. As philosophy is awarded almost undisputed sovereignty over questions of right in the prevailing division of
labor, philosophical considerations are sometimes expected
to be decisive where questions of right are concerned. The
division of labor leaves the study of coalition and compromise to the empirical disciplines, and the question of what
would be done if only we would do the best that we could to
the philosophers. If one does not give the proposition too
much scrutiny, this seems to imply that philosophers' ideal-
ization of political concepts such as justice and legitimate authority aims at criteria that define a kind of policy optimum.
Optima are action guiding in that any choice leading to suboptimal outcomes is deficient.

Vague as it is, this perception creates a series of expectations that are seldom fulfilled. First, philosophers apply the
classroom standard that the proper conclusion must not only

be accepted, but for the right reasons. Politicians, however, are not anxious to save the souls of political allies, particularly when no visible political consequences arise from failure to do so (Brock, 1987). Second, compromise and negotiation, which are essential to democratic politics, become devalued; compromises generally lead to suboptimal choices when measured by idealized criteria. A compromise, however, may well be the best that can be done, and reaching a compromise may involve an appeal to principles of right, as well as the art of the deal. Finally, high expectations imply that philosophical considerations must do more than indicate plausible suggestions about the direction of policy. If philosophical arguments are not entirely successful in enrolling the reader/audience in the political cause, they are, somehow, regarded as worthless (Weisbard, 1987). These unrealistic expectations reinforce the prevailing division of labor within the political world, as political theorists, whether affiliated with philosophy or political science, are unlikely to satisfy their own demands, let alone those of policy analysts.

The traditional political economy practiced by Adam Smith, Montesquieu, and John Stuart Mill predated this division of labor. These political economists both analyzed how private interests converge and diverge with respect to a policy question and attempted to articulate and defend a vision of public interest that would serve as a standard for judging policy outcomes. Early political economists were simultaneously actors and observers in the policy process. Their prescriptive claims were proactive in forming political alliances. The political effectiveness of the political economists is evidence that ideas about how policy decisions should be made influence the way that they are made. Even the most casual student of U.S. political rhetoric today cannot fail to recognize that advocates who attempt to garner popular support for public policies, even among small groups of interested parties, present normative arguments. That is, they offer reasons why the policy should be enacted, and why doing so is consistent with principles of democracy, public morality, and the public good. Although the rhetoric of democracy is admittedly elastic, it is not infinitely so, and an advocate's use of ethical language puts forward a set of principles that can function as constraints on policy, as well as licenses. To be sure, on some occasions this rhetoric is neither sincere nor particularly sturdy, nevertheless, it succeeds in the sense that the advocate's preferred course of action ensues. On other occasions, ethical considerations, principles of justice and democracy, are crucial either in assembling political action groups, or in activating existing groups by increasing the strength of their convictions. The national debate over abortion is surely an instance of this phenomenon, and any adequate empirical analysis of its politics requires some sensitivity to the way that shared moral concepts and values have shaped existing political alliances on either side.

Contrary to the current practice of separating policy analysis and political theory, ethics and political philosophy can be employed as instruments of policy analysis whenever interest groups need to build consensus and support for their views beyond the corridors in which they hold absolute power. Theoretical ideas serve as conceptual resources that can be captured and used by skillful advocates. Analysis of the Bumpers Amendment shows how social contract theory can bind American food producers into an advocacy group with a claim on the national agenda. Hegel noted a poetic justice in the capture of ideas for pursuit of personal interest; interested parties become vehicles for the notions of progress in the rhetoric they employ. Contract theory figures in the explanation of the policy controversy in that interested parties committed themselves to political positions legitimated by contractual arguments; their commitment to contractual rhetoric establishes public terms for debate that must be met by demonstrating either that the contract tradition is inapplicable, or that it does not support the preferred policy, as alleged. In the absence of dominating power groups that can unequivocally determine events, the

politics of the debate reflect alternative philosophical re-
sponses to the conceptual issues posed by the social contract
tradition.

Philosophical political theory generally aims at a singular
account of key notions such as justice and right, yet the
climate of political ideas is varied. That any systematic theory will score a decisive blow against its competitors is unlikely. Little enough of this happens among political
theorists, where people are paying close attention to the arguments, and that a conceptual advance will affect the general political culture of modern democratic societies seems
even less likely. Political ideas are advanced when carried
along by personal interests, not by academic debate. Hegel
seemed sanguine in the opinion that whatever ideology was
advanced by the contest of interest would ultimately conform to the right. Contemporary theorists do not share Hegel's faith, so defending the singular account can seem
necessary, no matter how much it is at odds with political
process.

Rawls has been profoundly aware of this dilemma and
has repeatedly attempted to develop a theory of procedural
justice that respects a plurality of more fundamental philosophies for the application of state power. He has made
his most pointed statement of this goal in "Justice as Fairness: Political Not Metaphysical" (1985), "The Idea of an
Overlapping Consensus" (1987), and "The Priority of Right
and Ideas of the Good" (1988). Joseph Raz (1990) published
an extensive critical analysis of the position developed in
these articles. Raz finds two key philosophical presumptions
in Rawls's new work on the political theory of justice. One is
autonomy from moral theory: Rawls hopes that his theory
does not depend on more foundational moral theory; the
second is epistemic abstinence: Rawls does not claim that
theory is true. The motivation for both presumptions is that
individuals in democratic societies have sharp and deeply
held differences of opinion on both moral theory and
epistemology. Rawls hopes that his theory of justice can

provide a framework for ameliorating conflict and for providing policy direction for democratic societies. If it is to do so, it must not depend on fundamental claims that are not widely shared.

Raz finds a serious problem with Rawls's new view:

> To recommend [a theory] as a theory of justice for our societies is to recommend a just theory of justice, that is, as a true, or reasonable, or valid theory of justice. If it is argued that what makes it *the* theory of justice for us is that it is built on an overlapping consensus and therefore secures stability and unity, then consensus-based stability and unity are the values that a theory of justice, for our society, is assumed to depend on. (Raz, 1990, p. 15)

Rawls's new work is, in short, self-defeating. One cannot make statements about middle-level, political justice that simultaneously withdraw all claims to truth and to moral authority. To make such statements faithfully, which Raz rightly assumes is Rawls's intent, is to posit the truth claims they state or imply; to offer them as principled norms, rather than merely as unfounded or manipulative commands, is to imply a view of right.

Raz's criticism of Rawls puts to a point the crucial theoretical problem of the social contract tradition. Hobbes and Locke represent the main alternatives to its solution. For Hobbes, the social contract story makes a foundational moral claim that entails conventionalist moral theory, at least, and a rationalist theory of truth for claims about human nature. For Locke, the contract is a middle-level agreement that reflects deeper moral values only when public consensus happens to coincide on them. While Hobbes's conventionalism escapes the self-defeating paradox of middle-level political philosophy, once Hobbes's a priori characterization of human nature falls, so does the critical authority of theory. Locke's strategy is more attractive in that it promises to provide an account of political authority that can accommodate substantial disagreement over matters of moral theory and epistemology. At least ten centuries of religious warfare have demonstrated the need to do this, but Raz's arguments, again, question its possibility.

Rawls's version of the social contract aims to accommodate a good deal more diversity than Locke's, for Locke assumed that natural law provided a warrant for the protection of life, liberty, and property. Like Rawls, Locke thought that one could forge agreement on these rights based only on assumption of self-interested rationality among contracting parties, but unlike Rawls, Locke is not inclined to conceal the more fundamental warrant for rights in divine authority. If references to God and to natural law are discounted, however, the criticism that Raz levels against Rawls can be applied as squarely to Locke. Accounts of rationality and self-interest can no longer be interpreted as middle-level arguments; they are no longer autonomous from moral theory and epistemic commitment. Therefore, middle-level arguments cannot be sustained; the necessity of falling back on foundational views is inevitable.

Although Raz wants to press Rawls's argument to a foundational level, he does not want to alter its substantive claims. Societies that tolerate opinion that deviates from their own founding principles are good societies; societies that are intolerant are bad. The theorist's role is to say why deviant opinions are wrong in the light of the true theory of justice. Raz correctly notes that this role does not require the theorist to assume a mantle of infallibility, only that statements of theory are proved wrong by being shown false or morally ungrounded, rather than by their inability to win consensus. Precisely this perspective, however, establishes the theorist's role in political economy's current division of labor, for only theory, and not politics, can now force a modification of theory. As such, though Rawls's position is philosophically self-defeating, Raz's position is politically self-neutering. Theorists talk primarily to one another; the coarser terms of political debate are consigned to media consultants and pollsters.

At this juncture the analysis of aid and trade issues may have a modest lesson for political theory. The dispute over whether actions of the U.S. Agency for International Development may sacrifice trade interests of some U.S. farmers revolves around AID's mandate. AID does not discharge the full range of a government's duties, but possesses a limited authority to act on the sovereign people's behalf. The multiplicity of interests and values in American society provides a mandate for AID's activity, and also for the limits to AID's legitimate agency. This mandate is more than a modus vivendi because it is a principled rationale, as well as a means of rapprochement between potentially competing interest groups. It is, however, much less than a full theory of justice, for it leaves untouched many points that opposed parties would dispute.

On many issues the primary political conflict will have much more to do with what an agency of government can and cannot do than with the fundamental principles of justice that underlie democratic society. A tradition of political economy that ignores or devalues the philosophical components of these issues does not serve truth or democracy, for the mandates that create limited forms of state agency are at least somewhat principled, even when the individuals who advance principled reasons do so out of personal interest. Perhaps all problems for which we need a middle-level philosophy arise in connection with limited mandates. Rawls's notion of overlapping consensus makes a great deal of sense when applied to the formation of a mandate for a specific agency or a piece of authorizing legislation. Furthermore, there is no reason to think that middle-level contract theory would be self-defeating in a limited context, as it is with regard to the theory of justice for society as a whole. Such an application of middle-level theory would seek compromise on the basis of principled reasons that relate back to moral theory and the theory of justice. Middle-level theory would seek common themes in alternative principled accounts and might rely on procedural arguments or appeals to presumptive goods to ameliorate areas of disagreement at a more fundamental level. This application of middle-level theory would not be justified unless compromise and appeal to overlapping consensus are justified at a more fundamental level – but Raz, for one, wishes to endorse exactly this sort of justification in his recent work. The possibility, then, is that social contract theory, understood as a middle-level, political enterprise is primarily aimed at specific political issues, at the constitution of society as it relates to particular policies and to limited application of state power. The way to prove such a hypothesis is to examine the political issues that divide the citizens of a democracy on a case-by-case basis, and to determine whether the conceptual incompatibility implied by debate and disagreement is at the root of political impasse, or whether it is a simple unwillingness to examine an issue at the level of policy, of limited warrant and authority, where overlapping consensus might produce compromise. Although no reason has been presented here to think that middle-level analysis can be directed to any level of political tension and disagreement, that it can be directed at the conflicts between aid and trade has been established.

SAILING SHIPS AND SEALING WAX

Stressing national interest, rather than rights or utility, may seem a philosophically retrograde strategy. Some readers will doubtless regard this strategy as yielding to popular attitudes that should be resisted. These readers, who may celebrate the opinions of the working class on other topics, may regard American farmers' suspicion of foreign aid as an example of backward parochialism, as a paradigm of the case in which common opinions should not be taken seriously. Although methodologically inclined to take such opinions seriously, this author has not done so purely as sophistry. The resort to the concept of national interest is substantive. The concept of national interest informs the mandate for foreign agricultural assistance, not humanitarian aid. The case for direct feeding programs may be different, but when we propose to apply foreign assistance to the improvement of agriculture, it should be as a cooperative and forward-looking venture, one that will lead to mutually beneficial partnerships.

This is not to deny the rights claims made on behalf of the foreign poor, nor to substitute an egoistic principle for the utilitarian's commitment to the welfare of all. Neither rights theory nor utilitarianism captures the mandate for foreign assistance. Rights and welfare claims provide good, general reasons for caring about the foreign poor, but when helping them threatens the implied agreements that legitimate government action, the advancement of rights or utility arguments threatens to undo the social consensus that makes official aid possible. In this attempt to fasten the bonds of the implicit contract a little tighter by appealing to national interest, contract theory is considered a middle-level language for describing and advocating consensus. Emphasis of interest claims mitigates conflict, and serendipitously points toward policies that should be more deeply consistent with the goals of rights and welfare advocates than they are currently. Such serendipities have always been the stuff of contract arguments.

Notes

INTRODUCTION: OF CABBAGES AND KINGS

1   There continues to be a significant degree of confusion regarding the views of foreign policy specialists such as Hans Morgenthau (1962) or George Kennan (1951; 1985) on this point. Both were opposed to linking separable policy issues, such as pursuit of arms control and international human rights. They were particularly concerned that moralistic insistence on achieving the latter goal might force negotiators to reject agreements on the former that were clearly in U.S. interests. Morgenthau more than Kennan argued for a general principle asserting the primacy of bilateral security relations over U.S. interests in securing privileges or benefits for foreign nationals, but neither ever wished to deny existence of normative international political obligations entirely. The nature of realism in international relations is discussed effectively in Beitz (1979) and Cohen (1984). This subject is also taken up in Chapter 8.

2. THE BUMPERS AMENDMENT

1   U.S. Senate, Report 99-301, "Urgent Supplemental Appropriations Bill 1986," May 15, 1986, p. 56.
2   *Congressional Record – Senate*, June 6, 1986, S7028.
3   See the comment by Honorable R. W. Daniel, Jr., "Grant by Agency for International Development Adds Insult to Injury," *Congressional Record – House*, September 24, 1982, H7565.
4   This figure is listed in a newsletter mailed to members of the American Soybean Association, the soybean producers' trade

association, August 1, 1985. Other soybean association reports state that AID "spent $341 million in FY84 . . . much was used to expand foreign agricultural production," and yet another letter to members states that AID spent "$341 million last year, much of which was used to improve *soybean* and agricultural production in foreign countries [emphasis added]." This figure, plus reports of World Bank activities described in ASA correspondence to members surface in many inquiries to government officials, and became part of the folklore on foreign agricultural assistance. (See Baize, 1985.)

5 The critical literature is quite extensive. In its broadest scope, it includes the work of Amin (1976) and Goulet (1977). For sources that target aid programs in particular see Teresa Hayter, *Aid as Imperialism* (1971); Francis Moore Lappe and Joseph Collins, *Food First* (1977); Susan George, *How the Other Half Dies: The Real Reasons for World Hunger* (1977); Barbara Dinham and Colin Hines, *Agribusiness in Africa* (1983).

6 The critical literature is reviewed and summarized in Thompson and Stout (1991). For sources influential in the decade before Bumpers see Erik Eckholm, *Losing Ground: Environmental Stress and World Food Prospects* (1975); and Kenneth Dahlberg, *Beyond the Green Revolution* (1980).

3. DOES HELPING FOREIGN INDUSTRIES VIOLATE A BASIC PRINCIPLE OF GOVERNMENT?

1 For a literature review see James Griffin, 1982, "Modern Utilitarianism," *Revue Internationale de Philosophie* 36:331–375; also Griffin, *Well Being: Its Meaning, Measurement and Moral Importance* (1981). Important philosophical literature is found in the following anthologies: J. C. C. Smart and B. Williams, eds., *Utilitarianism: For and Against* (1973); A. Sen and B. Williams, eds., *Utilitarianism and Beyond* (Cambridge: 1982); S. Scheffler, ed., *Consequentialism and Its Critics* (1988).

2 In my reading of the history of philosophy, the classical utilitarians are Jeremy Bentham, *Introduction to the Principles of Morals and Legislation* (1789, republished 1948); John Stuart Mill, *Utilitarianism* (1863, republished 1987); and Henry Sidgwick, *The Methods of Ethics* (1907).

4. INTERNATIONAL AGRICULTURAL ASSISTANCE AND THE INTERESTS OF U.S. AGRICULTURE

1 See Lappe, 1983; Jackson, 1985; Strange, 1988; for a review of the issue see Madden and Thompson, 1987; Jeffrey Burkhardt, 1988; and Woycik, 1989.

6. HUMANITARIANISM, HUNGER, AND MORAL THEORY

1 This aspect of Singer's argument, the question of supererogation, not surprisingly attracted attention from many philosophers who had little interest in hunger per se. Readers interested in the question are advised to consult Urmson (1958) for the seminal treatment of the last decade, and Fishkin (1982) for a more extended discussion of the literature, including Singer.

2 Such a claim must be qualified. Sneed (1977) has a utilitarian contribution to the literature, and many nonphilosophers continue to use both implicit and explicit utilitarian frameworks in presenting normative arguments. Nevertheless, there is little of philosophical interest in the repeated applications of the utilitarian framework. All action on the utilitarian side has to do with ascertaining the facts, and the difficulty of doing so is adequately grasped by examining the contrast between Singer and Hardin.

3 Although the literature supporting this point is extensive, this criticism has never been understood, much less internalized, by development specialists as a group. This is a subject for another book altogether. A representative sample of the critical literature includes Goulet (1976), Bedau (1979), Greenberg (1982), and Crocker (1991).

4 Readers who are unfamiliar with the basic pattern of Kantian moral philosophy will, no doubt, find this statement of O'Neill's position opaque. Further development of Kantian moral theory would, however, be entirely out of place in the present context. O'Neill's theory is interesting to philosophers because she resolves conceptual problems in human rights theory by retreating to an analysis of the concept of agency, but human rights theory is most typically given a

Kantian foundation similar to the one O'Neill provides for agency (see Gewirth, 1982).

5 A less technically complex argument for this claim which is primarily applied to corporations rather than governments is made by Peter French (1984).

7. MORALITY AND THE MYTH OF SCARCITY

1 The entire literature of the late sixties and early seventies on global disaster is relevant, but Paddock and Paddock (1967) and Ehrlich (1968) are probably most important for the world hunger literature. Hardin had been a long-standing contributor to the Cassandra literature (see 1959, 1968).

2 There is an important difference between normative utilitarianism and the preference analysis of an individual's charitable contribution that might be given by a neoclassical economist. The latter analysis might assume that charity is but one good (along with fine clothes and a meat diet) that goes into the bundles available to any given individual. Presumably an individual is willing to include some amount of charity in the consumption bundle, and individuals might, indeed, be willing to move from a point on their indifference curve with lots of meat and clothing, to another with less of these goods, but more charity. This is not what Singer is asking them to do, for by definition, individuals are indifferent to the consumption bundles all along the curve; going from one bundle to another does not cost the consumer anything. Singer's normative utilitarianism claims that the cost to the rich is outweighed by the benefit to the poor. The claim implies a rejection of the assumption that interpersonal comparisons of utility cannot be made, but it also implies that real costs and benefits are at stake.

3 This is less true for a utilitarian such as Singer, but Singer is the one philosopher in this group who has attempted to modify his position in the light of the facts (see Singer, 1977).

References

Addo, Herb. 1984. *Transforming the World Economy? Nine Critical Essays on the New International Economic Order.* Boulder, Colo.: Westview Press.

Aiken, William. 1977. "The Right to Be Saved from Starvation." In *World Hunger and Moral Obligation,* edited by William Aiken and Hugh LaFollette. Englewood Cliffs, N.J.: Prentice-Hall.

——— 1982. "The Goals of Agriculture." In *Agriculture, Change and Human Values,* edited by R. Haynes and R. Lanier. Gainesville, Fl.: University of Florida, pp. 29–54.

——— 1984. "Ethical Issues in Agriculture." In *Earthbound,* edited by T. Reagan. New York: Random House.

——— 1986. "On Evaluating Agriculture Research." In *New Directions for Agriculture and Agricultural Research,* edited by K. Dahlberg. Totowa, N.J.: Rowman & Allanheld, pp. 31–41.

Aiken, William, and Hugh LaFollette, eds. 1977. *World Hunger and Moral Obligation.* Englewood Cliffs, N.J.: Prentice-Hall.

Amin, Samir. 1976. *Unequal Development: An Essay on the Social Formations of Peripheral Capitalism.* New York: Monthly Review Press.

——— 1977. "Self Reliance and the New International Economic Order." *Monthly Review* 29, no. 3:1–22.

Amin, Samir, Giovanni Arrighi, Gunder Frank, and Immanuel Wallerstein. 1980. *Dynamics of Global Crisis.* New York: Monthly Review Press.

Anonymous. 1982. "Administration Undercuts Peanut Farmers." *Southeast Farm Press* 9, no. 37 (September 15): 1.

——— 1987. "World Bank Loans Stir Ire of U.S. Farm Groups." *New York Times* (June 5): A9.

References

Arendt, Hannah. 1963. *Eichmann in Jerusalem: A Report on the Banality of Evil.* New York: Viking Press.

Arthur, John. 1977. "Rights and the Duty to Bring Aid." In *World Hunger and Moral Obligation,* edited by William Aiken and Hugh LaFollette. Englewood Cliffs, N.J.: Prentice-Hall.

ASA Newsletter (June 1, 1985, and August 1, 1985).

Avery, Dennis. 1985. "U.S. Farm Dilemmas: The Global Bad News Is Wrong." *Science* 230:408–412.

Bachman, K. L., and L. A. Paulino. 1979. *Rapid Food Production Growth in Selected Developing Countries: A Comparative Analysis of Underlying Trends.* Washington, D.C.: International Food Policy Research Institute.

Baize, John. 1985. "Farmers Must Fight for World Market Share." *Pennsylvania Farmer* (September 14):48.

Banfield, Edward C. 1963. *American Foreign Aid Doctrines.* Washington, D.C.: American Enterprise Institute.

Barry, Brian. 1978. "Circumstances of Justice and Future Generations." In *Obligations to Future Generations,* edited by Brian Barry and R. I. Sikora. Philadelphia: Temple University Press, pp. 204–248.

Batie, Sandra S., and Robert G. Healy. 1980. *The Future of American Agriculture as a Strategic Resource.* Washington, D.C.: Conservation Foundation, pp. 3–7.

Baum, Warren C., and Stokes M. Talbert. 1985. *Investing in Development.* New York: Oxford University Press, pp. 89–92.

Bedau, Hugo Adam. 1979. "Human Rights and Foreign Assistance Programs." In *Human Rights versus Foreign Policy,* edited by Peter G. Brown and Douglas MacLean. Lexington, Mass.: Lexington Books.

Beegle, Philip H. 1982. "Letter to the Editor." *Atlanta Journal and Constitution* (August 22).

Beitz, Charles R. 1975. "Justice and International Relations." *Philosophy and Public Affairs* 4, no. 4:360–389.

———. 1979. *Political Theory and International Relations.* Princeton, N.J.: Princeton University Press.

———. 1983. "Cosmopolitan Ideals and National Sentiment." *Journal of Philosophy* 80, no. 10:591–600.

Bentham, Jeremy. 1789. Repub. 1948. *Introduction to the Principles of Morals and Legislation.* New York: Hafner Publishing.

Berardi, Gigi M., ed. 1985. *World Food, Population and Development.* Totowa, N.J.: Rowman and Allanheld.

References

Blatz, Charles V. 1991. *Ethics and Agriculture*. Moscow, ID: University of Idaho Press.

Blitz, Mark. 1982. "Human Rights Policy and the Doctrine of Natural Rights." *Human Rights and American Foreign Policy*, edited by Fred E. Baumann. Gambier, Ohio: Kenyon College Public Affairs Conference Center.

Boxill, Bernard R. 1987. "Global Equality of Opportunity and National Integrity." *Social Philosophy and Policy* 5, no. 1 (Autumn 1987):143–168.

Brandt, Willy. 1986. *North-South: A Programme for Survival*. Cambridge, Mass.: MIT Press.

Brock, Dan W. 1987. "Truth or Consequences: The Role of Philosophers in Policy-Making." *Ethics* 97, no. 4:786–791.

Brown, Lester R. 1988. *The Changing World Food Prospect: The Nineties and Beyond*. Worldwatch Paper 85. Washington, D.C.: Worldwatch Institute.

Brown, Peter, and Henry Shue. 1977. *Food Policy: The Responsibility of the United States in Life and Death Choices*. New York: Free Press.

Browne, William P. 1988. *Private Interests, Public Policy and American Agriculture*. Lawrence, Kansas: University of Kansas Press.

Bumpers, Dale, quoted in Glenn L. Johnson. 1987. "Objectivity in Public Decision Making." Ethical Aspects of Food Agriculture and Natural Resource Policy, Workshop Module 1, June.

Burke, Edmund. 1982. "Excerpts." In *The Conservative Reader*, edited by Russell Kirk. New York: Penguin, pp. 1–48.

Burkhardt, Jeffrey. 1988. "Crisis, Argument and Agriculture." *Journal of Agricultural Ethics* 1:123–138.

Carty, Anthony. 1988. "Liberal Economic Rhetoric as an Obstacle to the Democratization of the World Economy." *Ethics* 98, no. 4:742–756.

Christiansen, C., H. Lofchie, and L. Witucki. 1987. "Agricultural Development in Africa: A Comparison of Kenya and Tanzania." *United States Agricultural Exports and Third World Development: The Critical Linkage*. Boulder, Colo.: Lynn Reiner.

Christiansen, Robert E. 1987. *The Impact of Economic Development on Agricultural Trade Patterns*. Economic Research Service Staff Report No. AGES861118. Washington, D.C.: U.S. Department of Agriculture.

Clark, Lindsey H., Jr. 1981. "Grain Embargo: Let's Declare Victory and Quit." *Wall Street Journal* (Feb. 10):27.

References

Cohen, Marshall. 1984. "Moral Skepticism and International Relations." *Philosophy and Public Affairs* 13, no. 4:299–346.

Crocker, David A. 1991. "Toward Development Ethics," *World Development* 19:457–483.

Dahlberg, Kenneth. 1980. *Beyond the Green Revolution*. New York: Plenum Press.

Dalrymple, Dana G. 1980. "The Demand for Agricultural Research: A Columbian Illustration: Comment." *American Journal of Agricultural Economics* 62:594–596.

de Janvry, Alain, and Elizabeth Sadoulet. 1986. "The Conditions for Harmony between Third World Agricultural Development and U.S. Farm Exports." *American Journal of Agricultural Economics* 68:1340–1346.

Dinham, Barbara, and Colin Hines. 1983. *Agribusiness in Africa*. London: Earth Resources Research.

Dower, Nigel. 1983. *World Poverty: Challenge and Response*. York, England: Jackson Monley Sessions.

Eberstadt, Nick. 1980. "Malthusians, Marxists, and Missionaries." *Society* 17, no. 6:29–35.

Eckholm, Erik. 1975. *Losing Ground: Environmental Stress and World Food Prospects*. Washington, D.C.: Worldwatch Institute.

ERS (Economic Research Service). 1974. "World Food Situation and Prospects to 1985." FAER-98. Washington, D.C.: U.S. Department of Agriculture.

1985. "World Food Needs and Availabilities, 1985." Washington, D.C.: U.S. Department of Agriculture.

1986. *Embargoes, Surplus Disposal, and U.S. Agriculture*. Staff Report No. AGtS860910. Washington, D.C.: U.S. Department of Agriculture.

Ehrlich, Paul R. 1968. *The Population Bomb*. New York: Ballantine.

Field, John Osgood, and Mitchell B. Wallerstein. 1977. "Beyond Humanitarianism: A Developmental Perspective on American Food Aid." *Food Policy*, edited by Peter G. Brown and Henry Shue. New York: Free Press, pp. 234–258.

Fishkin, James. 1982. *The Limits of Obligation*. New Haven: Yale University Press.

Fletcher, Joseph. 1976. "Feeding the Hungry: An Ethical Appraisal." *Lifeboat Ethics: The Moral Dilemmas of World Hunger*, edited by George R. Lucas, Jr., and Thomas Ogletree. New York: Harper & Row, pp. 52–69.

References

1977. "Give If It Helps, But Not If It Hurts." *World Hunger and Moral Obligation*, edited by W. M. Aiken and H. LaFollette. Englewood Cliffs, N.J.: Prentice-Hall, pp. 104–114.

French, Peter A. 1984. *Collective and Corporate Responsibility.* New York: Columbia University Press.

Galston, William. 1982. "Defending Liberalism." *The American Political Science Review* 76:621–629.

George, Susan. 1977. *How the Other Half Dies: The Real Reasons for World Hunger.* Totowa, N.J.: Allanheld, Osmund.

1984. *Ill Fares the Land.* Washington, D.C.: Institute for Policy Studies.

Gewirth, Alan. 1982. *Human Rights Essays on Justification and Applications.* Chicago: University of Chicago Press.

Goodin, Robert E. 1988. "What Is So Special about Our Fellow Countrymen?" *Ethics* 98, no. 4:663–686.

Gorovitz, Samuel. 1977. "Bigotry, Loyalty, and Malnutrition." *Food Policy: The Responsibility of the United States in the Life and Death Choices*, edited by Peter G. Brown and Henry Shue. New York: Free Press.

Goulet, Denis. 1976. *World Interdependence: Verbal Smokescreen or New Ethic?* ODC paper no. 21. Washington, D.C.: Overseas Development Council.

1977. *The Uncertain Promise: Value Conflicts in Technology Transfer.* New York: IDOC/North America.

Greenburg, Edward S. 1982. "In Order to Save It, We Had to Destroy It: Reflections on the United States and International Human Rights." *Human Rights and American Foreign Policy*, edited by Fred E. Baumann. Gambier, Ohio: Kenyon College Public Affairs Conference Center.

Griffin, James. 1981. *Well Being: Its Meaning, Measurement and Moral Importance.* Oxford, England: Clarendon Press.

1982. "Modern Utilitarianism." *Revue Internationale de Philosophie* 36:331–375.

Hamilton, John Maxwell. 1990. *Entangling Alliances: How the Third World Shapes Our Lives.* With Nancy Morrison. Washington, D.C.: Seven Locks Press.

Hardin, Garrett. 1959. *Nature and Man's Fate.* New York: Holt.

1968. "The Tragedy of the Commons." *Science* 162:1243–1248.

1971. "Lifeboat Ethics: The Case Against Helping the Poor." *Psychology Today* 8, no. 4:38–43, 123–126.

References

1974. "Living on a Lifeboat." *Bioscience* 24 (October 1974):561–568.

1976. "Carrying Capacity as an Ethical Concept." *Lifeboat Ethics: The Moral Dilemmas of World Hunger*, edited by George R. Lucas, Jr., and Thomas Ogletree. New York: Harper & Row, pp. 120–140.

1977. "Ethical Implications of Carrying Capacity." *Managing the Commons*, edited by Garrett Hardin and John Baden. San Francisco: W. H. Freeman.

Hardin, Garrett, and John Baden, eds. 1977. *Managing the Commons*. San Francisco: W. H. Freeman.

Harris, Nigel. 1986. *The End of the Third World: Newly Industrializing Counties and the Decline of an Ideology*. Middlesex, England: Penguin.

Hayter, Teresa. 1971. *Aid as Imperialism*. Harmondsworth, England and Baltimore, Md.: Penguin.

Healy, Robert G., and Sandra S. Batie, eds. 1980. *The Future of American Agriculture as a Strategic Resource*. Washington, D.C.: Conservation Foundation.

Hill, Thomas E., Jr., 1989. "Kantian Constructivism in Ethics." *Ethics* 99, no. 4:752–770.

Hobbes, Thomas. 1651. Rep. 1950. *Leviathan*, edited by C. B. MacPherson. New York: Penguin.

Hoffman, Stanley. 1981. *Duties Beyond Borders: On the Limits and Possibilities of Ethical International Politics*. Syracuse, N.Y.: Syracuse University Press.

Holmes, Robert L. 1989. *On War and Morality*. Princeton, N.J.: Princeton University Press.

Houck, James P. 1986. *A Note on the Link Between Agricultural Development and Agricultural Imports*. Department of Agricultural and Applied Economics Staff Paper 86-26. University of Minnesota.

1987. "Foreign Agricultural Assistance: It's Mostly a Good Thing for U.S. Farmers." *Choices* 2, no. 1:19.

Huddleston, Barbara. 1987. "Trends in Trade and Food Aid." *Food Policy: Integrating Supply, Distribution and Consumption*, edited by J. Price Gittinger, Joanee Leslie, and Caroline Hoisington. Washington, D.C.: World Bank.

Hume, David. 1751. Rep. 1983. *An Enquiry Concerning the Principles of Morals*, edited by J. B. Schneewind. Indianapolis, IN: Hackett Publishing Co.

References

1986. "Of the Original Contract." *Readings in Social and Political Philosophy*, edited by Robert M. Stewart. New York: Oxford University Press, pp. 32–41.

IFPRI (International Food Policy Research Institute). 1976. *Meeting Food Needs*. Research Report no. 1 Washington, D.C.: IFPRI.

Jackson, Wes. 1985. *New Roots for Agriculture*. New Edition. Lincoln, Neb.: University of Nebraska Press.

Johnson, D. Gale. 1984. "World Food and Agriculture." In *The Resourceful Earth: A Response to Global 2000*, edited by Simon, Julian L., and Herman Kahn. Oxford, England: Basil Blackwell, pp. 66–111.

Johnson, Glenn L. 1987. *Objectivity in Public Decision Making: Soybeans and Pickles*. Lexington, Ky: Committee for Agricultural Research Policy, University of Kentucky.

Jones, E. L. 1981. *The European Miracle: Environments, Economies and Geopolitics in the History of Europe and Asia*. Cambridge, England: Cambridge University Press.

Kavka, Gregory. 1978. "Some Paradoxes of Deterrence." *Journal of Philosophy* 75:285–302.

Kellogg, Earl, Richard Godl, and Philip Garcia. 1986. "The Effects of Agricultural Growth on Agricultural Imports in Developing Countries." *American Journal of Agricultural Economics* 68, no. 5:1347–1352.

Kennan, George F. 1951. *American Diplomacy: 1900–1950*. Chicago: University of Chicago Press.

1985. "Morality and Foreign Policy." *Foreign Affairs* 64, no. 2:205–218.

Kennedy, John F. 1957. "A Democrat Looks at Foreign Policy." *Foreign Affairs* 36, no. 1:44, 53–54.

1962. Rep. 1971. "Foreign Aid, 1961." In *Why Foreign Aid?* edited by R. A. Goldwyn. Freeport, N.Y.: Books for Libraries Press, pp. 1–9.

Kennedy, Paul. 1987. *The Rise and Fall of the Great Powers*. New York: Random House.

Klosko, George. 1987. "Political Obligation and Consent." *Philosophy and Public Affairs* 16, no. 3:247–259.

1987. "Presumptive Benefit, Fairness and Political Obligation." *Philosophy and Public Affairs* 16:241–259.

Krickus, Richard J. 1979. "On the Morality of Chemical/Biological War." *War, Morality and the Military Profession*, edited by M. M. Wakin. Boulder, Colo.: Westview Press, pp. 487–503.

References

Krishna, Raj. 1967. "Agricultural Price Policy and Economic Development." *Agricultural Development Growth*, edited by H. Southworth and B. Johnston. Ithaca, N.Y.: Cornell University Press, pp. 497–540.

Lappe, Frances Moore. 1971. Rep. 1982. *Diet for a Small Planet*. New York: Ballantine.

1983. *Diet for a Small Planet*. Tenth anniversary edition, revised and updated. New York: Ballantine.

Lappe, Frances Moore, and Joseph Collins. 1977. *Food First*. New York: Ballantine.

1979. *World Hunger: Ten Myths*. 4th ed. San Francisco: Institute for Food and Development Policy.

Lappe, Frances Moore, Joseph Collins, and Cary Fowler. 1977. *Food First: Beyond the Myth of Scarcity*. Boston: Houghton Mifflin.

Lappe, Frances Moore, Joseph Collins, and David Kinley. 1980. *Aid as Obstacle: Twenty Questions about Our Foreign Aid and the Hungry*. San Francisco: Institute for Food and Development Policy.

Lee, Thomas H., and Proctor P. Reid, eds. 1991. *National Interests in an Age of Global Technology*. Washington, D.C.: National Academy Press.

Levin, Michael E. 1981. "Equality of Opportunity." *The Philosophical Quarterly* 31:110–125.

Locke, John. 1690. Rep. 1980. *Second Treatise of Government*, edited by C. B. Macpherson. Indianapolis: Hackett Publishing.

Lucas, George R., Jr. 1976. "Political and Economic Dimensions of Hunger." *Lifeboat Ethics: The Moral Dilemmas of World Hunger*, edited by George R. Lucas, Jr., and Thomas Ogletree. New York: Harper & Row, pp. 1–28.

1990. "African Famine: New Economic and Ethical Perspectives." *The Journal of Philosophy* 87, no. 11:629–641.

Lucas, George R., Jr., and Thomas Ogletree, eds. 1976. *Lifeboat Ethics: The Moral Dilemmas of World Hunger*. New York: Harper & Row.

Luper-Foy, Steven, ed. 1988. *Problems of International Justice*. Boulder, Colo.: Westview.

McCay, Bonnie J., and James M. Acheson, eds. 1987. *The Question of the Commons: The Culture and Ecology of Communal Resources*. Tucson, Ariz.: Univ. of Arizona Press.

References

McClennen, Edward. 1986. "The Tragedy of National Sovereignty." *The Nuclear Weapons and the Future of Humanity: The Fundamental Question,* edited by Axner Cohen and Steven Lee. Totowa, N.J.: Rowman & Allanheld.

Mack, Eric. 1988. "The Uneasy Case for Global Redistribution." In *Problems of International Justice,* edited by Steven Luper-Foy. Boulder, Colo.: Westview Press, pp. 55–66.

Mackie, Arthur B. 1983. *The U.S. Farmer and World Market Development.* Economic Research Service Staff Report no. AGES 830810. Washington, D.C.: U.S. Department of Agriculture.

McNeil, William. 1982. *The Pursuit of Power.* Chicago: University of Chicago Press.

Madden, Patrick, and Paul B. Thompson. 1987. "Ethical Aspects of Changing Agricultural Technology in the United States." *Notre Dame Journal of Law, Ethics, and Public Policy* 3, no. 1:85–116.

Mayer, Jean. 1979. "Ten Nutritional Myths." *Family Health* 11 (May 11):36.

Mellor, John W. 1972. *The Economics of Agricultural Development.* Ithaca, N.Y.: Cornell University Press.

1989. "Agricultural Development in the Third World: The Food, Poverty, Aid, Trade Nexus." *Choices* (Spring):4–29.

Mellor, John W., and Bruce F. Johnston. 1984. "The World Food Equation." *Journal of Economic Literature* 22, no. 2:531–574.

Mellor, John W., and Raisuddin Ahmed, eds. 1988. *Agricultural Price Policy for Developing Countries.* Baltimore, Md.: Johns Hopkins Press.

Mill, John Stuart. 1863. Rep. 1987. *Utilitarianism.* London: Penguin.

Miller, David. 1988. "The Ethical Significance of Nationality." *Ethics* 98:647–662.

Millikan, Max F. 1962. Rep. 1971. "The Political Case for Economic Development Aid." *Why Foreign Aid?* edited by R. A. Goldwyn. Freeport, N.Y.: Books for Libraries Press, pp. 90–108.

Mintz, Sidney W. 1985. *Sweetness and Power: The Place of Sugar in Modern History.* New York: Penguin Books.

Morgan, Dan. 1979. *Merchants of Grain.* New York: Viking Press.

Morgenthau, Hans. 1962. "A Political Theory of Foreign Aid." *American Political Science Review* 56, no. 2:301–309.

Murdoch, William W., and Allen Oaten. 1975. "Population and Food: Metaphors and the Reality." *Bioscience* 25, no. 9:561–567.

References

Nagel, Thomas. 1977. "Poverty and Food: Why Charity Isn't Enough." In *Food Policy,* edited by P. Brown and H. Shue. New York: Free Press, pp. 54–62.

Narveson, Jan. 1977. "Morality and Starvation." *World Hunger and Moral Obligation,* edited by William Aiken and Hugh LaFollette. Englewood Cliffs, N.J.: Prentice-Hall.

Newman, Barry. 1982. "Bangladesh Provides Ammunition for Critics of Food Aid." *Food and People,* edited by D. Kirk and E. K. Eliason. San Francisco: Boyd and Fraser.

Nichols, Bruce, and Gil Loescher, ed. 1989. *The Moral Nation: Humanitarianism and U.S. Foreign Policy Today.* Notre Dame, Ind.: University of Notre Dame Press.

Nickel, James W. 1987. *Making Sense of Human Rights.* Berkeley, Calif.: Univ. of California Press.

Niebuhr, Reinhold. 1932. *Moral Man and Immoral Society.* New York: Scribner.

Nielson, Kai. 1983. "Global Justice and the Imperative of Capitalism." *Journal of Philosophy.* 80, no. 10:608–610.

Norris, Frank. 1901. Rep. 1964. *The Octopus.* New York: New American Library.

Nozick, Robert. 1974. *Anarchy, State and Utopia.* New York: Basic Books.

ODC (Overseas Development Council). 1987. *What Americans Think: Views on Development and U.S.–Third World Relations.* New York: Inter Action.

O'Neill, Onora. 1975. "Lifeboat Earth." *Philosophy and Public Affairs* 4, no. 3:273–292.

    1980. "The Moral Perplexities of Famine Relief." *Matters of Life and Death: New Introductory Essays in Moral Philosophy,* edited by Tom Regan. New York: Random House.

    1986. *Faces of Hunger: An Essay on Poverty, Justice and Development.* Boston: Allen & Unwin.

    1988a. "Children's Rights and Children's Lives." *Ethics* 98, no. 3:445–463.

    1988b. "Ethical Reasoning and Ideological Pluralism." *Ethics* 98, no. 4:705–722.

    1988c. "Hunger, Needs and Rights." *Problems of International Justice,* edited by Steven Luper-Foy. Boulder, Colo.: Westview Press, pp. 67–83.

Osgood, Robert E. 1953. *Ideals and Self-Interest in America's Foreign Relations.* Chicago: University of Chicago Press.

References

Osterlund, Peter. 1986. "Congress Tightens Foreign Aid Screws." *Christian Science Monitor* (September 18).

Paarlberg, Robert L. 1980. "Lessons of the Grain Embargo." *Foreign Affairs* 59, no. 1:144–162.

——— 1986. "Farm Development in Poor Countries: The Disputed Consequences for U.S. Farm Trade." *American Journal of Agricultural Economics* 68:1353–1357.

Paddock, William, and Paul Paddock. 1967. *Famine 1975! America's Decision Who Will Survive?* Boston: Little Brown.

Peterson, E. Wesley F. 1986. "Third World Development and Trade: Discussion." *American Journal of Agricultural Economics* 68:1360–1361.

Pimentel, David, and Marcia Pimentel. 1979. *Food, Energy and Society.* New York: John Wiley.

Pogge, Thomas W. 1989. *Realizing Rawls.* Ithaca, N.Y.: Cornell University Press.

Poleman, Thomas T. 1977. "World Food: Myth and Reality." *World Development* 5:389–394.

Ponte, Lowell. 1982. "Food: America's Secret Weapon." *Reader's Digest* (May): 65–72.

Purcell, Randall B. 1987. "Develop Their Agriculture to Save Ours." *Wall Street Journal* (January 23):22.

Purcell, Randall B., and Elizabeth Morrison, eds. 1987. *U.S. Agriculture and Third World Development: The Critical Linkage.* Boulder, Colo.: Lynne Rienner.

Rachels, James. 1977. "Vegetarianism and "The Other Weight Problem." *World Hunger and Moral Obligation,* edited by William Aiken and Hugh LaFollette. Englewood Cliffs, N.J.: Prentice-Hall.

Rawls, John. 1971. *A Theory of Justice.* Cambridge, Mass.: Belknap Press of Harvard University Press.

——— 1975. "A Kantian Conception of Equality." *Cambridge Review* (Feb.):94–99.

——— 1980. "Kantian Constructivism in Moral Theory." *The Journal of Philosophy* 77, no. 9:515–573.

——— 1985. "Justice as Fairness: Political Not Metaphysical." *Philosophy and Public Affairs* 14:223–251.

——— 1987. "The Idea of An Overlapping Consensus." *Oxford Journal of Legal Studies* 7:1–24.

——— 1988. "The Priority of Right and Ideas of the Good." *Philosophy and Public Affairs* 17:251–276.

References

Raz, Joseph. 1990. "Facing Diversity: The Case of Epistemic Abstinence." *Philosophy and Public Affairs* 19:3–46.

Riddell, Roger C. 1987. *Foreign Aid Reconsidered.* Baltimore, Md.: Johns Hopkins University Press.

Rosecrance, Richard. 1986. *The Rise of the Trading State.* New York: Basic Books.

Rosenberg, Nathan, and L. E. Birdzell, Jr. 1986. *How the West Grew Rich: The Economic Transformation of the Industrial World.* New York: Basic Books.

Rossmiller, George E., and M. Ann Tutwiler. 1987. "Agricultural Trade and Development: Broadening the Horizon." *United States Agricultural Exports and Third World Development: The Critical Linkage.* Boulder, Colo.: Lynn Reiner for the Curry Foundation, pp. 265–293.

Rostow, W. W. 1986. *Eisenhower, Kennedy, and Foreign Aid.* Austin, Tex.: University of Texas Press.

Rothschild, Emma. 1976. "Food Politics." *Foreign Affairs* 54, no. 2:285–302.

Royce, Josiah. 1908. Repr. 1969. *The Philosophy of Loyalty.* Repr. in *The Basic Writings of Josiah Royce,* edited by John J. McDermott. Chicago: University of Chicago Press.

Runge, Carlisle Ford. 1977. "American Agricultural Assistance and the New International Economic Order." *World Development* 5, no. 8:725–746.

Ruttan, Vernon W. 1983. *Agricultural Research Policy.* Minneapolis, Minn.: Minnesota University Press.

——— 1986. "Toward a Global Agricultural Research System: A Personal View." *Research Policy* 15:307–327.

Sahlins, Marshall. 1972. *Stone Age Economics.* Hawthorne, N.Y.: Aldine de Gruyter.

Scheffler, S., ed. 1988. *Consequentialism and Its Critics.* Oxford, England: Oxford University Press.

Schuh, G. Edward. 1987. "The Changing Context of Food and Agricultural Policy." In *Food Policy: Integrating Supply, Distribution and Consumption,* edited by J. Price Gittinger, Joanee Leslie, and Caroline Hoisington. Washington, D.C.: World Bank.

——— 1986. "Some Healthy Competition for U.S. Farmers." *Washington Post* (September 4): A17.

Schultz, Theodore W. 1978. *Distortions of Agricultural Incentives.* Bloomington, Ind.: Indiana University Press.

Scobie, Grant M. 1979. "The Demand for Agricultural Research: A Columbian Illustration." *American Journal of Agricultural Economics* 61:540–45.

Sellers, James. 1976. "Famine and Interdependence." *Lifeboat Ethics: The Moral Dilemmas of World Hunger,* edited by George R. Lucas, Jr., and Thomas Ogletree. New York: Harper & Row, pp. 100–119.

Sen, Amartya. 1981. Repr. 1984. *Poverty and Famines: An Essay on Entitlement and Deprivation.* Oxford, England: Clarendon Press.

    1987. *On Ethics and Economics.* Oxford, England: Basil Blackwell.

    1990. "Individual Freedom as a Social Commitment." *New York Review of Books* 37, no. 10:49–53.

Sen, Amartya, and Bernard Williams, eds. 1982. *Utilitarianism and Beyond.* Cambridge, England: Cambridge University Press.

Shaughnessy, Daniel E. 1977. "The Political Uses of Food Aid: Are Criteria Necessary?" *Food Policy,* edited by P. G. Brown and H. Shue. New York: Free Press, pp. 94–102.

Shue, Henry. 1977. "Distributive Criteria for Development Assistance." *Food Policy,* edited by Peter G. Brown and Henry Shue. New York: Free Press, pp. 305–318.

    1980. *Basic Rights.* Princeton, N.J.: Princeton University Press.

    1983. "The Burdens of Justice." *Journal of Philosophy* 80, no. 10:600–605.

    1988. "Mediating Duties." *Ethics* 98, no. 4:687–704.

    1989. "Morality, Politics, and Humanitarian Assistance." *The Moral Nation: Humanitarianism and U.S. Foreign Policy Today,* edited by Bruce Nichols and Gil Loescher. Notre Dame, Ind.: University of Notre Dame Press.

Shuman, Charles B. 1977. "Food Aid and the Free Market." In *Food Policy,* edited by P. Brown and H. Shue. New York: Free Press, pp. 145–163.

Sidgwick, Henry. 1907. *The Methods of Ethics.* London: Macmillan.

Simon, Arthur. 1975. *Bread for the World.* New York: Paulist Press, pp. 116–119.

Simon, Julian L. 1980. "Resources, Population, Environment: An Oversupply of False Bad News." *Science* 208:1431–1437.

Simon, Julian L., and Herman Kahn, eds. 1984. *The Resourceful Earth: A Response to Global 2000.* Oxford, England: Basil Blackwell.

References

Sinclair, Wade. 1986. "U.S. Farm Program Goes Awry." *Washington Post* (June 24).

Singer, Peter. 1972. "Famine, Affluence, and Morality." *Philosophy and Public Affairs* 1:229–243.

———. 1977. "Reconsidering the Famine Relief Argument." In *The Responsibility of the United States in the Life and Death Choices*, edited by Peter G. Brown and Henry Shue. New York: Free Press.

Smart, J. C. C., and B. Williams, eds. 1973. *Utilitarianism: For and Against*. Cambridge, England: Cambridge University Press.

Smith, Brian. 1990. *More Than Altruism: The Politics of Private Foreign Aid*. Princeton, N.J.: Princeton University Press.

Smith, Rogers M. 1989. "Morality, Humanitarianism, and Foreign Policy: A Purposive View." *The Moral Nation: Humanitarianism and U.S. Foreign Policy Today*, edited by Bruce Nichols and Gil Loescher. Notre Dame, Ind.: University of Notre Dame Press.

Sneed, Joseph D. 1977. "A Utilitarian Framework for Policy Analysis in Food Related Foreign Aid." *Food Policy: The Responsibility of the United States in the Life and Death Choices*, edited by Peter G. Brown and Henry Schuh. New York: Free Press.

Strange, Marty. 1985. *Family Farming*. Lincoln, Neb.: University of Nebraska Press.

Thompson, Paul B. and Bill A. Stout. 1991. *Beyond the Large Farm: Ethics and Research Goals for Agriculture*. Boulder, Colo.: Westview Press.

Todaro, Michael P. 1985. "Ethics, Values and Economic Development." *Ethics and International Relations*, edited by Kenneth W. Thompson. New Brunswick, N.J.: Transaction Books, pp. 75–97.

U.S. Congress. 1986. *Urgent Supplemental Appropriations Act*. United States Statutes at large 100, PL 99-349, July 2, 1986, p. 710.

U.S. House. 1982. Honorable R. W. Daniel, Jr. "Grant by Agency for International Development Adds Insult to Injury." *Congressional Record* 128, pt. 18 (September 24).

U.S. Senate. 1986a. "Urgent Supplemental Appropriations Bill, 1986." Committee on Appropriations Report 99-301, May 15, p. 56.

———. 1986b. Senator Dale Bumpers (Arkansas). *Congressional Record* 132, no. 75 (June 6): S7028.

———. 1985. Senator Dale Bumpers (Arkansas). *Congressional Record* 131, no. 162, (November 22): S16269

References

USDA (U.S. Department of Agriculture). 1987. *World Food Needs and Availabilities, 1986/87.* Washington, D.C.: USDA, p. 10.

Upton, Michael, Jean-Pierre Godding, and Martin Godfrey. 1984. *International Perspectives on Rural Development.* Institute for Development Studies Discussion Paper no. 197 (November 1984). Brighton, England: Institute of Development Studies at the University of Sussex.

Urmson, J. O. 1958. "Saints and Heroes." *Essays in Moral Philosophy,* edited by A. I. Melden. Seattle, Wash.: University of Washington Press.

Van Wyk, Robert N. 1988. "Perspectives on World Hunger and the Extent of Our Positive Duties." *Public Affairs Quarterly* 2, no. 2:75–90.

Verghese, Paul. 1976. "Muddled Metaphors." *Lifeboat Ethics: The Moral Dilemmas of World Hunger,* edited by George R. Lucas, Jr., and Thomas Ogletree. New York: Harper & Row, pp. 151–156.

Walzer, Michael. 1981. "The Distribution of Membership." *Boundaries,* edited by P. G. Brown and H. Shue. Totowa, N.J.: Rowman and Littlefield, pp. 1–35.

Watson, Richard A. 1977. "Reason and Morality in a World of Limited Food." *World Hunger and Moral Obligation,* edited by William Aiken and Hugh LaFollette. Englewood Cliffs, N.J.: Prentice-Hall.

Wayne, J. C. 1983. "NCSU Involvement in the International Peanut Program." *Virginia-Carolina Peanut News* 29, no. 1:13–18.

Weisbard, Alan J. 1987. "The Role of Philosophy in the Public Policy Process: A View from the President's Commission." *Ethics* 97, no. 4:776–785.

White, T. Kelly, and Charles E. Hanrahan, eds. 1986. *Consortium on Trade Research, Agriculture, Trade, and Development: A Comparative Look at U.S., Canadian, and European Community Policies.* ERS Staff Report No. AGES850208. Washington, D.C.

Witt, Lawrence. 1977. "Food Aid, Commercial Exports, and the Balance of Payments." *Food Policy: The Responsibility of the United States in the Life and Death Choices,* edited by Peter G. Brown and Henry Schuh. New York: Free Press, pp. 79–93.

World Commission on Environment and Development. 1987. *Our Common Future.* New York: Oxford University Press.

Woycik, Jan. 1989. *The Arguments of Agriculture.* West Lafayette, Ind.: Purdue University Press.

Index

Index